Know Thyself:
Ideologies of Black Liberation

Know Thyself:
Ideologies of Black Liberation

Gwinyai H. Muzorewa, Ph.D.

Editor

Resource *Publications*

An imprint of *Wipf and Stock Publishers*
199 West 8th Avenue • Eugene OR 97401

KNOW THYSELF: IDEOLOGIES OF BLACK LIBERATION

ISBN: 1-59752-317-8

Manufactured in the U.S.A.

DEDICATION

This book is dedicated to all the oppressed people of African descent both in Diaspora and in their own land, who are facing double jeopardy: one, they are struggling with their identity; two, they are struggling to get from underneath the yoke of oppression and marginalisation.

CONTENTS

FOREWORD

DEAR READER,

As students at Lincoln University, we have the invaluable opportunity to learn about ourselves by acknowledging our history. As a people, Blacks have evolved into a complex race of differing classes, viewpoints, and goals. Despite our differences, our past links us closely together as we continue in the incessant struggle to liberate ourselves from the present-day consequences of slavery and oppression. We, as students of this prestigious institution, have been granted the opportunity to learn from each other in a curriculum focused strongly on our history, our present state, and our bright future.

Ideologies of Black Liberation encourages the student to further his or her acquiring of knowledge while appreciating the scholarly works of various theoreticians within the field. In addition, the Black student learns that he or she is not alone in the journey toward intellectual enlightenment. Beyond the classroom, this course calls for a new wave of young, Black intellectuals that will break the recurring cycle of complacency. While bringing relevant, current issues to life, the course also forces the student to first look inwardly for solutions to the problems that plague the Black community as a whole.

An ideology of Black liberation begins with knowledge. The continual accumulation of knowledge perpetuates liberation or freedom. As students fighting an ongoing struggle, we must allow knowledge to flow from our very beings permeating our minds, hearts, and actions if we hope for a better tomorrow. However, we cannot hope for a better tomorrow without taking appropriate action. We have the power within us to create a greater, more challenging intellectual atmosphere at this university. This journey toward greatness will allow us to eagerly approach all facets of life in hopes to grow in knowledge and understanding while abandoning mediocrity.

To know yourself is to understand the direction in which you are going. Rather than your direction being a result of futuristic plans or goals, your direction is clear because of where you've been. To know yourself is to understand that you are part of an intellectual body that need only recognize the power within to manufacture change. To know thyself is to understand that you set the example each day in all that you do. Finally, to know yourself is to understand that you are an invaluable member of a society that has neither historically nor currently willed for you to prosper or succeed. **But, to <u>Know Thyself</u> is to know that despite such opposition, you will succeed nonetheless.**

WITH YOU IN THE STUGGLE,

Erin K. Melton
Lincoln University
Class of 2006

ACKNOWLEDGMENTS

I wish to thank several classes at Lincoln University who took the course I taught on "Ideologies of Black Liberation" because it was they who inadvertently put pressure on me to compile this monogram. The students' interest in what select authorities on the subject have said, led me searching, until I found the chapters compiled here.

Among the students, I want to give special thanks to Ms. Erin Melton, A Religion/Political Science Major [double], who actually assisted me with some of the research. Her academic thoroughness with grammar, punctuation and the like, gives this book special qualities as a joint venture between faculty and scholarly students.

Many thanks go to Ms. Janice Fay-Walker, the Philosophy and Religion Department secretary, who constantly urged me to do this book because its message, though "old, will always speak to the young people of African descent." Then Janice went further and worked on the actual typing and all that was necessary to give this book its present form.

I thank God who sustains me in all that I do, inspires me in all my academic endeavors, and simply gives me more days on earth to make a modest contribution, first to my race and then to all others.

Chapter 1

Ideology: Definition and Application

By Gwinyai H. Muzorewa

The word "ideology" has been defined in various ways according to the authors' intended goals. Sometimes it is assigned a specific meaning. For example, in *Government by Constitution*, Herbert Spiro says: "an ideo-logy must have both ideas and logic. It is a comprehensive, consistent, closed system of knowledge, to which its adherents turn to get answers to all their questions, solutions to all their problems" (Spiro 1959 180). Spiro goes on to explain three main types of ideology based on what they intend to emphasize:

    (a) An ideology of knowledge
    (b) An ideology of recrimination
    (c) An ideology of goals

Types of Ideology

The best example of the ideology of knowledge can be seen in Marxism.

a.   Ideology of Knowledge

Committed Marxists are totally convinced that what people like Karl Marx, Friedrich Engels, and Nicolai Lenin have written "contain a complete interpretation of all reality, that this interpretation is wholly consistent internally, and that all criticism of any of its parts have been definitely refuted" (Spiro 1959 180). Thus a committed Marxist will always turn to the writings by the aforementioned authors and nowhere else. Such an ideology is what Spiro has designated as an *ideology of knowledge*. However, there are some problems with such a mindset. It is so exclusivistic that it tends to self-destruct through the vehicle of *socio-politico-religio narcissism*. There is no room for innovation, exploration, or openness to new discoveries, not to mention possible errors the "fathers" might have made and also possible misinterpretation on the part of the adherents. Furthermore, the ideology of knowledge will eventually become irrelevant and possibly harmful when the system or principle is distorted by the adherents as is bound to happen. A closed system of knowledge is a potential time bomb. Given that the globe is a shrinking village, and that change is inevitable, an ideology of knowledge will certainly and ultimately not serve a good purpose indefinitely. For one thing, as the community population increases, it will eventually not receive sufficient ideological nourishment from

1

"a rigid ideology." The situation is made worse if the ideology itself is unrealistic.

There is further danger in the ideology of knowledge namely, *anachronism*. In the event that such knowledge is exported to other communities or nations, it is most certain that it becomes the thinking of a few, imposed on the wish of the many, with the result that soon or later the ideology is either totally distorted, corrupted or rejected not only by the new community but also its very adherents.

b. Ideology of Recrimination

Next, we briefly examine the *ideology of recrimination*. When a political system has failed to deliver, or solve some of its problems that have been lingering for long, the leadership may have to be called to the carpet. Spiro also understands historical recrimination as arising out of the failure of a political system to solve some of its problems. Such failure is then blamed on "the failure on the part of some of its members to accept a 'solution' imposed upon them by procedures, such as force, whose authority they did not recognize" (Ibid 180). By way of elaborating recriminatory ideologism, Spiro cites the issue of the Revolution in French debates over colonial policy. He also cites the use of church-school problem; in the context of Germany, the issue of Nazi persecution of the church into discussions and debates all illustrate what historical recrimination refers to.

In the U.S.A. the issue of slavery surfaces often in Senate debates. Interestingly, it even surfaced in President George W. Bush's recent inaugural address in January 2005. Mr. Bush used this slavery rhetoric as reverse recrimination because he used the issue to portray the goodness of his government policy by attending to the nation's ever-unfinished business. Actually, President Bush was aware that the Democrats would use the issue of slavery and racism against his administration. Instead of succumbing to Democratic pressure, he simply intended to pre-empt such thinking. Some skeptics even argue that the appointment of Dr. Condolezza Rice – a black female – is intended to create a positive "perception," with the further effect of what I would call reverse recrimination. Reverse recrimination is intended to create the opposite effect of recrimination. It should enhance rather than reduce "the system's capacity to deal with the real and more urgent problems" confronting the nation. In the case of Mr. Bush, the real problem confronting the U.S.A. demanding his urgent attention is the Iraqi war and the continual count of U.S. soldiers losing their lives on foreign soil.

Regarding both an ideology of knowledge and ideology of recrimination, Spiro cautions that whenever there is competition "between an ideology and more realistic interpretation of reality, ideological style will also reduce the effectiveness of the of the constitution and of the policies under it" (Ibid 188).

In Southern Africa, the former British colony Zimbabwe, President Robert Mugabe still shouts at the British who since left the country over 25 years ago. Every four years, just before the parliamentary elections, and every five years, just prior to the Presidential election, Mr. Mugabe makes a chronic verbal attack

2

on the British. He intends to divert the masses' attention from the present reality to the liberation struggle in which the freedom fighters played a major role. By so doing, he received the sympathies of most voters, even if by intimidation. Unfortunately, such recriminatory ideologism has back-fired on Mugabe because the populace now knows that this attack on the British is a political tactic, referred to as "the old man's trick" to steal (i.e. rig) the vote from the more progressive opposition parties. Furthermore, Mugabe's utterances have actually incapacitated rather than enhanced his government. He chooses to live in the past, using this with the hope to control future events. Well, by using both the ideology of knowledge and of recrimination, both of which have negative effects, Mugabe has dug his own political grave.

    c.   An Ideological Historical Goal

The third and final type of ideology which Spiro discusses is ideologism with emphasis on historical goals. This "switches the orientation in time from the past to the future" (Spiro 1989 180). When some past, unrealistic goal is elaborated into a comprehensive, consistent, closed system as a guide to action, we have what Spiro calls an *ideological historical goal*. A good example of this is the establishment of a classless society according to Communist rhetoric. In the U.S.A. the Prohibitionism is also a perfect example. It was hoped that these arguments would solve the world's problems, but in reality they did not. At the international level, the argument that a complete universal disarmament and the idea of elaborating a system of international law could serve as the first step toward bringing about world peace did not deliver what it purported to do. Anytime one attempts to impose one ideology upon an entire population one simultaneously threatens to deprive the people of the opportunity to consider other alternatives or viable courses of action.

To sum, ideological tactic always has the tendency to hinder success, prosperity and true creativity. At the same time, it creates serious conditions of irresponsibility. Human beings as political animals do not thrive intellectually under rigid conditions. Hence, the adage, "you cannot fool all the people all of the time." To understand ideologism better, let us now briefly examine its exact opposite, namely *pragmatism*.

Pragmatism

Pragmatism simply defined means "practical." A pragmatic person is one who does whatever works best, and hopefully yields best results. While the ideologist operates from a set body of knowledge, or recrimination, and/or goals, the pragmatist does not have a closed system of knowledge to rely on at all. The pragmatist makes his or her decisions in response to the momentarily felt practical necessities. Of course, there can not be a perfect pragmatist just as there is no perfect human being.

Conclusion

Political responsibility involving making decisions must be undoubtedly based upon the best knowledge available about their consequences. Political responsibility also involves an awareness of the limitations that confine the scope and certainty of that knowledge.

The danger that most national leaders create for themselves is alienating the politically conscious masses. The exclusion of a large community of politically conscious and ambitious groups from participating in political decision-making process at the early stages of national growth, is a prescription for political and societal suicide. Such alienation by exclusion often leads to passionate resentment which, in turn, may lead to recrimination. In Zimbabwe, it has contributed to a mass exodus of the middle management, the blue collar and anyone who can leave the country in search of not only "green pastures" but also ordinary political freedom and human dignity both of which have become a scarce commodity in countries like Zimbabwe.

In Brazil, there is a slightly different scenario. The ruling class has its own ideology at the exclusion of the ideology of the populace. In some instances, the scenario is still more complex, where one individual has own ideology, at the total exclusion of the rest of the nation. In each case, the results are lack of true peace, distortion of democracy and ruinous corruption.

Chapter 2

Toward a Constructive Definition of Black Power

By James H. Cone

> If there is no struggle, there is no progress. Those who profess to favor freedom, and yet depreciate agitation, are men who want crops without plowing up the ground. They want rain without thunder and lightning. ... This struggle may be a moral one; or it may be a physical one; or it may be both moral and physical; but there must be a struggle.   *Frederick Douglas*

What is Black Power?

There has been and still is much debate among the critics of Black Power regarding the precise meaning of the words. The term "Black Power" was first used in the civil rights movement in the spring of 1966 by Stokely Carmichael to designate the only appropriate response to white racism.[1] Since that time many critics have observed that there is no common agreement regarding its definition. In one sense this fact is not surprising, since every new phenomenon passes through stages of development, and the advocates of Black Power need time to define its many implications. But in another sense, this criticism is surprising, since every literate person knows that imprecision, the inability of a word to describe accurately the object of reality to which it points, is characteristic of all languages. The complexity of this problem is evident in the development of modern analytical philosophy. We are still in the process of defining such terms as "democracy," "good," "evil," and many others. In fact the ability to probe for deeper meanings of words as they relate to various manifestations of reality is what makes the intellectual pursuit interesting and worthwhile.

But if communication is not to reach an impasse, there must be agreement on the general shape of the object to which a term points. Meaningful dialogue is possible because of man's ability to use words as symbols for the real. Without this, communication ceases to exist. For example, theologians and political scientists may disagree on what they would consider "fine points" regarding the precise meaning of Christianity and democracy, but there is an underlying agreement regarding their referents.

The same is true of the words "black Power." To what "object" does it point? What does it mean when used by its advocates? It means *complete emancipation of black people from white oppression by whatever means black people deem necessary.* The methods may include selective buying, boycotting, marching, or even rebellion. Black Power means black freedom, black self-determination, wherein black people no longer view themselves as without human dignity but as men, human beings with the ability to carve out their own destiny. In short, as Stokley Carmichael would say, Black Power means T.C.B., Take Care of Business- black folk taking care of black folks' business, not on the terms of the oppressor, but on those of the oppressed.

Black Power is analogous to Albert Camus's understanding of the rebel. The rebel says No and Yes. He says No to conditions considered intolerable, and Yes to that "something within him which 'is worthwhile' ... and which must be taken into consideration."[2] To say No means that the oppressor has overstepped his bounds, and that "there is a limit beyond which [he] shall not go."[3] It means that oppression can be endured no longer in the style that the oppressor takes for granted. To say No is to reject categorically "the humiliating orders of the master" and by so doing to affirm that something which is placed above everything else, including life itself. To say No means that death is preferable to life, if the latter is devoid of freedom. *"Better to die on one's feet than to live on one's knees."*[4] This is what Black Power means.

It is in this light that the slogan "Freedom Now"[5] ought to be interpreted. Like Camus's phrase, "All or Nothing," Freedom Now means that the slave is willing to risk death because "he considers these rights more important than himself. Therefore he is acting in the name of certain values which. ... he considers are common to himself and to all men."[6] That is what Henry Garnet had in mind when he said "rather *die freemen, than to live to be slaves."*[7] This is what Black Power means.

A further clarification of the meaning of Black Power may be found in Paul Tillich's analysis of "the courage to be," which is "the ethical act in which man affirms his being in spite of those elements of his existence which conflict with his essential self-affirmation."[8] Black Power, then, is a humanizing force because it is the black man's attempt to affirm his being, his attempt to be recognized as "Thou," in spite of the "other,"[9] the white power which dehumanizes him. The structure of white society attempts to make "black being" into "nonbeing" or "nothingness." In existential philosophy, nonbeing is usually identified as that which threatens being; it is that ever-present possibility of the inability to affirm one's existence. The courage to be, then, is the courage to affirm one's being by striking out at the dehumanizing forces which threaten being. And, as Tillich goes on to say, "He who is not capable of a powerful self-affirmation in spite of the anxiety of non-being is forced into a weak, reduced self-affirmation."[10]

The rebellion in the cities, far from being an expression of the inhumanity of blacks, is an affirmation of their being despite the ever-present possibility of death. For the black man to accept the white society's appeal to wait or to be orderly is to affirm "something which is less than essential ... being."[11] The black man prefers to die rather than surrender to some other value. The cry for death is, as Rollo May has noted, the "most mature form of distinctly human behavior."[12] In fact, many existentialists point out that physical life itself is not fully satisfying and meaningful until one can consciously choose another value which he holds more dear than life itself."[13] To be human is to find something worth dying for. When the black man rebels at the risk of death, he forces white society to look at him, to recognize him, to take his being into account, to admit

6

that he *is*. And in a structure that regulates behavior, recognition by the other is indispensable to one's being. As Franz Fanon says: "Man is human only to the extent to which he tries to impose his existence on another in order to be recognized by him."[14] And "he who is reluctant to recognize me opposes me. In a savage struggle I am willing to accept convulsions of death, invincible dissolutions, but also the possibility of the impossible."[15]

Black Power, in short, is an *attitude*, an inward affirmation of the essential worth of blackness. It means that the black man will not be poisoned by the stereotypes that have of him, but will affirm from the depth of his soul: "Get used to me, I am not getting used to anyone."[16] And "if the white man challenges my humanity, I will impose my whole weight as a man on his life and show him that I am not that 'sho good eatin' that he persists in imagining."[17] This is Black Power, the power of the black man to say Yes to his own "black being," and to make the other accept him or be prepared for a struggle.

> I find myself suddenly in the world and I recognize that I have one right alone: That of demanding human behavior from the other. One duty alone: That of not renouncing my freedom through my choices.[18]

Black Power and Existential Absurdity

Before one can really understand the mood of Black Power, it is necessary to describe a prior mood of the black man in a white society. When he first awakens to his place in America and feels sharply the absolute contradiction between *what is* and *what ought to be* or recognizes the inconsistency between his view of himself as a man and America's description of him as a thing, his immediate reaction is a feeling of absurdity. The absurd

> is basically that which man recognizes as the disparity between what he hopes for and what seems in fact to be. He yearns for some measure of happiness in an orderly, a rational and reasonably predictable world; when he finds misery in a disorderly, an irrational and unpredictable world, he is oppressed by the absurdity of the disparity between the universe as he wishes it to be and as he sees it.[19]

This is what the black man feels in a white world.

There is no place in America where the black man can go for escape. In every section of the country there is still the feeling expressed by Langston Hughes:

> I swear to the Lord
> I still can't see
> Why Democracy means
> Everybody but me.

I can remember reading, as a child, the Declaration of Independence with a sense of identity with all men and with a sense of pride: "We hold these truths to be self-evident: that all men are created equal; that they are endowed by their creator with certain unalienable rights; that among them is life, liberty and the pursuit of happiness." But I also read in the Dred Scott decision, not with pride or identity, but with a feeling of inexplicable absurdity, that blacks are not human.

> But it is too clear for dispute, that the enslaved African race were not intended to be included, and formed no part of the people who framed and adopted this declaration; for if the language, as understood in that day, would embrace them, the conduct of the distinguished men who framed the Declaration of Independence would have been utterly and flagrantly inconsistent with the principles they asserted; and instead of the sympathy of mankind ... they would have deserved and received universal rebuke and reprobation.

Thus the black man *"had no rights which the white man was bound to respect."*[20]

But many whites would reply: "The Negro is no longer bought and sold as chattel. We changed his status after the Civil War. Now he is free." Whatever may have been the motives of Abraham Lincoln and other white Americans for launching the war, it certainly was not on behalf of black people. Lincoln was clear on this:

> My paramount object in this struggle is to save the Union, and is not either to save or to destroy slavery. If I could save the Union without freeing any slave, I would do it; and if I could save it by freeing some and leaving others alone, I would also do that.[21]

If that quotation still leaves his motives unclear, here is another one which should remove all doubts regarding his thoughts about black people.

> I will say then that I am not, nor ever have been in favor of bringing about in any way the social and political equality of the black and white races- that I am not nor ever have been in favor of making voters or jurors of Negroes, nor of qualifying them to hold office, nor to intermarry with white people; and I will say in addition to this that there is a physical difference between the white and black races which I believe will forbid the two races living together on terms of social and political equality. And inasmuch as they cannot so live, while they do remain together, there must be the position of superior and inferior, and I as much as any other man am in favor of having the superior position assigned to the white race.[22]

And certainly the history of the black-white relations in this country from the Civil War to the present unmistakably shows that as a people, America has never intended for blacks to be free. To this day, in the eyes of most white Americans, the black man remains subhuman.

Yet Americans continue to talk about brotherhood and equality. They say that this is "the land of the free and the home of the brave." They sing: My country 'tis of thee, sweet land of liberty." But they do not mean blacks. This is the black man's paradox, the absurdity of living in a world with "no rights which the white man [is] bound to respect."

It seems that white historians and political scientists have attempted, perhaps subconsciously, to camouflage the inhumanity of whites toward blacks.[23] But the evidence is clear for those who care to examine it. All aspects of this society have participated in the act of enslaving blacks, extinguishing Indians, and annihilating all who question white society's right to decide who is human.

I should point out here that most existentialists do not say that "man is absurd" or "the world is absurd." Rather, the absurdity arises as man confronts the world and looks for meaning. The same is true in regard to my analysis of the black man in a white society. It is not that the black man is absurd or that the white society as such is absurd. Absurdity arises as the black man seeks to understand his place in the white world. The black man does not view himself as absurd; he views himself as human. But as he meets the white world and its values, he is confronted with an almighty No and is defined as a thing. This produces absurdity.

The crucial question, then, for the black man is, "How should I respond to a world which defines me as a non-person?" That he is a person is beyond question, not debatable. But when he attempts to relate as a person, the world demands that he respond as a thing. In this existential absurdity, what should he do? Should he respond as he knows himself to be, or as the world defines him?

The response to this feeling of absurdity is determined by a man's ontological perspective. If one believes that this world is the extent of reality, he will either despair or rebel. According to Camus's The Myth of Sisphus, suicide is the ultimate act of despair. Rebellion is epitomized in the person of Dr. Bernard Rieux in The Plague. Despite the overwhelming odds, Rieux fights against things as they are.

If, perchance, a man believes in God, and views this world as merely a pilgrimage to another world, he is likely to regard suffering as a necessity for entrance to the next world. Unfortunately Christianity has more often than not responded to evil in this manner.[24]

From this standpoint the response of Black Power is like Camus's view of the rebel. One who embraces Black Power does not despair and take suicide as an out, nor does he appeal to another world in order to relieve the pains of this one.[25] Rather, he fights back with the whole of his being. Black Power believes that blacks are not really human beings in white eyes, that they never have been and never will be, until blacks recognize the unsavory behavior of whites for what it is. Once this recognition takes place, they can make whites see them as humans. The man of Black Power will not rest until the oppressor recognizes him for what he is- man. He further knows that in this campaign for human dignity, freedom is not a gift but a right worth dying for.

Is Black Power a Form of Black Racism?

One of the most serious charges leveled against the advocates of Black Power is that they are *black* racists. Many well-intentioned persons have insisted that there must be another approach, one which will not cause so much hostility, not to mention rebellion. Therefore appeal is made to the patience of black people to keep their "cool" and not get too carried away by their feelings. These men argue that if any progress is to be made, it will be through a careful, rational approach to the subject. These people are deeply offended when black people refuse to listen and place such white liberals in the same category as the most adamant segregationists. They simply do not see that such reasoned appeals merely support the perpetuation of the ravaging of the black community. Black Power, in this respect, is by nature *irrational*, i.e., does not deny the role of rational reflection, but insists that human existence cannot be mechanized or put into neat boxes according to reason. Human reason though valuable is not absolute, because moral decisions- those decisions which deal with human dignity- cannot be made by using the abstract methods of science. Human emotions must be reckoned with. Consequently, black people must say No to all do-gooders who insist that they need more time. If such persons really knew oppression- knew it existentially in their guts- they would join black people in their fight for freedom and dignity. It is interesting that most people do understand why Jews can hate Germans. Why can they not understand why black people, who have been deliberately and systematically dehumanized or murdered by the structure of this society, hate white people? The general failure of Americans to make this connection suggests that the primary difficulty is their inability to see black men as men.

When Black Power advocates refuse to listen to their would-be liberators, they are charged with creating hatred among black people, thus making significant personal relationship between blacks and whites impossible. It should be obvious that the hate which black people feel toward whites is not due to the creation of the term "Black Power." Rather, it is a result of the deliberate and systematic ordering of society on the basis of racism, making black alienation not only possible but inevitable. For over three hundred years black people have been enslaved by the tentacles of American white power, tentacles that worm their way into the guts of their being and "invade the gray cells of their cortex." For three hundred years they have cried, waited, voted, marched, picketed, and boycotted, but whites still refuse to recognize their humanity. In light of this, attributing black anger to the call for Black Power is ridiculous, if not obscene. "To be a Negro in this country," says James Baldwin, "and to be relatively conscious is to be in rage almost all the time."

In spite of this it is misleading to suggest that hatred is essential to the definition of Black Power. As Camus says, "One envies what he does not have, while the rebel's aim is to defend what he is. He does not merely claim some good that he does not possess or of which he is deprived. His aim is to claim recognition for something which he has."[26] Therefore it is not the intention of the black man to repudiate his master's human dignity, but only his status as master.[27] The rebellion in the cities, it would seem, should not be interpreted as a few blacks who want something for nothing but as an assertion of the dignity of all black people. The black man is assuming that there is a common value which is recognizable by all as existing in all people, and he is testifying to that *something* in his rebellion. He is expressing his solidarity with the human race. With this in view, Camus' reinterpretation of the Cartesian formula, " think, therefore I am," seems quite appropriate: "" rebel, therefore *we* exist."

It is important to make a further distinction here among black hatred, black racism, and Black Power. Black hatred is the black man's strong aversion to white society. No black man living in white America can escape it. Even a sensitive white man can say: "It is hard to imagine how any Negro American, no matter how well born or placed, can escape a deep sense of anger and a burning hatred of things white."[28] And another non-black, Arnold Rose, is even more perceptive:

> Negro hatred of white people is not pathological- far from it. It is a healthy human reaction to oppression, insult, and terror. White people are too often surprised at the Negro's hatred of them, but it should not be surprising.
>
> The whole world knows the Nazis murdered millions of Jews and can suspect that the remaining Jews are having some emotional reaction to that fact. Negroes, on the other hand, are either ignored or thought to be so subhuman that they have no feelings when one of their number is killed because he was a Negro. Probably no week goes by in the United States that some Negro is not severely beaten, and the news is reported in the Negro press. Every week or maybe twice a week almost the entire Negro population of the United States suffers an emotional recoil from some insult coming from the voice or pen of a leading white man. The surviving Jews had one, big, soul-wracking "incident" that wrenched them back to group identification. The surviving Negroes experience constant jolts that almost never let them forget for even an hour that they are Negroes. In this situation, hatred of whites and group identification are natural reactions.[29]

And James Baldwin was certainly expressing the spirit of black hatred when he said:

> The brutality with which Negroes are treated in this country simply cannot be overstated, however unwilling white men may be to hear it. In the beginning- and neither can this be overstated- a Negro just cannot *believe* that white people are treating him as they do; he does not know what he has done to merit it. And when he realizes that the treatment accorded him has nothing to do with anything he has done, that the attempt of white people to destroy him- for that is what it is- is utterly gratuitous, it is not hard for him to think of white people as devils.[30]

This feeling should not be identified as black racism. Black racism is a myth created by whites to ease their guilt feelings. As long as whites can be assured that blacks are racists, they can find reasons to justify their own oppression of black people. This tactic seems to be a favorite device of white liberals who, intrigued by their own unselfish involvement in civil rights *for* the "Negro," like to pride themselves on their liberality toward blacks. White racists who are prepared to defend the outright subjugation of blacks need no such myth. The myth is needed by those who intend to keep things as they are, while pretending that things are in fact progressing. When confronted with the fact that the so-called progress is actually nonexistent, they can easily offer an explanation by pointing to the "white backlash" caused by "black racism."

But the charge of black racism cannot be reconciled with the facts. While it is true that blacks do hate whites, black hatred is not racism. Racism, according to Webster, is "the assumption that psychocultural traits and capacities are determined by biological race and that races differ decisively from one another, which is usually coupled with a belief in the inherent superiority of a particular race and its rights to dominance over others." Where are the examples among blacks in which they sought dominance over others because of a belief in black superiority? The only possible example would be the Black Muslims; and even here there is no effort of Black Muslims to enslave whites. Furthermore, if we were to designate them as black racists, they certainly are not dangerous in the same sense as white racists. The existence of the Black Muslims does not entitle whites to speak of black racism as a serious threat to the American society. They should be viewed as one possible and justifiable reaction to white racism. But in regard to Black Power, it is not comparable to white racism. Stokely Carmichael, responding to the charge of black supremacy, writes:

> There is no analogy- by any stretch of definition or imagination- between the advocates of Black Power and white racists. ... The goal of the racist is to keep black people on the bottom, arbitrarily and dictatorially as they have done in this country for over three hundred years. The goal of black self-determination and black self-identity- Black Power- is full participation in the decision making process affecting the lives of black people.[31]

Modern racism is European in origin, and America has been its vigorous offspring. It is the white man who has sought to dehumanize others because of his feelings of superiority or for his economic advantage. Racism is so embedded in this country that it is hard to imagine that any white man can escape it.

Black Power then is not black racism or black hatred. Simply stated, Black Power is an affirmation of the humanity of blacks in spite of white racism. It says that only blacks really know the extent of white oppression, and thus only blacks are prepared to risk all to be free. Therefore, Black Power seeks not understanding but conflict; addresses blacks and not whites; seeks to develop black support, but not white good will. Black Power believes in the utter determination of blacks to be free and not in the good intentions of white society. It says: If blacks are liberated, it will be blacks themselves who will do the liberating, not whites.

12

Whites are not only bothered about "black racism" but also about the rejection of integration implied in Black Power. They say, "Now that we have decided to accept the Negro, he will have no part of it. You see, we knew he really preferred segregation." What, then, does Black Power say about integration?

One Black Power advocate, when a newsman asked, "What about integration?" responded, "Integration of what?" The implication is clear. If integration means accepting the white man's style, his values, or his religion, then the black man must refuse. There is nothing to integrate. The white man, in the very asking of the question, assumes that he has something which blacks want or should want, as if being close to white people enhances the humanity of blacks.[32] This question- What about integration?- also completely ignores the beastly behavior of the "devil white man" (Malcolm X's designation). Black people cannot accept relationship on this basis.

On the other hand, if integration means that each man meets the other on equal footing, with neither possessing the ability to assert the rightness of his style over the other, then mutual meaningful dialogue is possible. Biblically, this may be called the Kingdom of God. Men were not created for separation, and color is not the essence of man's humanity. But we are not living in what the New Testament called the consummated Kingdom, and even its partial manifestation is not too obvious. Therefore, black people cannot live according to what ought to be, but according to what *is*. To be sure, men ought to behave without color as the defining characteristic of their view of humanity, but they do not. Some men can verbally rise above color, but existentially they live according to it, sometimes without even being conscious of it. There are so few exceptions to this that the universal assertion is virtually untouched. Therefore, to ask blacks to act as if color does not exist, to be integrated into white society, is asking them to ignore both the history of white America and present realities. Laws may be passed, but only whites have the power to enforce them.

Instead, in order for the oppressed blacks to regain their identity, they must affirm the very characteristic which the oppressor ridicules- *blackness*. Until white America is able to accept the beauty of blackness ("Black is beautiful, baby"), there can be no peace, no integration in the higher sense. Black people must withdraw and form their own culture, their own way of life.

Integration, as commonly understood, is nothing but "'a subterfuge for white supremacy;' i.e., as always involving only a token number of Negroes integrated into 'white institutions on the white man's terms.'"[33] As Professor Poussaint shows, this means blacks accepting the white man's view of himself, blacks saying, "Yes, [we are] inferior."[34]

Any careful assessment of the place of the black man in America must conclude that black self-hatred is the worst aspect of the legacy of slavery.[35] "The worst crime the white man has committed," writes Malcolm X, "has been to teach us to hate ourselves." During slavery, black people were treated as animals, and were systematically taught that such treatment was due them because of their blackness. "When slavery was abolished, the Negro had been stripped of his culture and left with this heritage: an oppressed black man in a white man's world."[36] When blacks were rewarded, it was because they behaved according to the stereotypes devised by whites. Coupled with this was the belief that "white is right" and "black is evil." Therefore, "lighter Negroes" were given better opportunities, while "darker Negroes" had doors closed to them, giving credence to the idea that the closer you are to being white, the more nearly human you are. Unfortunately, even many of our black institutions and media promoted the idea. As Elijah Muhammad, the leader of the Black Muslims, rightly says: "The Negro wants to be a white man. He processes his hair. Acts like a white man. He wants to integrate with the white man, but he cannot integrate with himself or his own mind. The Negro wants to lose his identity because he does not know his own identity."

In the present situation, while many of the mainline civil rights workers have promoted black identity by courageously fighting an apparent, immovable status quo, the idea of integration, at this stage, too easily lends itself to supporting the moral superiority of white society.

> Negro parents in the south never speak of sending their children to the "integrated school;" they say, "My child is going to the *white* school." No white children are "integrated" into Negro schools. Since integration is only a one-way street that Negroes travel to a white institution, then inherent in the situation itself is the implied inferiority of the black man."[37]

What is needed, then, is not "integration" but a sense of worth in being black, and only black people can teach that. Black consciousness is the key to the black man's emancipation from his distorted self-image.

As previously noted, some have called this racism in reverse. But this is merely a social myth, created by the white man to ease his guilt by accusing blacks of the same brutalities he has himself inflicted. The withdrawal of blacks is a necessary counterattack to overt, voluntary white racism. Furthermore, there is no way for blacks politically to enforce their attitudes, even if they were destructive of whites, but whites can and do enforce their attitudes upon blacks. Black identity is survival, while white racism is exploitation.

Black Power, then must say No to whites who invite them to share in their inhumanity toward black people. Instead, it must affirm the beauty of blackness and by so doing free the black man for a self-affirmation of his own being as a black man. Whites cannot teach this.

Is There an Appropriate Response to White Racism?

The asking of this question is inevitable. Whites want to know whether Black Power is an appropriate response to their bigotry. It is indeed interesting that they, the oppressors, should ask this question, since whatever response blacks make is nothing but a survival reaction to white oppression. It is time for whites to realize that the oppressor is in no position whatever to define the

14

proper response to enslavement. He is not the slave, but the enslaver. And if the slave should choose to risk death rather than submit to the humiliating orders of the master, then that is his right. Bigger Thomas in Richard Wright's *Native Son* demonstrates this choice when interrogated by white policemen who wanted him to confess raping a white girl:

> "Come on, now, boy. We've treated you pretty nice, but we can get tough if we have to, see? It's up to *you*! Get over there by the bed and show us how you raped and murdered that girl!"
> "I didn't rape her," Bigger said through stiff lips.
> "Aw, come on. What you got to lose now? Show us what you did."
> "I don't want to."
> "You *have* to!"
> "Well, we'll *make* you."
> "You can't make me do nothing but die!"[38]

You can't make me do nothing but die! That is key to an understanding of Black Power. Any advice from whites to blacks on how to deal with white oppression is automatically under suspicion as a clever device to further enslavement.

Furthermore, it is white intellectual arrogance which assumes that it has a monopoly on intelligence and moral judgment. How else can one explain the shocked indignation when the Kerner Report declared that race prejudice has shaped our history decisively. After all, Baldwin, Wright, Du Bois, and a host of other black writers had been saying for decades that racism is woven into the whole pattern of American society. Evidently the judgments of black people are not to be taken seriously (if, indeed, Whitey reads them at all).

The real menace in white intellectual arrogance is the dangerous assumption that the structure that enslaves is the structure that will also decide *when* and *how* this slavery ought to be abolished. The sociological and psychological reports, made by most white scholars, assume that they know more about *my* frustration, *my* despair, *my* hatred for white society than I do. They want to supply the prescriptions to my problems, refusing to recognize that for over three hundred years blacks have listened to them and their reports and we are still degraded. The time has come for white Americans to be silent and listen to black people. Why must the white man assume that he has the intellectual ability of the moral sensitivity to know what blacks feel or to ease the pain, to smooth the hurt, to eradicate the resentment? Since he knows that he raped our women, dehumanized our men, and made it inevitable that black children should hate their blackness, he ought to understand why blacks must cease listening to him in order to be free.

Since whites do not know the extent of black suffering, they can only speak from their own perspective, which they call "reason." This probably accounts for white appeals to nonviolence and Christian love. White people should not even expect blacks to love them, and to ask for it merely adds insult to injury. "For the white man," writes Malcolm X, "to ask the black man if he hates him is

15

just like the rapist asking the *raped* ... "Do you hate me?" The white man is in no moral position to accuse anyone else of hate." Whatever blacks feel toward whites or whatever their response to white racism, it cannot be submitted to the judgments of white society.

When a white man asks, "Is Black Power the answer?" or says, "It takes time," "Wait, let's talk it over and solve this problem together," "I feel the same way you do, but ... ," I must conclude that he is talking from a different perspective. There is no way in the world I can get him to see that he is the problem, not me. He has shaped my response. Bennett, then, is right when he states:

> We do not come up with the right answers to our problems because we seldom ask ourselves the right question. *There is no Negro problem in America; there has never been a Negro problem in America- the problem of race in America is a white problem.* To understand that problem and to control it, we must address ourselves to the fears and frailties of white people. We learn nothing really from a study of Harlem. To understand Harlem we must go not to Harlem but to the conscience of "good white people"; we must ask not what is Harlem but what have you made of Harlem? Why did you create it and why do you need it?[39]

Therefore, when blacks are confronted by whites who want to help with the "black problem" by giving advice on the appropriate response, whites should not be surprised if blacks respond, "We wish to plead our own cause. Too long have others spoken for us."[40] I am not prepared to talk seriously with a man who essentially says, "I sit on a man's back, choking him and making him carry me, and yet assure myself and others that I am very sorry for him and wish to lighten his load by all possible means- except by getting off his back."[41] Blacks must demand that whites get off their backs.

If whites do not get off the backs of blacks, they must expect that blacks will literally throw them off by whatever means are at their disposal. This is the meaning of Black Power. Depending on the response of whites, it means that emancipation may even have to take the form of outright rebellion. No one can really say what form the oppressed must take in relieving their oppression. But if blacks are pushed to the point of unendurable pain, with no option but a violent affirmation of their own being, then violence is to be expected. "Violence is a personal necessity for the oppressed," writes John Reilly in his analysis of Richard Wright's *Native Son*. "When life in a society consists of humiliation, one's only rescue is through rebellion. It is not a strategy consciously devised. It is the deep, instinctive expression of a human being denied individuality. ... Yet expression of the rebellion can be liberating."[42] Or again, as Bennett says: "The boundary of freedom is man's power to say 'No!' and whoever refuses to say 'No' involves himself tragically in his own degradation."[43] Black Power says No!

How Does Black Power Relate to White Guilt?

When white do-gooders are confronted with the style of Black Power, realizing that black people really place them in the same category with the George Wallaces, they react defensively, saying, "It's not my fault" or "I am not responsible." Sometimes they continue by suggesting that their town (because of their unselfish involvement in civil rights) is better or less racist than others.

There are two things to be said here. First, there are no degrees of human freedom or human dignity. Either a man respects another as a person or he does not. To be sure, there may be different manifestations of inhumanity, but that is beside the point. The major question is: Is the black man in white society a "Thou" or an "It?" Fanon puts it this way: "A given society is racist or it is not. ... Statements, for example, that the north of France is more racist than the south, that racism is the work of underlings and hence in no way involves the ruling class, that France is one of the less racist countries in the world are the product of men incapable of straight thinking."[44] Racism, then, biologically is analogous to pregnancy, either she is or she is not, or like the Christian doctrine of sin, one is or is not in sin. There are no meaningful "in betweens" relevant to the fact itself. And it should be said that racism is so embedded in the heart of American society that few, if any, whites can free themselves from it. So it is time for whites to recognize that fact for what it is and proceed from there. Who really can take it upon himself "to try to ascertain in what ways one kind of inhuman behavior differs from another,"[45] especially if one is a direct participant? "Is there in truth any difference between one racism and another? Do not all of them show the same collapse, the same bankruptcy of man?"[46]

Second, all white men are responsible for white oppression. It is much too easy to say, "Racism is not my fault," or "I am not responsible for the country's inhumanity to the black man." *The American white man has always had an easy conscience.* But insofar as white do-gooders tolerate and sponsor racism in their educational institutions, their political, economic, and social structures, their churches, and in every other aspect of American life, they are directly responsible for racism. "It is a cold, hard fact that the many flagrant forms of racial injustice North and South could not exist without their [whites'] acquiescence,"[47] and for that, they are responsible. If whites are honest in their analysis of the moral state of this society, they know that all are responsible. Racism is possible because whites are indifferent to suffering and patient with cruelty. Karl Jasper's description of metaphysical guilt is pertinent here.

> There exists among men, because they are men, a solidarity through which each shares responsibility for every injustice and every wrong committed in the world, and *especially for crimes that are committed in his presence or of which he cannot be ignorant.* If I do not do whatever I can to prevent them, I am an accomplice in them. If I have not risked my life in order to prevent the murder of other men, if I have stood silent, I feel guilty in a sense that cannot in any adequate fashion be understood juridically, or politically, or morally. ... That I am still alive after such things have been done weighs on me as a guilt that cannot be expiated.[48]

In contrast, injustice anywhere strikes a sensitive note in the souls of black folk, because they know what it means to be treated as a thing. That is why Fanon says, "Anti-Semitism hits me head-on: I am enraged, I am bled white by an appalling battle, I am deprived of the possibility of being a man. I cannot disassociate myself from the future that is proposed for my brother."[49] Yes, when blacks in Chicago hear about blacks being lynched in Mississippi, they are enraged. When they heard about Martin Luther King's death, they burned, they looted, they got Whitey. In fact, when blacks hear about any injustice, whether it is committed against black or white, blacks know that their existence is being stripped of its meaning. Aimé Césaire, a black poet, put it this way:

> When I turn on my radio, when I hear that Negroes have been lynched in America, I say that we have been lied to: Hitler is not dead; when I turn on my radio, when I learn that Jews have been insulted, mistreated, persecuted, I say that we have been lied to: Hitler is not dead; when, finally I turn on my radio and hear that in Africa forced labor has been inaugurated and legalized, I say that we have been lied to: Hitler is not dead.[50]

White America's attempt to free itself of responsibility for the black man's inhuman condition is nothing but a protective device to ease her guilt. Whites have to convince themselves that they are not responsible. That is why social scientists prefer to remain detached in their investigations of racial injustice. It is less painful to be uninvolved. White Americans do not dare to know that blacks are beaten at will by policemen as a means of protecting the latter's ego superiority as well as that of the larger white middle class. For to know is to be responsible. To know is to understand why blacks loot and riot at what seems slight provocation. Therefore, they must have reports to explain the disenchantment of blacks with white democracy, so they can be surprised. They must believe that blacks are in poverty because they are lazy or because they are inferior. Yes, they must believe that everything is basically all right. Black Power punctures those fragile lies, declaring to white America the pitiless indictment of Francis Jeanson: "If you succeed in keeping yourself unsullied, it is because others dirty themselves in your place. *You hire thugs*, and, balancing the accounts, it is you who are the real criminals: for without you, without your blind indifference, such men could never carry out deeds that damn you as much as they shame those men."[51]

Black Power and the White Liberal

In time of war, men want to know who the enemy is. Who is for me and who is against me? That is the question. The asserting of black freedom in America has always meant war. When blacks retreat and accept their dehumanized place in white society, the conflict ceases. But when blacks rise up in freedom, whites show their racism.

In reality, then, *accommodation* or *protest* seems to be the only option open to the black man. For three hundred years he accommodated, thereby giving credence to his own enslavement. Black Power means that he will no longer accommodate; that he will no longer tolerate white excuses for enslavement; that he will no longer be guided by the oppressor's understanding of justice, liberty, freedom, or the methods to be used in attaining them. He recognizes the difference between theoretical equality and great factual inequalities. He will not sit by and wait for the white man's love to be extended to his black brother. He will protest, violently if need be, on behalf of absolute and immediate emancipation. Black Power means that black people will cease trying to articulate rationally the political advantages and moral rightness of human freedom, since the dignity of man is a self-evident religious, philosophical, and political *truth*, without which human community is impossible. When one group breaks the covenant of truth and assumes an exclusive role in defining the basis of human relationship, that group plants the seed of rebellion. Black Power means that blacks are prepared to accept the challenge and with it the necessity of distinguishing friends from enemies.

It is in this situation that the liberal white is caught. We have alluded to him earlier, but now we intend to take a closer look at his "involvement" in this war for freedom. To be sure, as Loren Miller says, "there are liberals and liberals, ranging from Left to Right." But there are certain characteristics identifiable in terms of attitudes and beliefs.

> Simply stated, [liberalism] contemplates the ultimate elimination of all racial distinctions in every phase of American life through an orderly, step-by-step process adjusted to resistance and aimed at overcoming such resistance. In the field of constitutional law, the classic liberal position, exemplified in the Supreme Court's "all deliberate speed" formula of school-segregation cases, requires and rationalizes Negro accommodation to, and acquiescence in, disabilities imposed because of race and in violation of the fundamental law.[52]

The liberal, then, is one who sees "both sides" of the issue and shies away from "extremism" in any form. He wants to change the heart of the racist without ceasing to be his friend; he wants progress without conflict. Therefore, when he sees blacks engaging in civil disobedience and demanding "Freedom Now," he is disturbed. Black people know who the enemy is, and they are forcing the liberal to take sides. But the liberal wants to be a friend, that is, enjoy the rights and privileges pertaining to whiteness and also work for the "Negro." He wants change without risk, victory without blood.

The liberal white man is a strange creature; he verbalizes the right things. He intellectualizes on the racial problem beautifully. He roundly denounces racists, conservatives, and the moderately liberal. Sometimes, in rare moments and behind closed doors, he will even go so far as to make the statement: "I will let my daughter marry one," and this is supposed to be the absolute evidence that he is raceless.

But he is still white to the very core of his being. What he fails to realize is that there is no place for him in this war of survival. Blacks do not want his patronizing, condescending words of sympathy. They do not need his concern, his "love," his money. It is that which dehumanizes; it is that which enslaves. Freedom is what happens to a man on the inside; it is what happens to a man's being. It has nothing to do with voting, marching, picketing, or rioting- though all may be manifestations of it. No man can give me freedom or "help" me get it. A man is free when he can determine the style of his existence in an absurd world; a man is free when he sees himself for what he is and not as others define him. He is free when he determines the limits of his existence. And in this sense Sartre is right: "Man is freedom;" or, better yet, man "is condemned to be free." A man is free when he accepts the responsibility for his own acts and knows that they involve not merely himself but all men. No one can "give" or "help get" freedom in that sense.

In this picture the liberal can find no place. His favorite question when backed against the wall is "What can I do?" One is tempted to reply, as Malcolm X did to the white girl who asked the same question, "Nothing." What the liberal really means is, "What can I do and still receive the same privileges as other whites *and*- this is the key- be liked by Negroes?" Indeed the only answer is "Nothing." However, there are places in the Black Power picture for "radicals," that is, for men, white or black, who are prepared to risk life for freedom. There are places for the John Browns, men who hate evil and refuse to tolerate it anywhere.[53]

Black Power: Hope or Despair?

White racism is a disease. No excuse can be made for it; we blacks can only oppose it with every ounce of humanity we have. When black children die of rat bites, and black men suffer because meaning has been sapped from their existence, and black women weep because family stability is gone, how can anyone appeal to "reason?" Human life is at stake. In this regard black people are no different from other people. Men fight back, they grab for the last thread of hope. Black Power then is an expression of hope, not hope that whites will change the structure of oppression, but hope in the humanity of black people. If there is any expression of despair in Black Power, it is despair regarding white intentions, white promises to change the oppressive structure. Black people now know that freedom is not a gift from white society, but is, rather, the self-affirmation of one's existence as a person, a person with certain innate rights to say No and Yes, despite the consequences.

It is difficult for men who have not known suffering to understand this experience. That is why many concerned persons point out the futility of black rebellion by drawing a contrast between the present conditions of blacks in the ghetto and the circumstances of other revolutionaries in the past. The argument of these people runs like this: Revolutions depend on cohesion, discipline, stability, and the sense of a stake in society. The ghetto, by contrast, is relatively incohesive, unorganized, unstable, and numerically too small to be effective. Therefore, rebellion for the black man can only mean extermination,

20

genocide. Moreover, fact one is that many poor blacks, being poor so long, have become accustomed to slavery, feeling any form of black rebellion is useless. And fact two, that the black bourgeoisie, having tasted the richness of white society, do not want to jeopardize their place in the structure.

This analysis is essentially correct. But to point out the futility of black rebellion is to miss the point. Black people know that they comprise less than 12 per cent of the total American population and are proportionately much weaker with respect to economic, political, and military power. And black radicals know that they represent a minority within the black community. But having tasted freedom through an identification with God's intention for humanity, they will stop at nothing in expressing their distaste for white power. To be sure, they may be the minority in the black community but truth, despite democracy, can be measured by numbers. Truth is that which places a man in touch with the real; and once a man finds it, he is prepared to give all for it. The rebellion in the cities, then, is not a conscious organized attempt of black people to take over; it is an attempt to say Yes to truth and No to untruth even in death. The question, then, is not whether black people are prepare to die- the riots testify to that- but whether whites are prepared to kill them. Unfortunately, it seems that that answer has been given through the riots as well. But this willingness to die for human dignity is not novel. Indeed, it stands at the heart of Christianity.

NOTES

1. Richard Wright used the term as early as 1954 in reference to Africa.
2. Camus, *the Rebel*, trans. Anthony Bower (New York: Random House, 1956), p. 13.
3. *Ibid.*
4. *Ibid.*, p. 15. Emphasis added.
5. Most Black Power advocates have dropped the slogan because of its misuse by white liberals.
6. Camus, *The Rebel*, p. 16.
7. Quoted in Floyd B. Barbour (ed.), *The Black Power Revolt* (Boston: Porter Sargent, 1968), p.39.
8. Tillich, *The Courage to Be* (New Haven: Yale University Press, 1952), p. 3.
9. The word "other," which designates the neighbor, occurs frequently in Franz Fanon, *Black Skins, White Masks*, trans. C. L. Markmann (New York: Grove Press, 1967).
10. Tillich, *The Courage to Be*, p. 66.
11. *Ibid.*
12. Rollo May, *Psychology and the Human Dilemma* (Princeton: Van Nostrand, 1967), p. 73.
13. *Ibid.*
14. Fanon, *Black Skins*, p. 216.
15. *Ibid.*, p. 218.
16. *Ibid.*, p. 131.

17. *Ibid.*
18. *Ibid.*, p. 229.
19. W. R. Mueller and J. Jacobsen, "Samuel Beckett's Long Last Saturday: To Wait or Not to Wait" in Nathan Scott, Jr., *Man in Modern Theatre* (Richmond, Va.: John Knox Press, 1965), p. 77.
20. Quoted in L. H. Fischel, Jr., and Benjamin Quarles, *The Negro American* (Glenview, Ill.: Scott, Foresman and Co., 1967), pp. 204-205. Emphasis added.
21. "Reply to Horace Greeley," 1862, in *The American Tradition in Literature*, Vol. I; revised, S. Bradley, R. C. Beatty, and E. H. Long, eds. (New York: W. W. Norton, 1962), p. 1567.
22. Quoted in Charles Silberman, *Crisis in Black and White* (New York: Random House, 1964), pp. 92-93.
23. See John H. Franklin and Isadore Starr (eds.), *The Negro in Twentieth Century America* (New York: Random House, 1967), pp. 45-46. Here is an analysis by six American historians of how most scholars give a "white" twist to history.
24. A fuller discussion of Christianity and Black Power is found in the next chapter.
25. It should be pointed out here that another alternative for black people is to submit to the white view of blacks. The problem of self-hatred is discussed in this chapter under the heading, "Why Integration Is Not the Answer."
26. Camus, *The Rebel*, p.17.
27. *Ibid.*, p. 23.
28. Silberman, *Crisis in Black and White*, p.54.
29. Quoted in Lerone Bennett, *The Negro Mood* (New York: Ballentine Books, 1964), pp. 145-146.
30. James Baldwin, *The Fire Next Time* (New York: The Dial Press, 1963). Used with permission. Quotation is from the Dell paperback, pp. 94-95.
31. Stokely Carmichael and Charles Hamilton, *Black Power: The Politics of Liberation in America* (New York: Random House, 1967), p. 47.
32. In its crudest sense, it means black men want their women. Some psychologists have suggested that every inhuman act of white men toward black men is in part an act of sexual revenge. See Fanon, *Black Skins*.
33. Alvin Poussaint, "The Negro American: His Self-Image and Integration" in Barbour, *The Black Power Revolt*, p. 94.
34. *Ibid.*, p.96.
35. Fanon, Poussaint, and others agree.
36. Poussaint, in Barbour, *The Black Power Revolt*, p. 95.
37. *Ibid.* p. 99.
38. Wright, *Native Son* (New York: Harper & Row, 1966 ed.), pp. 311-312.
39. Lerone Bennett, *Confrontation: Black and White* (Baltimore: Penguin Books, 1966), pp. 254-255. Used with permission of Johnson Publishing Co., Chicago, the original publishers (copyright © 1965).
40. "Freedom's Journal," March, 1827, quoted in Silberman, *Crisis in Black and White*, p. 189.
41. Leo Tolstoy, quoted in *ibid.*, p.224.
42. Wright, *Native Son*, p. 395.
43. Bennett, *Confrontation*, p. 256.
44. Fanon, *Black Skins*, p. 85.
45. *Ibid.*, p.86.
46. *Ibid.*
47. Clark, *Dark Ghetto*, p. 229.

48. Quoted in Fanon, *Black Skins* (Copyright © 1967 by Grove Press), p. 89. Emphasis added. Used with permission.
49. *Ibid.*, pp. 88-89.
50. Quoted in *ibid.*, p. 90. Used with permission.
51. Quoted in *ibid.*, pp. 91-92.
52. Quoted in Francis L. Broderick and August Meier, *Negro Protest Thought in the Twentieth Century* (New York: Bobbs-Merill Co., 1965), p. 334.
53. For an analysis of John Brown by black writers, see W.E.B. DuBois, *John Brown* (New York: International Publishers, 1962); Bennett, *Confrontation* and *Negro Mood*.

24

Chapter 3

In the Absence of Ideology: Blacks in Colonial America and the Modern Black Experience

By Rhett S. Jones

In the Absence of Ideology:
Blacks in Colonial America and the Modern Black Experience

Despite the vast expansion in knowledge of black folk which came about as a result of the Black studies movement in the latter part of the 1960s, one part of Afro-American history remains comparatively understudied. While there are many works on nineteenth century Blacks and libraries are full of books on African Americans in the twentieth century, the colonial era remains comparatively understudied. Of course, a number of important works on this period have been published. 1978, the *William and Mary Quarterly*, regarded by most in the field as the premier scholarly journal on colonial America, published a special edition titled *Blacks in Early America*, which included essays not only on persons of African descent in the thirteen colonies, but in the West Indies as well.[1] The late Hoyt Fuller, while editor of *Black World*, also occasionally published articles on the Black experience in the colonial period.[2] Book-length works by Lorenzo Greene, Winthrop Jordan, A. Leon Higginbotham, and Peter Wood have contributed to understanding of the meaning of race in the Early American era.[3] Yet the period remains understudied as compared to more recent ones in Afro-American history. This is unfortunate for it was during this era that white Americans were reaching decisions about race, Africans, and race relations which were to have far reaching consequences first for Americans and later for the entire world. Black Americans were also working out issues of race at this time.

By the time of the Revolution, the vast majority of Blacks living in the thirteen colonies were the *grand-children* of black folk who had been born in North America. The Afro-American culture in the United States is therefore an old one and stands in sharp contrast to that of many "ethnic" American. The ancestors of most Irish Americans living in America did not come in large numbers until the nineteenth century, and those of most Italo-Americans until the twentieth. The North American Black experience also significantly differs from that of black peoples in Brazil and the Caribbean, where Africans continued to arrive in large numbers until well into the nineteenth century.[4] When compared to Brazil, the Caribbean, and some Spanish colonies on the mainland of South America, comparatively few Africans were transported to North America after the middle of the eighteenth century with the result that Blacks in the thirteen colonies began to carve out a culture of their own related to and yet distinct from that of Africa. The colonial era is an important one, not only for itself but for what it can contribute to an understanding of the problems which presently plague African Americans. This paper compares the different experiences of whites and Blacks during the colonial period – stretching roughly from 1619 (the date commonly given for the arrival of Africans in British North America) to 1783 (the formal acknowledgement of American independence) – and then examines the consequences of these experiences for black folk.

However, before turning to a systematic comparison of the experiences of white folk and Black in the thirteen colonies, some preliminary definitions are necessary. One way of viewing society is to divide it into three distinct, though related, levels. At the most abstract level are what sociologists call values, things which the society in question agrees are good, right, and proper. Things, in short, worth striving for. Some contemporary United States values are democracy, love, success, happiness – concepts with which few in the society would quarrel, and all would agree are important. Values, however, as these examples suggest, are by their very nature abstract, so that every society also has norms, rules which spell out how persons ought to behave in order to achieve the values. In the United States today in order to achieve democracy one *ought* to vote, and in order to achieve success one *ought* to work hard. At the lowest level of abstraction are social actions a term meant to refer to what people in a given society actually do, as distinct from what they ought to do in order to realize the values. For example, in the contemporary United States people may know they ought to work hard to become successful, but instead gamble or steal. While conceptually distinct from one another values, norms, and social actions are closely related.[5] For example, in the United States at the dawn of the twentieth century there was widespread agreement that in order to achieve the values associated with womanhood a married woman with children, *ought* not to go to work outside the home. Despite this widely agreed upon norm, over the course of the twentieth century millions of American women – for varied reasons – took jobs outside the home. Gradually their social actions had an impact on both the normative and the value level so that as the twentieth century draws to a close Americans no longer condemn a women who works outside the home.

Fusing Ideology and Reality: The White Experience in America

European migrants to North America arrived with a set of expectations about the New World which were grounded in Old World values, norms, and social actions, but found America very different from Europe. In their attempts to create an environment in which they could live the migrants had to resolve, in turn, five related problems. The first and most pressing set of issues confronted by the migrants was that posed by the strange and unfamiliar American environment itself. The colonists had no idea what American fruits and vegetables could be eaten, what they could expect of the climate, what materials were available for construction, or what resources might be used to make clothing. Throughout North America the colonists' first and most pressing need was to come to grips with the physical environment in which they were living. The settlers had to learn, often by trial and error, which European plants could be made to grow in the New World, and which European animals could thrive on this side of the Atlantic. There is widespread agreement among scholars that many migrants would not have survived without assistance from Native Americans. In the Caribbean, African slaves often helped the colonists to adjust to a tropical environment.[6] Throughout the hemisphere the colonists had to literally create a new physical world by constructing buildings, clearing land, laying out roads and creating shelter for their animals. They also had to adjust themselves to an existing ecosystem. Once they had mastered the physical environment, the settlers' next problem was mastery of one another. Or put in a slightly different way, they had to construct orderly societies, working social orders in which persons could live and have reasonable expectations as to what would happen to them in both the proximate and distant future.

There were two basic threats to order in colonial societies, one external, the other internal. External threats came from Native Americans and from the ongoing struggles for dominance of the New World by imperial powers themselves. Spain, Portugal, France, England, Holland, and Russia to say nothing of such minor powers as Denmark, Scotland, Sweden, and assorted German states struggled for control of one part of New World territory or another. The settlers also had to deal with rapidly shifting alliances. Holland and England, for example, might be allies at one time, and enemies at another.[7] The other external threat to the orderly working of colonial societies was that of Native Americans. Amerindian tribes differed of course, in size, sophistication, and their capacity to effectively respond to the threat posed by the Europeans.

As the Indians had no natural defenses against the diseases carried by Africans and Europeans, entire tribes were virtually eliminated. Among the coastal tribes of North America the death rate as the result of disease was not infrequently as high as eighty percent. Neither red folk nor white could explain why so many Indians died, but both were struck by the fact that whites moved immune through Native American communities while Indians died all about them. Indian beliefs were undercut because many of their traditional remedies for illness did not work. For example, gathering together family and friends around a sick person for community prayer only facilitated the spread of disease. While the Indians were disheartened, Europeans took the high death rate among Native Americans as proof of the fact that whites were indeed the favored of God and destined by him to rule over the entire New World. As Amerindian societies literally fell apart under the impact of the death rate many Indians became de-tribalized, disorganized, and confused presenting, yet, another problem to settlers who were attempting to construct working, predictable societies.[8] In addition to the external threats posed by Native Americans and other European powers, the English settlers in North America also had to cope with various internal threats. Few Englishmen had experience with multi-racial, multi-ethnic, multi-religious societies and, yet, many colonies consisted of Indians, Africans, Europeans of various nationalities, and persons holding a wide range of religious views. With the exception of England's larger cities most Britons lived in homogenous communities in which each person was much like each other and shared a common perspective on religious, economic, political and family issues. But in the American settlements migrants frequently lived alongside persons who had quite different values, norms, and patterns of behavior. While attempts were made in some colonies to enforce common religious orthodoxy, all the settlements were eventually characterized by religious diversity. Even Puritan Massachusetts and Pilgrim Plymouth grudgingly accepted a wide range of Protestants, to say nothing of Catholics and Jews. Similarly, most of the new communities included a variety of persons from diverse ethnic backgrounds. While the English colonies were part of the British empire they included large numbers of persons from Holland, Sweden, France, the Germanies, and other parts of Europe. Many of the settlements were also racially diverse as they included Indians, Africans, and Afro-American as well as mestizos, mulattos, zambos, and other persons of mixed racial ancestry.

Mastering these internal and external threats was not easy, particularly as most of the white migrants had fewer restrictions on their behavior than they had known back in England where their actions were circumscribed by church, by powerful ruling classes accustomed to rule, and by their own ingrained patterns of deference. But as Morgan and Frederickson make clear in writing of the New World, freed from many of these restraints the lower classes became especially troublesome.[9] In one sense problems around the issue of social control were never completely solved with some of them leading directly to the American Revolution. But in another sense the settlers were able to produce societies which were both orderly and predictable.

Having worked out ways of coping with the physical environment, one another, and the strange peoples they were both encountering and producing, the migrants next sought to persuade one another that these solutions were correct. In this they moved not only from the social level to the cultural level, out from the level of social actions to norms as they convinced one another that the things they had done were just and what they *ought* to have done. As Tannenbaum and Hoetink have demonstrated in quite different ways, compared to the Iberians the English had little contact with Africans, and so had no firm opinions on the meaning of Africanity.[10] But in North America they found Black labor not only useful but essential and so, very early, worked out a normative consensus as to how they ought to treat Blacks. Unfortunately for Africans and their Afro-American children, the colonists agreed that slaves should be cruelly handled in order to make them effective workers. The level of cruelty to which slaves were subjected has unfortunately been neglected by many recent students of the peculiar institution.[11] At the cultural level the settlers succeeded in convincing one another that the solutions they had worked out to problems of social order were correct.

The next step was among the most difficult of all undertaken by the colonists. Having mastered a series of problems at the physical, social, and cultural level they now had to persuade both their children and more recent arrivals from Europe to accept their solutions to these problems. This required the resolution of problems at the psychological level. In socializing their Euro-American children the migrants had the usual advantage that adults have over infants – these young people know no other way of life. The colonists were, therefore, successful in convincing their offspring that those born in America were different from, and superior to, those born in Europe. Or put in a slightly different way, the migrants successfully inculcated in their children a sense of American identity. The emergent American sense of self incorporated the solutions already worked out by the migrants to American environmental, social, and cultural problems. For example in the minds of most white Americans, Amerindians had failed to make good economic use of the lands on which they lived, were a threat to Anglo-American civilization and hence were a degenerate inferior group fit only to be pushed aside into separate enclaves, when they were allowed to live at all.[12] In addition to creating American children distinct from their European counterparts, the migrants persuaded most Europeans —even those who arrived as adults – to accept the differences between the two. To a remarkable extent, new immigrants accepted the American perspective on self. To be sure, they sometimes made minor modifications in this creole self-conception as when Catholics insisted on maintaining their religion in a protestant milieu, or when Germans attempted to keep their language while most around them spoke English. But, in general, the colonists succeeded in convincing both their own children and newcomers from Europe to become Americans, to become in effect a self-conscious distinctly different people. Once this consciousness of self had been achieved, and Anglo-Americans had come to believe they were different from the English, the next step, the resolution of issues at the political level, was virtually inevitable. White Americans, conscious of the separate behavioral, normative and value system they had created, sought political expression of this sense of difference. They concluded that as they were different from Britons, Great Britain had no right to rule over the thirteen colonies. They justified their break from England on the grounds that the government of Great Britain had no real understanding of America. As a consequence, they argued, the English government repeatedly blundered, placing the lives (and fortunes) of Anglo-Americans at risk. Moreover, it was the freedom the colonists had enjoyed and built into their own institutions, which enabled them to create solutions to their many problems. Constrained by Old World authoritative traditions, the English government was unable to freely respond to the many difficulties of the New World. In recognition of the limitations inherent in the English system, Anglo-Americans had no alternative but to establish independent governments of their own.

Of course, not all English settlers and their children accepted this argument and even in places where others did, they were not in a position to act on their beliefs.[13] Two observations need to be made on the migrants' successful handling of the various physical, social, cultural, psychological, and political issues which presented themselves in the colonial period. First, the settlers correctly perceived that their independence from English authority was a factor in their successful resolutions of problems. Settler solutions worked because they had sufficient autonomy to resolve issues on their own. Second, settlers seized eagerly on the values of the Enlightenment because it validated their own experience. As the migrants and the creole children saw it, Enlightenment theory claimed that free men were able to achieve more than those oppressed by tyrannical authority. In general, the European experience in North America had been one of freedom as compared to Europeans who remained at home as by migrating they had attained a significant degree of autonomy and independence. Whites had achieved much with this freedom and it was not, therefore, surprising that they eagerly embraced the ideology which legitimated it.

Using the Ideology of the Other: The Black Experience in America

The Black experience, however, was just the reverse. In most traditional West African societies – that is societies which operated independent of Islam and Christianity – men and women had a say in their governance. West Africans usually chose their leaders, could recall them under certain circumstances, and enjoyed community support in the expression of political views.[14] While the American colonial experience increased the political rights enjoyed by most whites the slave experience in the colonial Americas *decreased* the political rights of Blacks. While there is some debate among scholars over whether or not Africans and Afro-Americans were set apart from and discriminated against by the white population in the early part of the seventeenth century, there seems to be little doubt that slavery itself had become racially based a century later. In general slaves had no rights, and following American independence even free Blacks found their liberties in jeopardy. In sum, one race gained politically during the American colonial period, the other lost. Africans faced the same problems the migrants confronted as they had to master the environment, master one another, legitimate their solutions to these two issues, inculcate this legitimation into the minds of their children and new arrivals, and finally create an independent nation which would politically embody the solutions they had worked out. Because of slavery, however, neither Africans nor Afro-Americans were able to advance much beyond mastery of the environment. Slaves contributed much to the adjustment of whites and Blacks to the strange and unfamiliar American ecosystem. This was particularly true about the preservation and storage of food, the choice of clothing and the construction of dwellings were eagerly received by the migrants.[15] The Africans also served as useful-go-betweens in the contacts between Native Americans and colonists.[16] And they were often willing warriors in alliance with the English against Native Americans and against the other colonizing powers.[17]

But while Blacks were able to master the environment for the benefit of themselves and their owners, they were never able to master one another. The slaves were never able to construct orderly, working Black societies which would serve the Black folk who lived within them. The slave community was controlled not by the Blacks who lived in it, but by their owners. By virtue of their enslavement Blacks not only lost control over their own bodies, but over their communities as well. Slavery deprived Africans of the freedom they had known in traditional West Africa and made it impossible for them to construct working social orders which were responsive to the needs of Blacks. The many excellent studies of the slave community which appeared – as a part of the Black studies movement – over the course of the 1970s were important in that they demonstrated that despite the cruelties of slavery Blacks were able to achieve a great deal. These achievements, however, have been exaggerated. It is true, for example, as Levine has demonstrated, that Afro-Americans were able to forge a culture independent of that of white folk.[18] Gutman correctly demonstrates that Blacks were able to maintain a sense of family throughout the colonial era and beyond, and Raboteau provides a useful overview of the many autonomous Black religious traditions.[19] The many studies of the slave community itself, though for the most part focused in post-colonial nineteenth century slavery, clearly demonstrates the existence of an Afro-American culture. Africans and their Afro-American children accomplished much despite the brutalities of slavery. Yet in writing of slavery, Willie Lee Rose has argued, "Some historians have tried to have it both ways, describing a totally dehumanizing institution that dehumanized nobody."[20] Since the 1970s most scholars have continued to insist on the horrors of slavery – while publishing few works on its many cruelties[21] – but at the same time have cited the rich Afro-American culture as proof of the fact that Blacks triumphed over it. But Black folk were not the victors, they were the vanquished. Winthrop Jordan has written that it would surprise the migrants to learn their descendents spoke knowingly of the contended slave.[22] It would also doubtless surprise the slaves to learn their descendents spoke knowingly of the wondrous community bondsmen created. Blacks never gained control over their own communities. Lacking the freedoms the migrants enjoyed in North America, and deprived of the freedoms their ancestors had enjoyed in West Africa Blacks in North America were unable to create a social order able to celebrate Black achievement.

Put in a slightly different way, those who lived in the slave quarters were not able to sustain normative agreement on how they ought to behave. Bondsmen were able to create norms which reflected how they ought to treat one another, their children, Native Americans, and whites, but for two reasons were unable to maintain a permanent normative structure. The first reason was what Carmichael and Hamilton termed, some years ago, "white power."[23] The slave holder and his supporters penetrated the quarters at will and prevented bondsmen from continuing any kind of normative agreement which would have benefited the slave community as a whole. When the slave owner was not himself physically present to prevent slaves from behaving in ways calculated to serve their interest, he used Black spies. Most slave revolts failed because they were betrayed by a spy slave. The second reason slaves were unable to maintain agreement on how they ought to behave had to do with their inability to *publicly* celebrate individuals who contributed to their community or *publicly* discipline those who had injured it. In Carmichael and Hamilton's terms, this inability was a lack of "black power."[24] To be sure slaves were able to sometimes deceive the masters and his spies, and they were able to construct a world of their own "between sundown and sunup" as Rawick has titles his memorable work.[25] But their underground culture, their successful puttin' on of ole massa[26] was no substitute for an organized, disciplined society in which Black people could hold one another accountable for their behavior toward one another. In contrast, the migrants were able to publicly come together to honor those who had contributed to their communities and to punish those who worked against them. The ability of the settlers to assemble in public places to affirm the decisions they had made in mastering the environment and one another played no small role in their ability to create a culture self-declared to be better than that of Europe. The many ceremonies in which the migrant celebrated their culture and themselves, in turn, made it possible for them to declare independence and to fight war to achieve it. The slaves were never able to advance beyond mastery of the environment as unlike whites, *Blacks were unable to discipline one another for the good of the community.* Because they could not control the places in which they lived the slaves were unable (at the cultural level) to legitimate their lifestyles, nor able to then inculcate (at the psychological level) their children with a sense of achievement and pride in what Blacks had accomplished.[27] In the absence of such a sense of achievement political acknowledgement of blackness was beyond Afro-Americans. In other words, having failed to agree at the normative level there was little chance that Africans and their Afro-American offspring would be able to create a value system which could reflect the ways in which the Black experience differed from the white one in British North America.

Unable to carve out an ideology which would reflect their experience, Black Americans did the next best thing – they borrowed the ideology of white Americans. The post colonial history of Afro-Americans demonstrates that they were enormously successful in turning the Enlightenment ideology the colonists had used to justify their independence from England against Euro-Americans themselves. David Walker is perhaps the best known of the early nineteenth century political agitators having asked rhetorically of Euro-Americans, "Now, Americans! I ask you candidly, was your suffering under Great Britain, one hundredth part as cruel and tyrannical as you have rendered ours under you?"[28] But Walker was not alone among Afro-Americans in finding white Americans guilty of failing to measure up to their own values. In a July 4, 1852 speech aimed at Euro-Americans, Frederick Douglass said to those celebrating freedom while continuing slavery

> Your celebration is a sham; your boasted liberty, an unholy license; your national greatness, swelling vanity; your sounds of rejoicing are empty and heartless...a thin veil to cover up crimes which would disgrace a nation of savages.[29]

As these writings by Walker and Douglass demonstrate, Black Americans were successful in using Enlightenment beliefs against whites. If the country, Blacks argued, rested on the ideological basis that all men were equal and therefore entitled to freedom, liberty and justice, then America was false to

32

herself in denying Black rights routinely given whites. Lacking an ideology of their own, Blacks used the ideology of Euro-Americans against whites.[30]

Preventing the Growth of Afro-American Ideology: Two Public Fictions

In the years between the Revolutionary War and the Civil War, white folk faced a cruel dilemma. On the one hand they wished to present the nation to the world and to themselves as a democratic, egalitarian republic in which every man had equal opportunity. But on the other hand millions of them wished to continue slavery, and even those who did not seldom regarded the Black man as a social and political equal. In order to escape this dilemma, whites created a *public fiction* to the effect that all Black people were inferior physically, intellectually, culturally, and morally to all white people. By public fiction, it is meant here as the collective, civic acceptance and promulgation of something individual members of the society know and privately concede to be untrue. Slaveholders, who pushed most strongly for the public fiction of Black inferiority, knew very well it was not true. As the works of Blassingame, Fogel and Engerman, Genovese, and Miller make clear, masters did not treat their slaves as if they were all the same – stupid, docile, immoral brutes they publicly proclaimed them to be.[31] Instead, almost without exception, slave-owners drew careful distinctions among slaves, recognizing which were intelligent, strong, rebellious, and which were not. To have operated a plantation as though all its resident bondsmen were the grinning simpletons of the public fiction would have led to disaster. According to this white public fiction, because Blacks were inferior they could not be permitted free access to the economic marketplace, nor could they be given civil rights. As property restrictions on the franchise were gradually eliminated, whites agreed every white man was entitled to vote simply because he was white, and every black man could not simply because he was black. Of course, Euro-Americans were not fools they knew of black men who were morally superior to some white men, but they did not publicly acknowledge this reality. Indeed, white Southerners continue to insist on Black inferiority and to deny Blacks the vote even in the second half of the twentieth century. Faced with this white public fiction, Blacks had no choice but to construct one of their own. Since the colonial era the Black public fiction has been that Blacks are just like whites, and therefore, entitled to the same rights and privileges. But while most Blacks have publicly pushed for political equality with whites, few have believed that Blacks and whites are alike for the simple reason that their experiences have been so very different. Most whites who migrated to British North America came voluntarily, and by leaving the Old World gained a degree of freedom most of them had not known in Europe. Most Blacks were forcibly transported in the chains of slavery and on their departure from the Old World lost a freedom few of them were to know in America. Unlike whites, Blacks did not gain in the thirteen colonies experience in administering their own communities for the benefit of themselves and their children, but instead lived in communities which were administered, operated and controlled by slaveholders for the benefit of themselves and their children. Blacks lacked the freedom to experiment in government as did whites and to, thereby, learn first hand the patterns of cooperative responsibility necessary to successfully construct and maintain orderly communities. Afro-Americans had to be satisfied with hidden informal methods of social control. While whites were creating and celebrating white heroes, Blacks had to content themselves with feeble little tales about the doings of rabbits.[32] Yet, Black people have clung to their public fiction that they are like white people and, therefore, entitled to the same political status as whites, as stubbornly as whites have clung to their public fiction that all Blacks are inferior to all whites. Neither public fiction has any basis in reality, but because whites have had power in the United States they have been able to force Blacks to behave as simpletons and to terrorize them into accepting a situation in which Black folk accepted second class citizenship. Blacks, on the other hand, were not able to compel whites to accept their public fiction that Blacks were just like whites. At best they were able to make some whites feel guilty about their treatment of Blacks. In his now classic study, *An American Dilemma*, sociologist Gunnar Myrdal argued that white Americans found themselves caught in a dilemma between their democratic ideas and their treatment of Blacks.[33]

Blacks are different than whites. Their experience from the colonial era on has been different from that of whites, and the strategies they have devised to deal with slavery and racism have no counterparts in the Euro-American community.[34] Regardless of how much Blacks insist on their essential similarity to whites their own history has produced an Afro-American culture distinct from its Euro-American counterpart. As Blacks and whites occupy different positions, America's system of social stratification tends to reinforce the cultural differences between them. Most Blacks are members of the working class, with only a few of them having made their way into the middle classes, while the middle classes are almost exclusively populated by Euro-Americans.[35]

For Blacks the central problem remains their inability to construct an ideological structure which will reflect their experiences in North America, just as the Enlightenment ideology developed by whites reflects their experience in the New World. Black people have creatively adapted and pragmatically applied this white ideology. By using it Jim Crow has been destroyed, millions of Blacks have gained access to the franchise, and affirmative action programs have been established in a variety of institutions. Yet this ideology, reflective as it is of white realities, white aspirations, and white achievements cannot be an organic part of Afro-American experience. Black culture is distinct and different from that of whites but has, as yet, no ideology of its own. The failure of Blacks in the colonial period to build an ideology expressive of their experience has grave consequences for twentieth century Black Americans. So long as Blacks in the United States were able to use the white ideology of the Enlightenment and the public fiction that whites and Blacks were identical, Black failure to develop an ideology of their own went unnoticed save by a few intellectuals. Cruse, for example, called attention to absence of such an ideology, while Carmichael and Hamilton sought to build one on their own independent of and separate from the Black people it sought to serve.[36] Their Black power constructs failed as such ideas have to emerge naturally from the cultural history of a people, they cannot simply be grafted on by intellectuals. In a widely acclaimed work anthropologist John Gwaltney found in a northern ghetto strong, positive, Black folk, people who were both intellectually insightful and morally conscious.[37] As Gwaltney allows them to tell their own story the saga of a strong, confident, and shrewd Black people emerges, yet one looks in vain for an articulated, clear ideology. These people are in flight from ideology. They are intelligent enough to recognize that the political ideals of white people are not only frequently betrayed by whites themselves, but that they have done little for Black people. As a result Gwaltney's people content themselves with either relating to other Black folk on an individual basis or through churches, schools, community organizations and other non-political institutions. While none of the people Gwaltney interviewed expressed a need for an ideology which, derived from the Afro-American experience, would regulate and give purpose to their lives, almost all of them recognize the absence of such an ideology which pretty much doomed them to repeating patterns of behavior which have long been common in the Black community. Most were optimistic and while they expected nothing new from their Black neighbors themselves, were confident they could continue to build satisfying lives. None of the people Gwaltney interviewed expressed confidence in the dominant Euro-American ideology on which Blacks have long relied. Instead, many of them remarked on the lack of commitment whites had to their own ideology. Most of those interviewed by Gwaltney were persons of middle age and beyond. Few interviewed were in their twenties and none were in their teens. But it is on young Afro-Americans that the failure of Blacks to construct a political interpretation of the Black American experience falls most heavily. They do not accept the dominant Euro-American ideology as they know it does not work for Black people. At the same time there is no Black ideology which commands their allegiance and commits them to self-disciplined work. As a consequence these young people drift into teen-aged pregnancy, into drug addiction, into petty crime and into unemployment. The roots of such behavior lie not, as some would have it in the dislocation of Black communal life which came about as the result of the movement from southern rural areas to northern urban ones, but rather in the inability of Afro-Americans to construct a working communal life governed by political tenets which has grown naturally and normally out of the Black experience. During the slave era and for some decades beyond, Black Americans were constrained by two forces. The first was the power of white folk; the slave-owner and his successors needed disciplined Black labor and insisted that Afro-Americans who worked for them be regular and obedient. The second and weaker of these forces was that made by Blacks themselves in their effort to live up to the public fiction that Blacks were like whites and to conduct their lives accordingly. In recent decades, as the result of automation and other technological developments, whites have not needed disciplined Black workers on a large scale. This has placed the burden on Afro-Americans of disciplining themselves. But Black folk have, at least on this side of the

Atlantic, *a cultural tradition of disciplining one another for the good of the community.* With exception of maroon societies and a number of all Black towns, persons of African heritage in the Americas have no significant experience in running Black societies for the benefit of Black people.[38] During the slave era Black communities were operated for the benefit of the slave master, and after emancipation they were controlled so as to produce a reserve pool of workers to be drawn upon when whites needed them. Not only do Black Americans lack a tradition of self-governance, but they never created an ideological structure that would enable them to legitimate such a tradition. Older Blacks have nothing to offer the millions of young Blacks who are no longer subject to the discipline of white Americans. The day-to-day experiences of these young people renders the public fiction of each of the two races absurd. They do not believe Black people and white people are alike, nor do they accept the idea that they are all – simply by virtue of skin color – inferior to whites.

Conclusion

The experiences of whites and Blacks in the American colonial period were strikingly different, European migrants to North America gained freedoms had not known at home, while whites gained a measure of control over their newly established American settlements and solved in succession environmental, social, cultural, psychological, and political problems, Blacks were never able to gain control of their own communities. The Enlightenment ideology to which Euro-Americans were so committed reflected their experiences as a free people in British North America. Blacks used this ideology – with mixed success – against their white oppressors, but it was not part of their experience. The long Afro-American commitment to an ideology which reflected neither conditions in their community nor their ideas about themselves prevented Black people from developing a distinct political interpretation of their own experience. While some scholars see the Black community as suddenly fallen into disorganization, the current confusion characteristic of Black urban areas is the direct consequence of the inability of Blacks in the colonial era to create political structures capable of making sense of the Black experience.

Afro-Americans and Euro-Americans have, from the colonial period on, had such different experiences that it is unlikely that the majority of Black folk will ever fully accept a political ideology which has its roots in white life. Without a set of political guidelines in which they can believe, young Black Americans will continue to drift isolated, confused, and insecure. Black intellectuals must continue to energetically work at the difficult task of constructing an ideology that is reflective of the Afro-American experience, and capable of inspiring young Black people.

NOTES

1. *The William and Mary Quarterly*, Third Series 35 (April, 1978), pp. 185-420. See especially the introductory overview to this volume by Peter H. Wood, "'I Did the Best I Could for My Day:" The Study of Early Black History during the Second Reconstruction, 1960-1976,' pp. 185-225, which contains a useful bibliography.

2. See, for example, Rhett S. Jones, "blacks in Colonial America: Historical Perspectives, 1858-1969," *Black World* 21 (February, 1972), pp. 12-30, and Rhett S. Jones, "Slavery in the Colonial Americas," *Black World* 26 (February, 1975), pp. 23-39.

3. Lorenzo Greene, *The Negro in Colonial New England*. New York: Atheneum, 1974, (first published 1942); Winthrop D. Jordan, *White Over Black: American Attitudes Toward the Negro, 1550-1812*. Baltimore: Penguin Books, 1969 (first published 1968); Peter H. Wood, *Black Majority: Negroes in Colonial South Carolina from 1670 to the Stono Rebellion*. New York: Norton, 1975; A. Leon Higginbothan, Jr., *In the Matter of Color – Race and the American Legal Process: The Colonial Period*. New York: Oxford University Press, 1980 (first published, 1978).

4. For an interesting overview of the contrast between race relations in Brazil and the United States as the result of developments in the colonial period see Carl Degler, *Neither Black nor White:Slavery and Race Relations in Brazil and the United States*. New York: Macmillan, 1971, especially Chapter V. For the Caribbean see Orlando Patterson, *The Sociology of Slavery*. Rutherford, NJ: Fairleigh Dickinson University Press, 1969, especially Chapters III, VI, and IX; and Richard S. Dunn *Sugar and Slaves: The Rise of the Planter Class in the English West Indies, 1624-1713*. New York: Norton, 1973 (first published 1972), especially Chapters 3 and 8.

5. This model has been applied to the study of comparative Afro-American history in the colonial era by Rhett S. Jones, "Race Relations in the Colonial Americas: An Overview," *Humbolldt Journal of Social Relations* 1 (Spring/Summer, 1974), pp. 73-82.

6. Dunn, *Sugar*, Chapter 8.

7. During the early years of colonization, continuous warfare was characteristic of much of the New World. See Carl and Roberta Bridenbaugh, *No Peace Beyond the Line: The English in the Caribbean*. New York: Oxford University Press, 1972.

8. One perspective on the three-way encounter among the Amerindians, English, and French in North America is James Axtell, *The Invasion Within: The Contest of Cultures in Colonial North America*. New York: Oxford University Press, 1985.

9. Edmund S. Morgan, *American Slavery – American Freedom: The Ordeal of Colonial Virginia*. New York: Norton, 1975, Chapter 11; George M. Frederickson, *White Supremacy: A Comparative Study in American and South African History*. New York: Oxford University Press, 1982 (first published 1981), Chapter II.

10. Frank Tannenbaum, Slave and Citizen: The Negro in the Americas. New York: Vintage Books n.d. (first published, 1946), pp. 43-56; Harmannus Hoetink, *The Two Variants in Caribbean Race Relations*, translated from the Dutch by Eva M. Hooykaas. New York: Oxford University Press, 1967, pp. 164-175.

11. The classic statement on the role of cruelty in the slave system is Kenneth M. Stampp, *The Peculiar Institutions: Slavery in the Ante-Bellum South*. New York: Vintage Books, 1956. See especially Chapter IV, "To Make Them Stand in Fear."

12. The origin of this attitude toward Native Americans lies in the seventeenth century. See Francis Jennings, *The Invasion of America: Indians, Colonialism, and the Cant of Conquest*. New York: Norton, 1976 (first published 1975); also Neal Salisbury,

Manitou and Providence: Indians, Europeans, and the Making of New England, 1500-1643. New York: Oxford University Press, 1982.

13. Anglo-Jamaicans, for example, agreed whole-heartedly with their fellow colonists in North America that American governing bodies should enjoy more independence from London than the Crown was willing to grant, but because Anglo-Jamaicans needed the might of the British Army and Navy to maintain control of their slaves they dared not risk rebellion. See, on this subject, Edward Brathwaite, *The Development of Creole in Jamaica, 1770-1820.* Oxford: Claredon Press, 1978 (first published 1971), especially Chapters 5 and 8.

14. Compare on this issue W. E. Abraham, *The Mind of Africa,* Chicago: University of Chicago Press, 1962, Chapter 2; John S. Mbiti, *African Religions and Philosophy.* Garden City, NY: Anchor Books, 1970 (first published 1969), Chapters 15, 17; and Jacques Maquet, *Africanity: The Cultural Unity of Black Africa.* New York: Oxford University Press, 1972, pp. 56-66 and 76-88.

15. Chapter three of Leslie Howard Owens, *This Species of Property: Slave Life and Culture in the Old South.* New York: Oxford University Press, 1977 (first published 1976) demonstrates that when deprived of control of their diets, slaves frequently suffered from a variety of illnesses. Owens also suggests more attention be given to the relationship between slave diet and behavior in light of modern knowledge of nutrition.

16. Earl Spangler, *The Negro in Minnesota.* Minneapolis, MN: T. S. Davidson, 1961, p. 17 observes of the fur traders in Minnesota that they "always got a Negro if possible to negotiate for them with the Indians, because of their pacifying effect."

17. An overview of the many varieties of Black-Indian relationships during the colonial period is found in Rhett S. Jones, "Black and Native American Relations before 1800." *Western Journal of Black Studies* 1 (September, 1977), pp. 151-163.

18. Lawrence W. Levine, *Black Culture and Black Consciousness: Afro-American Folk Thought from Slavery to Freedom.* New York: Oxford University Press, 1978 (first published, 1977).

19. Herbert G. Gutman, *The Black Family in Slavery and Freedom, 1750-1923.* New York: Vintage Books, 1977; also Albert J. Raboteau, *Slave Religion: The "Invisible Institution" in the Antebellum South.* New York: Oxford University Press, 1970 (first published 1978).

20. Willie Lee Rose, *Slavery and Freedom,* edited by William W. Freehling. New York: Oxford University Press, 1982, p. 31.

21. See, however, Rhett S. Jones, "Structural Isolation, Race and Cruelty in the New World," *Third World Review* 4 (Fall, 1978), pp. 34-43.

22. Jordan, *White over Black.*

23. Stokely Carmichael and Charles V. Hamilton, *Black Power: The Politics of Liberation in America.* New York: Vintage Books, 1967, especially Chapter I.

24. Carmichael and Hamilton, *Black Power,* especially Chapter II.

25. George P. Rawick, *From Sundown to Sunup: The Making of the Black Community.* Westport, CT: Greenwood, 1972.

26. Gilbert Osofsky used this phrase as title for his edited collection of slave narratives, *Puttin' On Ole Massa.* New York: Harper and Row, 1969.

27. Rose, *Slavery and Freedom,* while conceding "we know much less than we ought to know about childhood in slavery," p. 39, makes a good case for its centrality in understanding of black experience. These issues are explored in her chapter, "Childhood in Bondage," pp. 37-48.

28. *David Walker's Appeal,* edited and with an Introduction by Charles M. Wiltse. New York: Hill and Wang, 1965, p. 75.

29. Cited in Rhett S. Jones, "Trifling Patriots and a Freeborn People," *Brown Alumni Monthly* 76 (December, 1975), p. 27.
30. Jones, "Trifling Patriots," Also Higginbotham, *In the Matter.*
31. John W. Blassingame, *The Slave Community: Plantation Life in the Antebellum South.* New York: Oxford University Press, Revised and Enlarged Edition, 1979, clearly demonstrates just this point in Chapter 6 and 7. The letters collected by Randall M. Miller (ed.) *"Dear Master:" Letters of a Slave Family.* Ithaca, NY: Cornell University Press, 1978, particularly those which appear in Part II, reveal the slaves themselves expected their masters to carefully distinguish among them and act accordingly. The watchful knowledge masters had of their slaves is one of the points on which Robert William Fogel and Stanley L. Engerman, *Time on the Cross: The Economics of American Negro Slavery.* Boston: Little, Brown, 1974, and Eugene D. Genovese, *Roll, Jordan, Roll: The World the Slaves Made.* New York: Vintage Books, 1976 agree.
32. Patterns of black resistance were influenced by the varying conditions of their enslavement as Genovese, *Roll*, and Blassingame, *Slave Community* make clear.
33. Gunnar Myrdal, *An American Dilemma: The Negro Problem in Modern Democracy.* New York: Harpers, 1944.
34. There are parallels, to be sure, between the strategies used by white ethnics and blacks to cope with discrimination, but racism has made them fundamentally different from one another. This difference, unfortunately, is sometimes obscured by the Euro-American scholarly establishment. Sociology departments, for example, routinely offer courses entitled "Race and Ethnics Relations," which typically blur race and ethnicity and fail to make clear how different the two are from one another.
35. See, for example, James E. Blackwell, *The Black Community: Diversity and Unity.* New York: Dodd, Mead, 1975, especially Chapter 3.
36. Harold Cruse, *The Crisis of the Negro Intellectual: From Its Origins to the Present.* New York: William Morrow, 1967, especially Chapter 1; Carmichael and Hamilton, *Black Power*, especially Chapters II and VIII.
37. John Langston Gwaltney, *Drylongso: A Self-Portrait of Black America.* New York: Vintage Books, 1981.
38. While a number of works have since been published on maroons – communities formed by runaway slaves – the best introductory overview to maroon life remains Richard Price (ed.), *Maroon Societies: Rebel Slave Communities in the Americas.* Garden City, NY: Anchor Books, 1973.

Chapter 4

The African-American Intellectual and the Struggle for Black Empowerment

By Charles Green and Basil Wilson

Within the realm of Black intellectual thought there exist four distinct schools of thought which have influenced the manner in which the Black community defines itself in relationship to white America. These contending schools of thought or tendencies within the Black community have enjoyed moments of hegemony at particular historical junctures. This essay looks at these tendencies from a development or historical perspective and seeks to explain their significance and ramification to the Black community.

The four schools of thought or major tendencies within the Black community are 1) accommodation to racism, 2) integration, 3) Black nationalism, 4) and the revolutionary tendency. Each tendency affects not only the way the Black community defines itself but alters or reinforces existing patterns of race relations. The writers will examine each school of thought and place it in some historical context.

Accommodation to Racism

In many respects, accommodation to racism has become anachronistic. It is difficult to find people who would defend this school of thought as constituting a viable response to the condition of an oppressed people. That does not necessarily mean that it has been non-existent. It has lost its organizational viability but lingers on in terms of individual conduct even though it represents a dying tendency.

Accommodation to racism emerged as the dominant school of thought after the collapse of Reconstruction governments in 1876. From the civil war period of 1876, this country agonized over the question of what should be the position of free Black people in American society. The war settled the issue of slavery and the Southern states begrudgingly passed the 13th Amendment to the constitution. But there was greater resistance on the question of whether Black men and women were entitled to social, political, and economic equality.

Frederick Douglass and other Black abolitionists spearheaded the struggle for these constitutional rights and received the support of the Republican Party not because the Republican Party was committed to these principles but because there was the realization that unless Blacks had the right to vote, the defeated South under the political guise of the Democratic Party would monopolize state power in that part of the country. From this early post civil war period, one can discern the genesis of the dependency on the federal government for the protection of civil rights of Black people in America.

One must recognize that despite the presence of federal troops in the South and the control of state power by the Republicans, white civil society remained violently against Blacks exercising the right to vote. A plethora of terrorist organizations emerged to beat back Black people into a position of subordination or acquiescence to racism. With the collapse of Reconstruction, this meant that white civil society now had control of state power and could use the state apparatus to systematically keep Black people in a position where they were economically and politically acquiescent to white racism. Slavery had ended, the 14th and the 15th Amendments had been passed but the super-ordinate racial relationship continued to be violently enforced.

Booker T. Washington and the rise of the accommodationist school of thought is an attempt to arrive at a rapprochement with white racism. What were the major precepts of this school of thought? Booker T. Washington was not only a conservative Black man, but one who matured in a world in which Christianity was synonymous with civilization. Washington understood capitalism; he understood the importance of education but was frightened of free intellectual inquiry; he recognized the importance of building Black institutions but remained throughout his life dependent on white philanthropy; he was committed to Black economic development but failed to grasp the connection between politics and economics; he believed in the good of white civil society even though there was no evidence, past or present to support this faith. Washington sought harmony, or preferably accommodation in a system which was specifically organized for his own destruction.

Washington attributed the racial troubles in the South to the alliance that had developed between white carpetbaggers, scalawags, and Blacks. He wrote quite gleefully about the loyalty of the Black slave and how in the midst of the civil war, slaves refrained from attacking the master's family in absence of the master. This appears to be too sweeping a generalization. Du Bois points out in *Black Reconstruction in America* that once Blacks in bondage recognized that the North was committed to the principle of emancipation rather than fighting a war to save the union, the bondsman engaged in a general strike. He stopped working or went behind the lines on the Union army.

Washington developed the notion of "black loyalty" to a further stage. He argued that it would serve the interest of Black people to extricate themselves from continued involvement in the political arena. The political system should remain the exclusive domain of whites and Black people should concentrate their efforts in excelling in the realms of the economy. This entailed setting up the necessary educational institutions to produce a disciplined, skilled labor force committed to developing a strong Black economy.

Booker T. Washington found himself betwixt a declining agrarian economy and an encroaching industrial revolution. The skills that Blacks had acquired during the ante-bellum south were rapidly disappearing and the future of Black people rested on industrial educational institutions that would lead to the acquisition of new skills critical to their survival in a changing world.

42

Washington saw the need to revitalize Black civil society. He was an advocate of race pride and saw the need to honor great Black men and study the Black historical experience. This is why some people argue that Washington could be classified as an early Black nationalist. But assertiveness is intrinsic to nationalism and Washington sought to build a Black nation subordinate to white racism. He naively felt that there was some mystical attachment between Blacks and whites and that the southern white would not feel threatened by the elevation of the Black man.

Washington was placed on a pedestal by the capitalist class. H. H. Rogers of Standard Oil, William H. Baldwin, Jr., of Southern Railway, Collis B. Huntingdon of Newport News, and Andrew Carnegie, cultivated a relationship with Washington. Having had access to wealth and power, Washington was recognized by white America as the leader of a 'bantustan' Black nation. Whites were never alarmed by Washington's alleged nationalism. Traditionally, white America has always treated Black America as a separate nationality and Washington's philosophy of accommodation fitted in well with the mainstream of American political thought.

The industrial educational institutions attempted to meet the need of an expanding capitalist regimentation and production although not much emphasis was placed on history, mathematics or science. The focus was on practical skills such as agriculture, dairying, horticulture, and stockraising. Students at the Black Tuskegee Institute received training in 26 industries including woodwork, iron, leather, tin, masonry, carpentry, etc.

Washington understood that the application of science to productivity was what was lacking in countries like Haiti and Liberia. He elaborated on this thesis when he stated:

> Although among the richest countries in natural resources in the world, are discouraging examples of what must happen to any people who lack industrial or technical training.[1]

The educational institution in these countries placed too much emphasis on liberal arts rather than industrial and scientific education. Washington's criticism of Haiti and Liberia was quite valid. But Washington defined education in dangerously narrow terms. Certainly there was a need for industrial education at this historical juncture but there was also a need for Black inquiring minds willing to critically analyze the racist nature of American society. Washington did not only seek a well trained Black labor force but, also, one that would be subservient to capital. He had no understanding of the exploitative historical past, and discouraged the Black labor force from being part of a nascent union movement getting ready to challenge the hegemony of industrial capital.

Washington sought to isolate black people from politics with the presumption that whites would enable Blacks to maneuver quite freely in the economic spheres and thus provide the opportunity to develop a viable economic system. He presumed economic empowerment was the antithesis of Black subjugation. White racists in charge of state power would not allow that kind of empowerment to take place. Washington failed to grasp the economic component of racism which comes both from the force of white labor and white capital to ensure there remains intact a reservoir of Black labor ready to be employed in periods of expansion and to be discharged in periods of contractions.

Washington presumed that goodwill was sufficient to fight the despicable system of racism. In his famous Atlanta address, Booker T. Washington demonstrated the absurdity of the accommodation to racism when he remarked:

> As we have proved our loyalty in the past, in nursing your children, watching by the sick-beds of your mothers and fathers, and often following them with tear dimmed eyes to their graves, so in the future, in our humble way, we shall stand by you with a devotion that no foreigner can approach, ready to lay down our lives, if need be, in defence of yours, interlacing our industrial, commercial, civil, and religious life with yours in a way that shall make the interests of both races one.[2]

Washington's pleading for harmony and his pledge of loyalty to the white South only resulted in the Black man having to accommodate to more entrenched and vicious forms of racism. Terrorism against Blacks continued unabated. Lynchings increased, political participation was reduced to negligible numbers, and the economic condition remained just as trying. In 1895, 113 Blacks were lynched.

Accommodation to racism did not lead to salvation but to more horrendous forms of oppression. To escape the racist dehumanization, Black people migrated out of the south with the expectation that civil society and state institutions in the north would be more willing to grant them political, economic, and social equality.

Washington died in November, 1915, but his spirit persisted. When the federal government sought expertise on the Black question during World War I, the appointments invariably went to Blacks who were advocates of the school of accommodation. Disciples of Washington, like Emmett J. Scott and Robert R. Moton were used by the federal government to ensure that the spirit of acquiescence remained the dominant tendency in the Black community. Even before Washington's death, opposition to accommodation to racism was mounted by the Niagara Movement. Ida B. Wells-Barnett and Monroe Trotter represented that spirit of defiance which Washington, with his access to power and wealth, tried hard to smother.

Accommodation to racism in organizational form is anachronistic. Yet, there is a spirit of acquiescence that has developed in the post-civil rights period which one finds in some sectors of the Black middle class. This form appears largely among affluent Blacks who are naive or unmindful that the material condition that they have risen to enjoy only came about because of the struggles waged in the 1960s.

The Integrationist Tendency

The Niagara Movement was formed in 1905 with a commitment to fight against racial injustice. There was also the need to form a Black autonomous interest group which would articulate and struggle for the interest of Black people. Yet, the Niagara Movement lost much of its vitality when the integrationist tendency came to the fore with the formation of the National Association for the Advancement of Colored People (NAACP), an integrationist organization committed to racial justice. The NAACP was dominated by liberal whites incensed at the racist nature of American society. Whereas accommodation to racism represented a sheepish form of "nationalism," the formation of the NAACP represented a commitment to building an interracial society.

The NAACP was committed to elimination of segregation, an integrated public educational system, and for Blacks to have the right to vote.[3] The strategy revolved around challenging the constitutionality of institutionalized racism through the federal courts. Although some of the founders of the NAACP were committed to socialism, the organization was not concerned with questioning the economic system of capitalism. The intent was not to challenge the economic or political system through the use of direct action or mass movement. The assumption was that this was a democratic society and if segregation was outlawed by the courts then the vicious monstrosity of racism in American life would disintegrate.

At the formation in 1910, the NAACP was dominated by liberal whites incensed at racism. W. E. B. Du Bois was the only Black officer in the early years and was responsible for the organization's journal, *The Crisis*. This journal had a circulation of 100,000 in 1918 and Du Bois attempted to use his editorials to expose the inhumanity of white racism.

There is a tendency for the present generation to dismiss the NAACP as an innocuous bourgeois organization which played an insignificant role in the struggle for liberation. The NAACP suffered from serious theoretical weaknesses. The organization was much too one-dimensional. It focused almost exclusively on undermining institutional racism through the court system. Maintaining the racist character of the state is critical to the continuity of institutionalized racism. State power helps to legitimize racism and uses the state's monopoly on violence to ensure the impervious nature of the system. If the state takes an anti-racist position, the racism that emanates from civil society is not as all encompassing and, thus, Black people are in a much better position to improve their lot.

The neutralization of the state is critical in the defeat of racism. In assessing some of the accomplishments of the NAACP, John Hope Franklin wrote:

> In 1915, in the case of Quinn v United States, the Supreme Court declared the grandfather clauses in Maryland and Oklahoma constitutions to be repugnant to the Fifteenth Amendment and therefore null and void. In 1917, in the case of Buchanan v Warley, the Court declared unconstitutional the Louisville

ordinance requiring Negroes to live in certain sections of the city. In 1923, in the case of Moore v Dempsey, the Court ordered a new trial in Arkansas courts for a Negro who had been convicted of murder. The representative of the NAACP had argued that the Arkansas peon had not received a fair trial because, among other things, Negroes were excluded from the jury.[4]

These victories may appear insignificant to the present era but they created cracks in the wall of a totalitarian system. Black people were heartened by these court victories and by 1921 there were over four hundred branches of the NAACP throughout the country.

The NAACP recognized the connection between politics, the judicial system, and racism. It emerged in the post World War I period as the dominant protest organization in the Black community and although not an advocate of direct mass movement, indeed, constituted a powerful organized force in the Black community. This alliance of liberal whites and middle class Blacks increased its influence in the body politic during the New Deal Administration.

Despite the tradition of activism during the 1930's, NAACP represented a conventional organization committed to overthrowing 'Jim Crow' by the judicial process. The NAACP represented the interest of the Black bourgeoise and the Black "middle class." Although the disciples of Booker T. Washington were instrumental in forming the Afro-American Realty Company, the real estate firm that encouraged the concentration of Blacks in Harlem, the Black bourgeoisie were not advocates of Black nationalism. African-American nationalism was perceived as a school of thought that was counterproductive to the interests of Black people. Whites had always imposed the concept that Blacks constituted a distinct nationality but the Black bourgeoisie was committed to pursuing the path of integration and were vehemently opposed to all forms of Black nationalism.

Any form of group or bloc activity was perceived as injurious to the long term interest of Black people. There was no necessity to form Black institutions or to mobilize the Black community as an autonomous political force. Obviously, that was seen as an activity that would alienate white sympathism. Harold Cruse points out in *The Crisis of the Negro Intellectual* that America is not a monolith but is comprised of ethnic blocs competing for political hegemony.

In his typical brusque manner Cruse argued:

> The Black bourgeoisie in the United States is the most politically backward of all the colored bourgeois classes in the non-Western world. It is a class that accepts the philosophy of whites whether radical, liberal progressive or conservative, without alteration or dissent and call it leadership. It is a class that absorbs very little from the few thinkers it has produced- Martin R. Delaney, W. E. B. Du Bois, Booker T. Washington, E. Franklin Frazier and Carter G. Woodson- men who left something behind them.[5]

The Black bourgeoise felt Blacks were on the periphery of the society and the only way they could terminate that condition of marginality is by integration and thus becoming an assimilated variant of the American core. But the competitive nature of American politics was such that the two dominant political parties, the Republican Party and the Democratic Party, were neither willing to fight against structural racism in the former Confederate states nor racism in the larger society. Although Blacks abandoned the Republican Party in increasing numbers for the Democratic Party during the height of the New Deal era, they became captives of a political party that was committed to welfare capitalism but condoned racism. The disfranchisement of Blacks in the post Reconstruction era had led to a one party apartheid system in the south, a region in the country that was critical to the Democratic Party in national elections. Any vigorous enforcement of the constitutional rights of Black people would endanger the regional alliance.

The white liberal/Black bourgeois alliance led to some changes in the state institutions of the north but could not get the Democratic or Republican Party to take a non-racist stand. Steady progress was made through the judicial system but none that threatened the very survival of the racist system.

Legal segregation was not crushed by the constitutional challenge. The integrationist school of thought did not have a national impact until people like Martin Luther King, Stokely Carmichael, et al. Seized the time and took the struggle to a higher stage. This entailed mobilizing the masses of Black people and directly engaging in confrontational politics.

Martin Luther King understood how state power was used to prop up the segregationist edifice. A system of this kind can only endure if those oppressed are willing to conform. Once resistance mounts, the system can only survive through naked coercion. What was a critical factor in Martin Luther King's strategy of mass civil disobedience was the fact that the state systems did not enjoy absolute power and the changing nature of the world system forced the federal government to take an anti-racist position.

It is quite clear that the mass movement for civil rights transformed the racist nature of national politics. The Civil Rights Bill of 1964 and the Voting Rights Act of 1965, led to the decline of de jure segregation and helped to change the power configuration of southern politics. Blacks now had the right to vote, so this bloc vote had to be factored in by those aspiring for state office.

Although the civil rights movement was a mass movement, like the NAACP it was still dependent on white paternalism. The leadership did not see any necessity for building Black institutions exclusively accountable to the Black community. A large portion of the funds that kept the civil rights organization alive came from white liberals who were ready to abandon the movement once it showed a willingness to step outside of the bourgeois paradigm or to incorporate Black nationalism.

The civil rights movement had a profound impact on the structure of racism but racism continues to permeate civil society in America. But even more critical, the material condition of the vast majority of the Black working class remains unaltered. Gains were made by the Black middle class to the extent that it created the illusion that a Black sociologist from the University of Chicago, William Julius Wilson could have written a book, *The Declining Significance of Race* in which he argued that racism was no longer the cause in the inability of the Black underclass to be upwardly mobile. Although not taking a Marxist position, William Julius Wilson argued that class not race was what was currently critical.

The alliance between the liberal wing of the Democratic Party and the Black community attained hegemony in the society under the Lyndon Johnson Administration. There was an economic underpinning to this alliance as the Great Society programs served as an extension of the New Deal era and attempted to alter the nature of the state in relationship to the poor. Welfare capitalism remained the dominant school of thought in America until the international crisis of capitalism led to a temporary revival of American conservatism, a school of thought much more hostile to incorporating the interest of Black people.

Although liberalism was dominant in the 1960s, it never rested on a sound theoretical or organizational footing. Liberal programs were enacted begrudgingly and in no way was the conservative mood altered. C. Wright Mills was aware of this liberal weakness even before the rise of the conservative school of thought assumed dominance. Mills wrote:

> The combination of the liberal rhetoric and the conservative mood, in fact, has obfuscated hard issues and made possible historical development without benefit of idea. The prevalence of this mood and this rhetoric means that thought, in any wide meaning of the term, has become largely irrelevant to such politics as have been visible, and that in postwar America mind has been divorced from reality.[6]

The shallow foundation of American liberalism was evident with the conservative resurgency which began in the Presidential election of 1968. The liberal concepts had not penetrated civil society. Although involved in this partnership, Blacks were not a part of the decision-making process. The Democratic Party demonstrated an unwillingness to share power, merely to have Blacks included in the machine and to externalize the right to vote. The right to vote is separate from the right to govern or to share power.

The Civil War had settled the question of emancipation. Reconstruction had settled the right of citizenship, and the civil rights movement had effectively settled the right to vote. The right to govern or to share power remained an unresolved issue and one that still petrifies the racist nature of the white civil society.

Blacks grew dissatisfied with the game of the civil rights movement because it did not alter the material conditions of the mass of the population and they were still distantly related to power. It is this dissatisfaction that gave rise to the Black Power Movement.

The integrationist school of thought emerged as a counterforce against Washington's accommodation to racism. In the initial stages, it was confined to challenging racism by testing the constitutionality of 'Jim Crow' legislation. Significant gains were made through this method but not sufficient to fundamentally alter the system. The integrationist school of thought moved to a more advanced stage when it incorporated itself into a mass movement willing to confront the amoral and illegal nature of the state apparatus. The new strategy brought about fundamental changes in the state and national politics. In the 1960s, one saw the expansion of the Black middle class but the material condition of the Black working class and underclass remained unaffected by the changes in the body politic. The changes in white civil society had been marginal but the civil rights movement had an enormous impact on Black civil society. An outgrowth of the civil rights movement was that it increased the political and cultural consciousness of Black people.

After the Civil Rights Bill of 1964 and the Voting Rights Act of 1965 were passed by the United States Congress, the Civil Rights Movement was forced to deal with issues that were quite unfamiliar. The nature of American capitalism could not accommodate the demands emanating from the Black community and white civil society was simply not willing at that historical juncture to share power with the Blacks.

The Black middle class have not moved beyond the bourgeois paradigm but there has developed a realization that empowerment is essential to the further development of Black people in this country. The collapse of American liberalism has not only exposed the non-viability of the integrationist school of thought but the emergence of the conservative credo has whittled away some of the gains made in the 1960s such as affirmative action.

The Black Nationalist School of Thought

The Integrationist school of thought has failed to produce a leading theoretician. James Weldon Johnson, Walter White, Martin Luther King, et al., have written on the matter but the propositions are inadequately developed. That is not the case with the Black nationalist school of thought. Although there are identifiable differences within the school of Black nationalist thought, the writings of Marcus Garvey have had a lasting impact on all Black nationalist organizations in the twentieth century. In this section we will assess Garvey's contribution and also the writings of a modern Black nationalist, Haki Madhubuti.

Garvey migrated to the United States in 1915 with the expectation that he would meet with Washington and acquire some expertise on building Black institutions. Garvey had hoped to return to Jamaica and construct educational institutions of the Tuskegee variant. Washington died before Garvey arrived and rather than returning to Jamaica, Garvey remained in the United States and built a large mass organization, the Universal Negro Improvement Association.

Unlike Washington, Garvey understood the connection between racism and organizational power. He understood the necessity to build autonomous institutions devoid of the financial entrapment of white philanthropy. He understood why the commercial and financial power of the United States enabled it to exercise so much influence in world politics. It was also clear to Garvey that command of the seas enabled Britain to be recognized as a major sea power.

Racism can only persist if Blacks are kept in a state of powerlessness. Garvey scoffed at the relevance of morality in national or international politics. He perceived that the strong would inevitably devour the weak. But Garvey was sufficiently sophisticated to grasp the multifaceted nature of power. Blacks had to seek power not only in the realm of politics but in education, science, and industry.

Garvey was convinced that the oppression of Black people could only be terminated by the emergence of Pan-African organization with sufficient power to engage enemies in a struggle of resistance. Yet, Garvey focused not on the national picture but on the global system.

In an era in which Europe dominated the world, Garvey argued that the liberation of Black people in America was intertwined with liberating the African continent from the yoke of imperialism. A united Africa would change the power configuration of world politics and be in a position to protect the interest of the Black nation in America and in other parts of the world.

Garvey thought it futile to appeal to the decency of white people. For him, the Ku Klux Klan was not an aberration of white civil society but the personification of that society. Garvey was quite ambivalent as to the future of Black people in America. At one point, he exhorted them to repatriate to Africa and in other passages he implored them to struggle for freedom. Garvey frequently made the case that racism was deeply ingrained in white civil society and any attempt to exorcise racism would be an exercise in futility. He felt the competitive nature of capitalism was such that Blacks would perennially occupy a marginal position in America. Yet on March 24, 1923 he indicated:

> To fight for African redemption does not mean that we must become disloyal to any government or to any country wherein we were born. Each and every race outside of its domestic national loyalty has a loyalty to itself, therefore, it is foolish for the Negro to talk about not being interested in his own racial, political, social and industrial destiny. We can be as loyal American citizens or British subjects as the Irishmen or the Jew and yet fight for the redemption of Africa, a complete emancipation of the race.[7]

Yet, Garvey pointed to Reconstruction as an example of the disastrous fate that Black people would inevitably experience in this society. Thus, much of Garvey's counseling recommended an abandonment of the American ship of State. The mission of the New World Black man was to take leave of western civilization and repatriate to Africa and contribute to building a mighty nation-state in Africa. In his inimitable manner, Garvey chorused:

> Awake! the day is upon you, go forth in the name of the race and build yourselves a nation redeem your country Africa, the land from whence you came and prove yourselves men worthy of the recognition of others.[8]

This new vision of Africa aroused the interest of the Black working class who in their quest of social justice had recently migrated from the farms in the south to the cities in the south and in the north. Garvey made them into believers when he painted his vision of Africa:

> I have a vision of the future, and I see before me a picture of a redeemed Africa; with her dotted cities with her beautiful civilization with her millions of happy children, going to and fro.[9]

The Garvey Movement burst on the stage of history during the second decade of the twentieth century, surged into mass movement in the third decade of the twentieth century, and was eclipsed as a vibrant historical force in the fourth decade of the twentieth century.

Cruse has argued that Black nationalism has been haunted by the ghost of Garvey. Nationalists have failed to come to terms with themselves "as American products created out of American conditions and ingredients, requiring in the final analysis, an American solution."[10]

Writing during the 1960s, Cruse was critical of the extreme fragmentation and romantic orientation that characterized the state of the Black nationalist school of thought. Nationalists could not decide

> ...whether they want to see the United States reformed or revolutionized, destroyed or democratized, abandoned, overthrown, or obliterated.

> The Afro-American nationalists cannot make up their minds whether they want to emigrate, separate, migrate or simply sit still in the ghettos admiring each other during the quiet lulls between uprisings... The black ghettos are in dire need of new organizations or parties of a political nature, yet it is a fact that most of the leading young nationalist spokesmen are apolitical.[11]

For Cruse, post-Garvey nationalism wallowed in phrenetic romanticism and brought very little intellectual clarity to the Afro-American experience. Cruse made a distinction between Back-to-Africa nationalism and Afro-American nationalism. He is critical of the former but an advocate of the latter. He further argued:

> As a result, the readiness of most Black Nationalist tends to lean heavily on the African past and the African image, is nothing but a convenient cover-up for an inability to come to terms with the complex demands of the American reality.[12]

Has Black nationalism in recent years come to terms with the complex demands of the American reality? One must turn to the work of Haki Madhubuti to answer this question.

Black nationalism renewed itself in the aftermath of the civil rights movement. The question of emancipation, the right of citizenship, and the right to participate in the political process have been settled. The critical question remaining is the empowerment of Black people, an objective continuously sought by the Black nationalist school of thought.

Black nationalism in the American context is a direct response to white nationalism and often lapses into a variant of American racism. Madhubuti and

Karenga place heavy emphasis on creating a Black value system to determine the world view of the Black community. Madhubuti speaks of Pan-Africanism and communalism as being at the root of this new Black ideology. He dismisses Marx's class analysis as irrelevant to the plight of Black people. Marx is perceived as a European philosopher who was not concerned with the Black question and represented a radical form of European entrapment.

Madhubuti is alarmed at the influence of Marxism on the Black intelligentsia and like Cruse finds the inadequacy of left-wing analysis as being responsible for the inability of the Black intellectual to understand the complex realities of American society. Madhubuti rejects the connection between capitalism and racism. He warns:

> It is important to understand that the ideology of white supremacy precedes the economic structure of capitalism and imperialism, the latter of which are falsely stated as the cause of racism.[13]

Madhubuti did not find support for this Black nationalist ideology when he attended the Sixth Pan-African Congress in Dar-es-Salaam, Tanzania. It was a rude awakening for Haki Madhubuti although he held fast to the efficacy of his position.

> One can also say at this point that the dominant line of thought that was adopted by the Congress was clearly Marxist and not Nationalist. In fact, Black nationalism was seen by most of the participants as provincial, racism in reverse, short-sighted and at best naive.[14]

This writer has seen no evidence in his writings that Haki Madhubuti learned anything from this experience. It demonstrates the theoretical weakness of Black nationalism with its attempts to consolidate the Black world as if it constitutes a monolith. Madhubuti quotes Cruse but he has not understood the distinction that Cruse makes between African nationalism and Afro-American nationalism.

The Afro-American condition is quite dissimilar from that of the people living in the throes of underdevelopment on the African continent. Nationalism is relevant to the African nation-state but the definition of nationalism goes beyond pigmentation. The critical question in Africa is not a value system but the task of development and any serious attempt to grapple with that question must deal with the ideological question. Africa is comprised of not only Black people, but Black people who occupy different positions in the division of labor. Nationalism can serve as a point of departure in Africa but the class question cannot be escaped. Thus, the politics of pigmentation must be understood for its glaring weaknesses.

Malcolm X had already seen the limited political value of a politics wedded solely to Black nationalism. Rather than creating something revolutionary, what Madhubuti had done is to construct an ideology which was consonant with the mainstream of white civil society. He alighted from the Sixth Pan-African Conference, flinched but adamant:

The major enemy of the Black race is the white race. White people operating out of white supremacist ideology which manifests itself the greatest in economic and social systems such as capitalism, communism and socialism have been able to co-opt and enslave Blacks from the left, the right and the in-between.[15]

Madhubuti's analysis is lacking in intellectual rigor. History is perceived as a carcass, not something in motion that can be assessed over time. He is ambivalent about whether to leave the United States at this point in time but he wants to extricate Blacks from any dependency on white people. Black labor constitutes an integral part of the American economy and any attempt at disengagement is indeed fanciful. Blacks have long since been "integrated" into American economy and the obligopolitic mature of the economy is such that it would be counter-productive to begin anew. The material condition of Black people would not improve but deteriorate.

One must make a distinction between integration and assimilation. It is in Black interest to work toward further integration of the labor force. The greatest threat to the Black community is the growing marginalization of Black labor in the present crisis of capitalism in America. But economic integration is compatible with cultural nationalism and this is where the contribution of the Black nationalist in recent years has been most useful. There is a need to recapture the autonomy of the Black mind, to develop a worldview free from the encumbrance of western civilization. There is a need to encompass the Black historical, cultural, and artistic experiences into viable institutions which can assist in the education of a new generation. Black people must understand the peculiarities of their condition in America. Nothing is more crucial to the survival of a people than to have the Black community erect and preserve its monumental contributions to American civilization. Afro-Americans do constitute a nation within a nation and these institutions must be cultivated for the enrichment and viability of the Black community. But like Malcolm X and Franz Fanon and W. E. B. Du Bois, one must know the limitations of Black nationalism. One must understand its cultural ramifications and its political limitations. At this historical juncture, the critical issue for the Black community is the sharing of power. A politics limited to skin pigmentation will only elevate the racist nature of conventional American politics to a new state at a time when even within official society, racism has become morally indefensible. Nonetheless, this does not prevent Black people from using the solidarity of their votes to bring about changes in the body politic.

Black nationalism as a school of thought has always been preoccupied with the question of empowerment. It has tended to think in global terms and often appears to be imitating the more vulgar tendencies of western civilization and failing to grasp the complexity of the American reality. It gets bogged down in the fundamental error of defining race as constituting the essence of man. Black nationalists have failed to develop a clear vision of the world. Racism is perceived as a permanent feature of the American landscape and, thus, Blacks have no other choice but to become adept at the art of racism.

Black nationalism's significance is its willingness to aggressively confront racism, to endow Black people with a sense of dignity. It has in recent years been untiring in its devotion to construct Black institutions that will contribute to the wholesomeness of the Black community. Yet, it remains politically underdeveloped although in recent years, it has been forced to take an anti-capitalist, anti-imperialist position in world affairs and has contributed to the task of Black empowerment in white America.

The inability of the civil rights movement to alter the material condition of Black people has triggered a revival of Black nationalism. The rise of the white backlash and the crisis of welfare capitalism in America has given a new credibility to Black nationalism. Even integrationist organizations like the NAACP have recognized the power of the bloc vote in local and in national elections. Nationalists are less apprehensive about political participation in America but are yet to become attuned to a kind of politics that will have trans-racial appeal.

The Revolutionary School of Thought

Harold Cruse's criticism of Marxism is based on the hostility of Marxist political parties to Black nationalism. Conventional Marxism attacked all forms of Black nationalism as being reactionary and helping to exacerbate the division within the working class movement. It is the influence of radical socialist theory that prevented people like Paul Robeson from understanding the significance of the Harlem Renaissance. They failed to understand the necessity to create cultural, political and economical institutions that would contribute to transforming the position of Black people in this society.

Cruse also depicted a certain strain of white paternalism coming from within the ranks of the Communist Party, U.S.A. The theoreticians within the United States Communist Party were quite receptive to the Jewish nationalism at the same time they were critical of Black nationalism. Cruse is concerned with the question of originality:

> Black experience in the United States has shown that it is dangerous and non-productive for blacks to adopt Marxism; just as it has been historically detrimental for blacks to have adopted Christianity. The reason is that blacks have been unable to add anything original to the intellectual patrimony not of blacks, but of whites. If blacks continue to adopt these philosophies in the form that they received them from whites, then blacks will forever remain subservient to whites, intellectually, ethically, morally, etc.[16]

One of the problems with Black intellectual thought is that Blacks create monuments to heroes, yet, seem unfamiliar with their intellectual insights. The philosophical thought of W. E .B. Du Bois, C. L. R. James or a Walter Rodney has been able to relate the theoretical precepts of Marxism to the peculiar condition of Black people in the New World. In assessing the radical tendency, the writers will concentrate for the purposes of this paper on the contribution of

54

Du Bois and Manning Marable. Du Bois was born in 1868 and died in 1963. In essence, his long life enabled him to encounter the four schools of Black intellectual thought. Du Bois had a working relationship with Booker T. Washington but recognized the futility of Washington's accommodation to racism when he unleashed a verbal attack on the gatekeeper in 1903. He was involved with the formation of the Niagara Movement in 1905 and the NAACP in 1910. Although he worked with the NAACP, it was from the beginning an uneasy alliance. This interlude of conventional intergrationism lasted from 1910 until 1934 when he resigned as editor of *The Crisis.*

Du Bois was a Pan-Africanist from the early decade of the twentieth century when the NAACP thought such a course was irrelevant to the problems of Black people in America. Du Bois was a Pan-Africanist who did not advocate repatriation. Nonetheless, he recognized that an independent Africa would contribute to the dignity of Black people everywhere.

Du Bois surmised that the NAACP was comprised of well-meaning people who refused to alter their perceptions of American society. The NAACP could not see beyond the lynching or challenging 'Jim Crow' in the courts.

> By 1930, I had become convinced that the basis policies and ideals of the Association must be modified and changed; that in a world where economic dislocation had become so great as in ours, a mere appeal based on the old liberalism, a mere appeal to justice and further effort at legal decisions was missing the essential need; that the chances of Negroes, educated and ignorant, to earn a living, safeguard their income, and raise the level of their employment. I did not see any contradiction between taking a Marxist position and recognizing the need to create black institutions.[17]

Du Bois was a member of the Socialist Party from 1911. Although recognizing the power of socialism, he was critical of the inability of socialists to confront the race question. The view of the socialists then was that the race problem should be subordinated to the class problem with the presumption that once capitalism was eclipsed and the socialist order was established, the race question would be solved.

The socialists were afraid to confront the issue of racism for fear that they would alienate the white working class. The Communist Party was more willing to confront the question of racism. They were adamant that a revolutionary party must adhere to the principle of class solidarity irrespective of the entrenched racism in civil society.

Although influenced by Marxism, Du Bois was not an advocate of violent revolution. In his early conceptualization of socialism, he saw the necessity of introducing socialist reform in an evolutionary manner. Du Bois felt the high percentage of foreign born in the Communist Party prevented them from understanding the realities of American politics.

Long before James Boggs proposed Blacks serving as a revolutionary vanguard, Du Bois argued against Blacks serving as shock troops in communist revolution. He surmised that if Blacks were to lead the revolutionary charge, the country would merely unite under the patriotic banner of white nationalism and crush the Black putschists.

Du Bois was influenced by Marxism but he never accepted it unconditionally. He recognized Marx wrote about a nineteenth century Europe and his theoretical propositions would not be applicable without modification to the specific conditions in America, especially in regards to the Afro-American.

Du Bois' analysis carried him along a different axis than conventional Marxism. Blacks were exploited both by white capitalists and the white working class. Despite his criticisms of capitalism, he felt the Black condition would be somewhat alleviated if a capitalist class was created in the Black community. Later on in the program that he developed, he encouraged the development of cooperatives rather than the expansion of a class of Black capitalists.

Whether they were recent immigrants or the sons of immigrants the white proletariat used racism to provide themselves with a modicum of security in a precarious capitalist environment. This meant that Blacks had no other choice but to develop autonomous Black institutions dedicated to struggle against naked racism found in the bourgeois and proletariat class.

Du Bois' first visit to the Soviet Union in 1926 left an indelible impression on him. He stated that "since that trip my mental outlook and the aspect of the world will never be the same."[18] Yet Du Bois never reached the point in his life where he looked at the Soviet Union uncritically. He never became a romantic or a true believer:

> I think it was the Russian Revolution which first illuminated and made clear this change in my basic thought. It was not that I at any time was concerned Bolshevik Russia as ushering in my present millennium. I was painfully sensitive to all its failures, to all the difficulties which it faced; but the clear and basic thing which appeared to me in unquestioned brightness, was that in the year 1917 and then, after a struggle with the world and famine ten years later, one of the largest nations of the world made up its mind frankly to face a set of problems which no nation was at the time willing to face, and which many nations including our own are unwilling to face even to this day.[19]

Du Bois believed that Black liberation could not take place without the economic system being forced under democratic control. Private ownership of capital increased the suffering of Black people while at the same time leading the world to disaster. C. L. R. James is fond of declaring that the choice before the world is quite a simple one. "It is socialism or barbarism." Du Bois declared in his later years:

> I have studied communism and capitalism long and carefully in lands where they are practiced and in conversation with their adherents and with wide reading. I now state my conclusion frankly and clearly. I believe in communism. I mean by communism a planned way of life in the production of wealth and work designed for building a state whose object is the highest welfare of its people and not merely the profit of a part.[20]

56

Much lip service has been paid to Du Bois but seldom does one find a critical analysis of his writings. Du Bois negates the Cruse thesis that radical theory has prevented Blacks from understanding the complex reality of America or that Blacks have not made a contribution to Marxism. Those comments are usually made by people unfamiliar with the complexities of Marxist political thought and by those who feel comfortable functioning outside of the historical process.

Manning Marable has also tried to fuse the revolutionary tendency with nationalism. Marable has engaged in this quest for Marxist originality.

> The Old Left's dependency on the Soviet Union as the sole theoretical basis for worldwide socialist development, and the New Left's uncritical acceptance of either Cuba, Albania, or China as the appropriate revolutionary structure to imitate, led to an infantile and a historical replication of inappropriate social models to the cultural and economic terrain of the United States. [21]

Marable tries to lift contemporary Black politics out of the morass of nothingness other than the acquisition of power. The key issues around which there can develop cooperation between white progressives and Black nationalists are 1) full employment, 2) a reduction in the work week, 3) greater unemployment and welfare benefits, 4) and elimination of the Taft-Hartley Law, particularly Section 14B. [22]

Marable sees the need to abolish capitalism but he also recognizes the need to develop Black institutions. He envisioned Black people living in a multi-racial socialist society but with Black people guaranteed the right of self rule. Marable argued for a National Assembly with regional and local components which would be symbolic of the quasi-independence Blacks would enjoy in this multi-racial socialist state. The quasi-political autonomy would not include an independent judiciary and there would be ties to the larger bodypolitic. Yet this "socialist constitution would have to guarantee the right of total territorial separation for any and all black Americans." [23] The other ethnic groups would also have this guaranteed clause.

For Marable, racism precedes capitalism. And under the rubric of a capitalist state there had to be constitutional guarantees that would not lead to a stifling of the cultural autonomy of Black people. So Marable skillfully attempts to synthesize two separate tendencies within Black intellectual thought, Black nationalism, and the revolutionary tendency.

The criticism of the revolutionary tendency by Cruse and others have failed to grasp the originality of Blacks who have been influenced by Marxism. C. L. R. James, W. E. B. Du Bois, Walter Rodney, Robert Allen and Manning Marable have not sought merely to echo nineteenth century Marxism but have related Marxism to the peculiar conditions of the New World Black man.

The revolutionary tendency has been traditionally quite weak within Black civil society. Heretofore, much of Black activism has revolved around conventional political thought. The integrationist tendency and Black nationalist tendency, one wanting in, the other wanting out, failed to raise the fundamental question of economic democracy. The search for community and political empowerment, the liberation struggles in the Third World, particularly in Africa and the Caribbean, have forced the Black nationalist to take an anti-capitalist; anti-imperialist position. The integrationist tendency, which has been the dominant school of thought now finds itself in a quandary in an America where there prevails not just a conservative mood but a conservative ideology which will exacerbate the already high levels of suffering within the Black community. Integrationists have come to realize that the sharing of power is indispensable to breaking the back or racism. That is where the mass movement finds itself today- engaged in the quest for empowerment. This constitutes another stage in the Black historical experience.

NOTES

1. Hugh Hawkins (ed.),*Booker T. Washington and His Critics: The Problem of Negro Leadership*, (Massachusetts, D.C., Heath & Co. 1962) p. 16.
2. Booker T. Washington, *The Future of the American Negro*, (Chicago, Afro-American Press, 1969) p. 70.
3. John Hope Franklin, *From Slavery to Freedom, A History of Negro Americans*, (Chicago, Alfred A. Knopf, Inc.) p. 328.
4. Ibid, p. 329.
5. Harold Cruse, *The Crisis of the Negro Intellectual*, (New York, William Morrow & Company, 1967) pp. 327-328.
6. C. Wright Mills, *The Power Elite*, (New York, Oxford University Press, 1959) p. 317.
7. Marcus Garvey, *Philosophy and Opinions of Marcus Garvey*, (New York, Atheneum Press, 1969) p. 35.
8. Ibid, p. 89.
9. Ibid, p. 78.
10. Harold Cruse, op. cit., p. 421.
11. Ibid, p. 441.
12. Ibid, p. 554.
13. Haki R. Madhubuti, *Enemies: The Clash of Races*, (Chicago, Third World Press, 1978) p. 46.
14. Ibid, p. 67.
15. Ibid., p. 15.
16. "Interview with Harold Cruse," *Blacks Books Bulletin*, Vol. 3, No. 4 Winter, 1975. p. 27.
17. W. E. B. DuBois, *Dusk of Dawn*, (New York, Schocken Books, 1971) pp. 295-296.
18. Ibid, p. 287.
19. Ibid, p. 284.
20. W. E. B. DuBois, *The Autobiography of W. E. B. DuBois*, (New York, International Publishers, 1968) p. 57.
21. Manning Marable, *Blackwater: Historical Studies in Race, Class Consciousness and Revoolution* (Ohio Black Praxis Press, 1981) p. 173.
22. Ibid, p. 183.
23. Ibid, p. 198.

Chapter 5

A Philosophical Basis for an Afrocentric Orientation

By Norman Harris

Background

By now, it is common knowledge that an Afrocentric orientation is one which places the interests and needs of African people at the center of any discussion. The awesome and ongoing intellectual contributions of Maulana Karenga; the works of several African American psychologists —particularly Wade Nobles, Asa Hilliard, Naim Akbar and Linda James Myers; and most certainly the work of Molefi Asante – all provide examples of how Afrocentric orientations structure ethical, psychological, socio-economic and cultural analyses. This paper proposes to indicate basic philosophical assumptions which seem to structure the application of all Afrocentric approaches. It does not critique the work of Afrocentric approaches. It does not critique the work of Afrocentric scholars – though such an essay would certainly be useful. Rather, the writer's assertions and observations about the philosophical underpinnings of Afrocentricity are a result of having for a number of years read, reflected and acted on the fundamental idea that Afrocentric philosophy ought to structure any discussion of African people.

This essay has three related sections. The first indicates how Afrocentricity interacts with what the writer asserts to be fundamental motivations within African American life. The second section is an overview of Afrocentric ontological and epistemological orientations, and those are developed in terms of conceptions of time and logic. The third section illustrates that the way one thinks about time determines the role history plays in social change.

I.

Situated within the nucleus of the Afrocentric orientation is an assumption that a central motivation in African American life is the desire to achieve freedom and literacy.[1] Freedom is the ability to conceptualize the world in ways continuous with one's history. Literacy is the application of historical knowledge as the confluence between personality and situation dictates.

Freedom is an idealized conception derived from historical knowledge. This definition is one which turns analytical activity away from the quantification of gross changes in the socio-political and economic position of African Americans at any point in time (an end to chattel slavery, the passage of civil rights legislation, an end to various forms of discrimination, etc.) and towards a look at the way Africans in America define themselves and the extent to which they are able to implement their definitions. This definition of freedom therefore encourages research which seeks to distinguish between an appearance of change and the reality of change.

Historically, African Americans have been encouraged to confuse a rearrangement of reality with fundamental changes in reality. This phenomenon is facilitated through the implementation of various modes of socialization which undercut or minimize African and African American humanity. These modes of socialization include everything from changes in law to the inclusion of African American images in the print and electronic media. To be sure, this process has never been entirely successful, and we are now living in an historical period characterized by increased attention to the role of Africa in shaping humanity.[2] In response to that attention, one might perceive an increased pathology in Eurocentric scholarship[3] as it seeks to displace and discount the African origins of humanity and the fundamental role of African peoples in shaping western civilization at its point of conception. The contention here is commonplace and it is that the fundamental antagonism of Whites toward Africans, be they on the continent or in the Diaspora, has not altered over time. What has altered in this relationship is the form and appearance which White pathology might take at any given point in time. The definition of freedom used here provides a basis for the African American consciousness to merge with the best traditions in African and African American culture in order to more fully contribute to the forward flow of human history than the current ideas, definitions and subsequent attempts to attain freedom now allow.

Literacy is the practical dimension of freedom and is defined as noted above for two reasons: first, the definition acknowledges the subjective dimension of the human experience which makes one-to-one correlations between being exposed to or deprived of any given stimuli and having a specific response to that exposure or deprivation impossible to predict. To be sure, there is a range of predictable behavior among African Americans that non-African Americans rely on in creating and perfecting the methods they use to maintain the myriad systems of oppression. Alluded to here is the stubbornness of African humanity; its unwillingness to do as objective circumstances dictate – that is to succumb to any number of limiting phenomenon. Secondly, literacy is materialist in its acknowledgement of differences over and within time relative to the situations people confront. More directly, the way literacy plays out in a given situation is in part a function of what the opportunities and limitations of the material conditions under question dictate. The most sublime expression of literacy is of course rhythm. Here in *Roots of Soul*,[4] Pasteur and Toldson describe the phenomenon:

> At the essence of man's basic nature, enveloping vital forces, rhythm is a critical factor in the organization of human behavior. It is required for the attainment and maintenance of monetary perfection in human performance, which is the platform for achieving happiness. To be in rhythm is popularly recognized as a form of human efficiency... At such moments, one does not

move in an analytical, step-by-step progression, one is the spontaneous, rhythmic unfolding of the progression. One does not try to do, one happens to be an instrument of the doing. During such moments, nothing is difficult, there is no anxiety. (76-77)

Literacy seeks to attain the state described above, and its attainment is dependent on the application of historical understanding as the confluence between personality and situation dictates. This writer's assertion is that all African American ethical, psychological, socio-economic, political and cultural activity is an attempt to attain freedom and literacy.

Afrocentricity places the needs of African people at the center of all discussions. The quest to achieve freedom and literacy operates from that center.

II.

While not anti-materialistic, an Afrocentric orientation is one which asserts that consciousness determines being. Consciousness in this sense means the way an individual (or a people) think about relationships with self, others, with nature, and with some superior idea or Being. Certainly, the idea that consciousness determines being or the definition this writer gives to consciousness are not new. A variety of expressions drawn from classical and vernacular African and African American culture speak to this phenomenon. For example, the ancient Egyptian assertion, "Man Know Thy Self," indicates that the way one sees (thinks about and conceptualizes) the world precedes and determines life chances more so than exposure to or deprivation from various material conditions. The popular refrain of the "Funkadelics": "Free your mind and your ass will follow," is an example from vernacular culture of the assumption that consciousness determines being. Put another way, changes in the material world are possible only after one is able to think freely about those changes. In like manner, one can understand Marcus Garvey's assertion that what man has done, man can do; or Maulana Karenga's assertion that the crisis in the African American community is a crisis of values; or Jesse Jackson's insistent refrain, "I am somebody." In each instance, the assertion is that new thought precedes new action.

The idea that consciousness determines being derives from an Afrocentric ontology and epistemology. The Afrocentric ontology is characterized by a communal notion of existence, and can be stated as follows: we are, therefore I exist. This communal orientation is in contrast to the Eurocentric orientation that is best characterized by Rene Descartes's assertion, "I think, therefore I am." The Afrocentric epistemology validates knowledge through a combination of historical understanding and intuition. What is known, what can be proven is demonstrated through the harmonization of the individual consciousness with the best traditions in the African past. Again, by way of contrast, the Eurocentric epistemology validates knowledge through a combination of objectivity and "scientific method" wherein it is assumed that similar results obtained through similar steps under similar conditions is an indication of reality. Carl Jung, not always known for forward thinking on matters of race,[5] says that "Scientific materialism has merely introduced a new hypostasis, and that is an intellectual sin. It has given another name to the supreme principle of reality and has assumed that this created a new thing and destroyed an old thing. Whether you call the principle of existence "God," matter, energy, or anything else you like, you have created nothing; you have simply changed a symbol" (xxxi)[6] Jung's observations humanize science by noting its arbitrariness, and, implicitly, its juvenile quality. More directly, unable to understand relationships among the various expressions of reality (an inability to attain the literacy that rhythm occasions), western science seeks to sub-divide reality into angry little parts that barely know how to converse with each other. One may understand current events as flowing from the disharmony of implemented Western science.

The significance of Afrocentric ontology and epistemology is profound. The way one constructs reality, one's place in it, and the way one validates' knowledge determine one's life chances. For example, the individualistic ontology into which we have all been socialized makes it all but impossible for many African Americans to conceptualize the idea of racial responsibility, particularly as it relates to racial empowerment. At worse, racial responsibility ends at the tip of one's nose, and at worse, racial responsibility is merely a romantic concept, a passing stage in the individual's development before one reaches maturity.

The Eurocentric notion of individualism rests on the assumption that being determines consciousness, and it is this assumption which infuses materialism with a spirit it could never have. A new or better job, more income, a car, an outfit, etc. Are all assumed to carry intrinsic meaning that will at the level of consciousness create a new person. As long as a Eurocentric ontology of individualism obtains in the African American community, one may expect casual and justified inhumanity. A Black brother might say, "After all, if it's good for me, it's good for me. So step off, chump." The gangster image of the individualistic African American just described is, if you will, the whiter side of an all-White philosophical phenomenon that is not derived from the Black World experience. The eloquent stasis of neo-conservatives[7] is but the other side. The writer has written elsewhere about their tendency to write as if history has no abiding force in the world;[8] more directly, they assume that history has little if any contemporary and ongoing significance, particularly the history of enslavement, the various racist assumptions that sought its justification, and the continued phenomenon of institutionalized racism. More will be said about the way one conceives time and the impact that it has on the role that history plays in social change in the next section. Suffice it here to say that those the writer labels as neo-conservatives conceptualize time in a linear fashion, have difficulty in seeing a contradiction between appearance and reality, and therefore assume that changes in appearance actually represent a change in reality.

To sum up, an Afrocentric ontology is one which is communal; therefore, individuals find their worth, and their most sublime expression of existence in relationship to a community, to nature, and in relationship to some supreme idea or being. The Afrocentric ontology seeks to use rhythm to harmonize with those forces which appear external to the individual, but are in point of fact, simply expressions of the individual's potential. Na'im Akbar makes this point in his essay "African American Consciousness and Kemet Spirituality, Symbolism and Duality,"[9] when he asserts that

> African people are concerned about the invisible more than they are about the visible... They are concerned about those forces that operate on a higher plane... That's the nature of the spiritual orientation of African people. African people are more concerned about the infinite than they are about the finite. (106)

The idea of the infinite is similar to what might be referred to as potential; both are without limit and cannot be known in the context developed here except in association with other positive forces in the African world. Thus we see again the holistic – indeed, the limitless – nature of humanity that is possible from an Afrocentric ontological stance.

The Eurocentric ontology is individualistic and in it, the individual finds his fullest expression of existence in isolation or in opposition to man, nature, or some supreme idea or being. In this model there is no transcendent order to which the individual can attach herself. Indeed, attachments are at best pragmatic, and at worse they are parasitic. Tragedy, outrage and imposition are the hallmarks of Eurocentric cultural achievement and these can be understood as flowing from a view of the world in which humanity knows no collective and nurturing tradition to which it can attach itself. Like a child in a tantrum, one must be amazed by the ferocity of its self-destruction, particularly when it is all so unnecessary. A comparison between the "creative" culture associated with a Eurocentric orientation would yield exciting psychological data about the way the African and the non-African think about reality.

An Afrocentric epistemology validates reality (or what it claims to know) through a combination of historical knowledge and intuition. In this epistemology, history is key because when the individual appropriately submerges himself in the reservoir of African history, then that submersion allows the individual to discover him or her self in the context of that history and thereby judge the reality of any given phenomenon. Wade Nobles[10] writes: "unlike the 'stand for' connotation of the symbolic utilized today, the symbolic of ancient African times, and the contemporary African as well, was a symbolism that went beyond the 'representational-sequential-analytic' mode to the transformation-synchonistic-analogic' mode" (100). The last mode about which Noble writes derives from holistic view of reality; it is an aspect of a communal ontology. From this perspective, knowing is both rational and supra-rational, for it incorporates both that which can be understood in terms of methods to measure the material world, and that which transcends the material. Implicit in what Nobles writes, and, indeed, in what one sees in the writings of a number of scholars who explore classical African civilizations[11] is that reality follows essence, and that if one really wishes to know, then one must go beyond what is possible by the measuring and cataloging of material reality.

In a remarkable, and perhaps overlooked essay, "Hunting is Not Those Heads on the Wall,"[12] Leroi Jones makes the point that hunting, like art, is a process and what is left – a dead head hung on the wall or the artifact – is not the reality; it is simply the artifact, the "leavings" of a process. So it is with reality as one has been taught to think about it: it is not the mere appearance of physical phenomenon; rather, reality is the essence which connects the multiple expressions of appearances.

This discussion could continue along these lines in terms of defining a relationship between how one validates claims to knowing (epistemology) and one's notion of what reality is (a version of ontology). But the purpose here is to pose what the writer sees as a fundamental difference between an Afrocentric epistemology and a Eurocentric epistemology. The Afrocentric epistemology assumes transcendent order in the world, and the Eurocentric epistemology assumes that the only order in the world is that which it can "scientifically" demonstrate and that which it can impose. An Afrocentric epistemology attempts to validate claims to knowledge through immersion while the Eurocentric epistemology seeks distance from what it attempts to know and understand.

The differences between Afrocentric and Eurocentric epistemologies have pronounced effects on the way this society is organized and on the life chances of Africans in America. The more Afrocentric the epistemology of the African American[13] the more profound will be his contribution to humanity. The less Afrocentric the orientation, the more narrow will be the contribution. To be sure, for an African American to have a Eurocentric epistemology is consistent with the way many Blacks have been socialized. That African Americans have not marched entirely into the various slave holes constructed for them is remarkable testament to the transcendent nature of our humanity.[14]

To sum up here, the Afrocentric epistemology assumes transcendent order in the world. It seeks to verify its claims to knowing through a combination of historical understanding and intuition. Its methods are both empirical and supra-empirical.[15] An Afrocentric ontology and epistemology are necessary to advance the quest for freedom and literacy.

The following discussion relates how the Afrocentric ontology and epistemology structure the way one thinks about time, and, as a consequence, the way one thinks about the relationship of history to social change.

III.

The way one thinks about time determines the role that history plays in social change. If time is conceptualized in a cyclical fashion, then history plays a fundamental, one might say, a definitional role in social change. If time is conceptualized in a linear fashion, then history has little if any role to play in social change.

Deriving from its ontology (view of the world), and epistemology (verifications of those views of the world), an Afrocentric orientation conceptualizes time in a cyclical fashion. It assumes that the appearance of phenomenon always changes, but that the underlying essence of phenomenon remains basically unchanged. Part of life's journey, part of the quest for freedom and literacy is to systematically discover meaning (connections) beneath the surface of appearance. One may say in this regard, that an Afrocentric conception of time is not impressed by progress, which, in the Euro-Western context, means the endless rearrangement of appearances for their own sake. No beauty here, only the unending march of progress.

The Eurocentric orientation of time is linear, and it assumes, at least at the level of the way it organizes its various socializing agents, that there is a one-to-one correlation between appearance and reality. But, as Public Enemy says, "Can't Trust It,"[16] meaning of course that the mere appearance of change does not signify actual change – that is, a change in the power relationships between African Americans and non-African Americans.

A cyclical conception of time encourages immersion in history at a level and in a way that marries individuality or personality to precedent. As is the way of education in classical African Civilizations, the immersion is consistent with and necessary to self transformation, or, in another fashion, it is consistent with being born again.[17] This transformation must happen not only for the individual African in America, but for all African Americans.

To clarify: the social transformation is possible from an Afrocentric conception of time, and that notion of time is cyclical. The transformation itself simultaneously involves immersion and expansion in Black World history; only then can the individual discover herself or himself; only then can the race discover itself. As outlined here, self-discovery is freedom; the ability to conceptualize the world in ways continuous with one's history. This self-discovery, this freedom, is again consistent with what the Ancients taught, "Man Know Thy Self." Finally, on this part of the discussion, there can be no social change without freedom.

Literacy is the implementation of freedom and, as noted, is possible only when one thinks of time in a cyclical fashion. Social transformation is what is being struggled for. This is not an essay intended to list specific items or accomplishments that would signify social transformation. The Urban League and like organizations routinely publish these kinds of things. Rather, it would be more useful here to repeat and elaborate upon what has been said: literacy is the implementation of freedom, and the increasing ability of African Americans to implement freedom does signify social transformation.

IV.

This essay has sought to indicate the philosophical infrastructure on which Afrocentric scholarship rests. This will, the author thinks, provide others with a way of operationalizing the definition of Afrocentricity.

NOTES

1. I have been working with and expanding these terms since I came across them a decade ago while writing my dissertation. My acquaintance with the concepts of freedom and literacy come from my reading of Robert Stepto's *From Behind the Veil*, and from a variety of things I have read by Northrop Frye. While African American literary analysis was the specific reason for my usage of these terms, further reading indicated that their philosophical basis rested in what Carl Jung calls the collective unconscious. Additional reading indicated that Jung's notion of a collective unconscious is consistent with Richard Wright's prosaic, yet profound observation of things unseen, and the more fundamental African orientation concerning death, ancestor veneration, and the role of the past (if indeed it is that) in structuring the present. In short, the idea that African American life is structured by predispositions that cannot be fully explained by reference to empirical data is the basis for what I am doing here. In effect, the desire to achieve freedom and literacy is a supra-rational desire that is consistent with the African philosophical assumption that consciousness determines being.

2. The systematic rescue of Nile Valley Civilizations by writers and scholars as diverse as Charles Fitch, Ivan Van Sertima, Asa Hilliard, Larry Williams, W. Joye Hardiman, Martin Bernal, Jacob Carruthers, and organizations like the Association for the Study of Classical African Civilizations are indicators of this fact.

3. See Daudi Azibo's article in the Spring 1992 issue of *Word*, "Eurocentric Psychology and the Issue of Race."

4. Ivory Toldson and Alfred D. Pasteur, *Roots of Soul* (Garden City, New York: Doubleday Anchor Books, 1982.)

5. Naim Akbar notes in a speech that Jung asserts that the problem with America is that it is more or less infected by the African.

6. W. Y. Evans-Wentz, *The Tibetan Book of the Great Liberation*, commentary by Carl Jung. New York: Oxford University Press, 1977.

7. I would include in this group those African Americans who are more concerned mashing what is unique in African and African American culture into existing paradigms than they are with indicating what is unique. See my essay, "Who's Zoomin Who: The New Black Formalist," for a criticism of Henry Louis Gates, Jr., Robert Stepto and Houston Baker; see also my forthcoming book, *Signposts* for more discussions.

8. See my review of Shelby Steele's *The Content of Our Character* in *Word* and also my review of *Reflections on An Affirmative Action Baby* in the Spring 1992 issue of *Word*.

9. This essay can be found in *Reconstructing Kemetic Culture, Papers, Perspectives, Projects*, edited by Maulana Karenga. (Los Angeles: University of Sankore Press, 1990), pp. 99-114.

10. Wade W. Nobles, "Ancient African Thought and the Development of African (Black) Psychology," in *Kemet and the African Worldview*, edited by Maulana Karenga and Jacob H. Carruthers.

11. See the works of Schwaller de Lubeitz, Na'im Akbar, Asa Hilliard, et. At. For each, reality is essence, that which is at the center of physical phenomenon and consequently that which does not change. One of the most remarkable elucidations of this is a speech that Louis Farrakhan gave on the Black Man (I heard on a colleague's tape machine and cannot give a specific reference) in which he discussed who and what the Black man is in term of what reality is.

66

12. See Leroi Jones, "Hunting is Not Those Heads on the Wall." *Home Social Essays*; see also his essay, "Black Ethos" in *Raise Race Rays Raze*.
13. It should be noted here that no one is necessarily born with full-blown Afrocentric orientation, complete with an articulated ontology and epistemology. It should also be noted that people more directly of African descent (by whatever combination of scientific and cultural measures that seem appropriate) are more likely to be predisposed to an Afrocentric direction than are those who are of European or Asian descent. Nonetheless, people who are of European descent – Count Volney, De Lubicz, Gerald Massey, Melville Herskovits, Martin Bernal, and others are examples – can have an Afrocentric orientation. And this rather unremarkable observation achieves its strength based on the tendency of mainline scholarship to deny or denigrate the intellectual influences that Africa has exerted over its offspring in Europe and Asia.
14. It would be interesting here to explore as an historical continuum the Kemetic idea found in all of Africa that the purpose of all education is the deification of humanity. Could the stubbornness of this aspect of Classical African Civilization account for the transcendent nature of our humanity? This would be an intriguing question to explore.
15. To demonstrate this claim requires an elaboration on Nobles' discussion of the symbolic quoted earlier – specifically, the difference between "representational-sequential-analytic" mode and the "transformation-synchronistic-analogic" mode. I would refer the reader to Nobles' article as a beginning discussion of the methods the ancients used to verify knowledge.
16. Their video of this song cuts between an enslaved African American whose female interest is raped by the White man, to a brother working in a factory whose female interest is harassed by a White man. The effect is to emphasize that the more things change the more they remain the same. "Can't Trust It!" What you cannot trust is the mere appearance of change. *Word*.
17. See Asa Hilliard's "Pedagogy in Ancient Kemet," in *Kemet and the African Worlview*; op. cit.

Chapter 6

What is Black Consciousness?

By Nyameko Pityana

Black people are notoriously religious. Religion permeates all the depth of life so fully that it is not easy or even possible sometimes to isolate it. It must be accepted then that a study of Black Theology is a study of black consciousness or self-awareness. In the context of the black community, the two themes are intertwined. To the black people, religion is their whole system of being. It is for this reason that the church (and consequently a study of Black Theology) has added significance to all those who are seeking avenues of self-expression and the assertion of humanity and self-awareness. Thus the theme of blackness is 'a quest for new values and definitions that are meaningful and appropriate for black people and which give substance and significance to their lives.'

The significance of this mood, this quest for new values, is well summarised by Lerone Bennett, a black American historian: "The overriding need of the moment is for us to think with our own eyes. We cannot see now, because our eyes are clouded by the concepts of white supremacy. We cannot think now, because we have no intellectual instruments save those which were designed expressly to keep us from seeing. It is necessary for us to develop a new frame of reference which transcends the limits of the white concepts, for white concepts have succeeded in making black people feel that they are inferior; they have wiped out their past history; or they have presented it in such a way that they feel not pride, but shame. They have successfully created the conditions that make it easy to dominate a people. The initial step towards liberation is to abandon the frame of reference to our oppressors, and create new concepts which will release our reality.'

It has become imperative for us today to speak about Blackness and Consciousness because of the unfortunate history of events between black and white in South Africa. It is a history of continuous plunder of land and cattle by the European invaders, of devastation and the decimation of peoples, followed by their economic enslavement. It is a story of treacherous deeds, rapacity seasoned with sanctimonious hypocrisy, of 'treaties' that were not treaties but the cynical legalising of plunder, or the policy of 'divide and rule' carried out with systematic cunning to turn one group of black people against the other.

It has been alleged with truth the trader and the settler followed the missionary, who was the agent of European imperialism, working hand in hand with the colonial powers for the subjugation of the black people and the territorial extension of the imperialist power. The coming of Christianity set in motion a process of social change involving rapid disintegration of the tribal set-up and the framework of social norms and values by which people used to order their lives and their relationships. The measure of one's Christian conviction, the extent of one's love and charity was in preserving the outer signs and symbols of the European way of life – whether you had acquired European good manners, dressed as the Europeans did, liked European hymns and tunes, etc. was all-important. The acceptance of the Christian church, the triumph of the missionary endeavor, meant the rejection of African customs. The tribal community was split widely asunder when Christianised blacks were encouraged to violate tribal customs. They were exempt from the morals and customs of the tribe which, in the light of Christian morality, were condemned as immoral. This meant the rejection of those values and rituals which held us together. European missionaries had attacked the primitive rites of the people, condemned our beautiful and soulful African tribal dances – the images of our gods – recoiling from their suggestion of sensuality. The black convert followed the same line, often with more zeal, for he had to prove how Christian he was through the rejection of his past and roots.

The coming about of Christianity brought with it a deep upheaval of African norms and values, a disintegration of families and tribes, and the cancerous money economy. The effect was to prepare blacks psychologically for the onslaught that was coming from the colonial rulers. They were dehumanised and had to accept their inferior status in the land of their birth. The early church in South Africa was never prepared to face up to the elements that stifled the national development and happiness of the black people. Black Consciousness has identified of the great myth designed to rob the black man of his soul and his human dignity, brought about by the white settlers with the able assistance of their handmaiden the Church, through blood and tears, in suppression and humiliation, through dishonest means, by force and subjugation of the sons of the soil. It is the liberating effect of this self-knowledge and awareness that we refer to as Black Consciousness.

I support Adam Small's definition of blackness; 'It is not colour of the skin in terms of which we see our blackness in the first place. It is, in the first place, a certain awareness, a certain insight.' He later on refers to this awareness as a phenomenon of pride and not inferiority. Ben Khoapa (Black director of Sprocas II [second phase inaugurated early in 1972].) supports this thesis when he says: 'The blackness we are talking about is not an emotional outburst – it speaks of a newly found self-love and self-affirmation.' No man can love another unless he loves himself; no group can value the truths maintained by others unless it perceives the essentials of its own truths. Khoapa further defines blackness in terms of 'developing a black perspective.' By this, he means 'searching for black identity, self-awareness and self-esteem and the rejection of white stereotypes and morals. It means stopping looking at things through white eyes and beginning to look at things through black eyes.'

These speakers come close to the S.A.S.O. definition of black consciousness. To us it is an attitude of the mind, a way of life. Consciousness goes a step further than mere awareness, for it seeks a positive and practical exhibition of one's awareness in deeds. It is way of life – you must live and practice your consciousness in order to make it real. The S.A.S.O. policy manifesto goes on:

> (i) the basic tenet of Black Consciousness is that the black man must reject all value systems that seek to make him a foreigner in the country of his birth and reduce his basic human dignity;
> (ii) the black man must build up his own value system, and see himself as self-defined and not as defined by others;
> (iii) the concept of Black Consciousness implies the awareness by the black people of the power they wield as a group, both economically and politically, and hence group cohesion and solidarity are important facets of Black Consciousness;
> (iv) Black Consciousness will always be enhanced by the totality of involvement of the oppressed people, hence the message of Black Consciousness has to be spread to reach all sections of the black community.

Black Consciousness calls for a decultured being in the black society. It means 'a whole new vision, a totally different perspective, a penetration to the depths beneath the depth of blackness' (Lerone Bennett). Black Consciousness implies a vision of the heritage of our forefathers. It is the beginning of a new search for roots to anchor us firmly in the midst of a military struggle. It is not only a search for humanity but is an assertion and affirmation of the worth and dignity of the black man. Black Consciousness is indeed a hunger for solidarity with the oppressed people of this world. The real black people are those who embrace the positive description 'black' rather than the negatives of others who set themselves up as the standard, the criterion and hallmark of value. It is a positive confrontation with the self. Black Consciousness seeks for a social content of the lives of the black people, and to involve the cornerstone of the traditional black community.

Having thus attempted to define and explain Black Consciousness, and to present the unfortunate activities of missionaries in the course of conquest, the stage is now set for a discussion of Black Theology. The need for a Black Theology must be seen in the context of the Church's role up to the present. The Churches are still an extension of the missionary ideal, being rooted in the white 'racist' system and dominated by whites and the values of white superiority. The Church is white and it tells us that 'white Caesar can do no wrong;' instead of fighting against the real anti-Christ, it fights vigorously against those who are prepared to lose their lives that many might live. We have come to live with the contrasts between theory and practice – the white Church whose basic doctrine is love and equality between men is still an integral part of that social force, a white baasskap (Afrikaans, overlordship. As an official South African Government policy, gave way to apartheid under Dr. Verwoerd.) on which is built the 'South African way of life,' with it the consequent hatred between men, and effective subjugation of the black masses. Christianity is rooted in an explosive, basically selfish cultural system.

Black Theology, then, is an extension of Black Consciousness. Theology is the study of God, but it also studies the relationship between man and man, and thus it must have an existential and social content. This will affect the ultimate good and shape the values of society. To black people the Church needs to be a haven where they can freely shed their tears, voice their aspirations and sorrows, present their spiritual needs, respond to the world in which they live and empty their souls out to God. Traditional belief provided psychological areas where uprooted men and women could find comfort, a sense of oneness and belonging together, and a recognition of being wanted and accepted. This is the true Church. But the Church, as at present constituted, is still foreign to the soul of the black man. He will not bring forth his love, fears, social relationships, thought-patterns, attitudes, philosophical dispositions, needs, aspirations, etc. The Church of the people must have its roots deeply established in the history and traditions of those who profess its doctrine. It is the black people themselves who must work out priorities in terms of their overriding aspirations, and their emotional and intellectual involvement in the struggles and sufferings of their people. They alone can do it.

If the Church is the greatest cause of the misshapen state of our country, the blackness of souls and culture alienation, it must in future work for the culture of liberation. It must go back to the roots of broken African forms of worship, marriage, sacrifice, etc., and discover why these things were meaningful and wholesome to the traditional African community.

The awareness of this challenge motivated black students at the S.A.S.O. conference in July 1971 to pass a resolution affirming the belief that Black Theology 'is an authentic and positive articulation of the black Christian' reflection on God in the light of their experience.' It sees Christ as liberating men not only from internal bondage, but also from external enslavement. With James Cone we define Black Theology as 'a theology of liberation' that emancipates black people from white racism, and thus provides an authentic freedom for both black and white people. It affirms the humanity of white people in that it says 'no' to white oppression. It is an awareness by black people of the failure of the white establishment to work selflessly towards the values and ethics which Christianity claims to uphold. It is the will of the blacks to get their house in order and work towards the realisation of their aspirations, and their emancipation from the entanglements of an immoral society. This is where 'the twain' meet. Black Consciousness is also an awareness by a particular social group of people of its own situation in the world, and its expression of it by means of a concrete image. Both Black Theology and Black Consciousness are instruments of construction. Blackness gives a point of reference, an identity and a consciousness.

Black Theology seeks to commit black people to the risks of affirming the dignity of black personhood. 'We do this as men and as black Christians,' writes Cone. It calls upon all black people to affirm with Eldridge Cleaver: 'We shall have it on the Earth. The Earth will be leveled by our efforts to gain it.' In a nutshell, then, Black Theology concerns itself with liberation, and liberation presupposes a search for humanity and for existence as a God-created being.

The relationship between Black Theology and Black Consciousness is that one is a genus of the other. To be real in our situation, Black Theology must say something positive and meaningful to the black people. One such suggestion comes from James Ngugi: 'I believe the Church could return to (or learn lessons from) the primitive communism of the early Christian church of Peter and Paul, and the communalism of the traditional African society. With this, and working in alliance with the socialist aspirations of the African masses, we can build a new society to create a new man freed from greed, competitive hatred, and ready to realise his full potential in humble co-operation with other men in a just socialist society.'

Chapter 7

Black Consciousness
and the Quest for a True Humanity

By Steve Biko

It is perhaps fitting to start by examining why it is necessary for us to think collectively about a problem we never created. In doing so, I do not wish to concern myself unnecessarily with the white people of South Africa, but to get to the right answers, we must ask the right questions; we have to find out what went wrong – where and when; and we have to find out whether our position is a deliberate creation of God or an artificial fabrication of the truth by power-hungry people whose motive is authority, security, wealth and comfort. In other words, the 'Black Consciousness' approach would be irrelevant in a colourless and non-exploitative egalitarian society. It is relevant here because we believe that an anomalous situation is a deliberate creation of man.

There is no doubt that the colour question in South African politics was originally introduced for economic reasons. The leaders of the white community had to create some kind of barrier between blacks and whites so that the whites could enjoy privileges at the expense of blacks and still feel free to give a moral justification for the obvious exploitation that pricked even the hardest of white consciences. However, tradition has it that whenever a group of people has tasted the lovely fruits of wealth, security and prestige it begins to find it more comfortable to believe in the obvious lie and to accept it as normal that it alone is entitled to privilege. In order to believe in this seriously, it needs to convince itself of all the arguments that support the lie. It is not surprising, therefore, that in South Africa, after generations of exploitation, white people on the whole have come to believe in the inferiority of the black man, so much so that while the race problem started as an offshoot of the economic greed exhibited by white people, it has now become a serious problem on its own. White people now despise black people, not because they need to reinforce their attitude and so justify their position of privilege but simply because they actually believe that black is inferior and bad. This is the basis upon which whites are working in South Africa, and it is what makes South African society racist.

The racism we meet does not only exist in an individual basis; it is also institutionalised to make it look like the South African way of life. Although of late there has been a feeble attempt to gloss over the overt racist elements in the system, it is still true that the system derives its nourishment from the existence of anti-black attitudes in society. To make the lie live even longer, blacks have to be denied any chance of accidentally proving their equality with white men. For this reason there is job reservation, lack of training in skilled work, and a tight orbit around professional possibilities for blacks. Stupidly enough, the system turns back to say that blacks are inferior because they have no economists, no engineers, etc., although it is made impossible for blacks to acquire these skills.

To give authenticity to their lie and to show the righteousness of their claim, whites have further worked out detailed schemes to 'solve' the racial situation in this country. Thus, a pseudo-parliament has been created for 'Coloureds' (Persons of mixed race, mostly living in Cape Province.), and several 'Bantu states' are in the process of being set up. So independent and fortunate are they that they do not have to spend a cent on their defense because they have nothing to fear from white South Africa which will always come to their assistance in times of need. One does not, of course, fail to see the arrogance of whites and their contempt for blacks, even in their well-considered modern schemes for subjugation.

The overall success of the white power structure has been in managing to bind the whites together in defense of the *status quo*. By skillfully playing on that imaginary bogey – *swart gevaar* (Black peril.) – they have managed to convince even diehard liberals that there is something to fear in the idea of the black man assuming his rightful place at the helm of the South African ship. Thus after years of silence we are able to hear the familiar voice of Alan Paton saying, as far away as London: "Perhaps apartheid is worth a try.' "At whose expense, Dr. Paton?' asks an intelligent black journalist. Hence whites in general reinforce each other even though they allow some moderate disagreements on the details of subjugation schemes. There is no doubt that they do not question the validity of white values. They see nothing anomalous in the fact that they alone are arguing about the future of 17 million blacks – in a land which is the natural backyard of the black people. Any proposals for change emanating from the black world are viewed with great indignation. Even the so-called Opposition, the United Party, has the nerve to tell the Coloured people that they are asking for too much. A journalist from a liberal newspaper like *The Sunday Times* of Johannesburg describes a black student – who is only telling the truth – as a militant, impatient young man.

It is not enough for whites to be on the offensive. So immersed are they in prejudice that they do not believe that blacks can formulate their thoughts without white guidance and trusteeship. Thus, even those whites who see much wrong with the system make it their business to control the response of the blacks to the provocation. No one is suggesting that it is not the business of liberal whites to oppose what is wrong. However, it appears to us as too much of a coincidence that liberals – few as they are – should not only be determining the *modus operandi* of those blacks who oppose the system, but also leading it, in spite of their involvement in the system. To us it seems that their role spells out the totality of the white power structure – the fact that though whites are our problem, it is still other whites who want to tell us how to deal with that problem. They do so by dragging all sorts of red herrings across our paths. They tell us that the situation is a class struggle rather than a racial one. Let them go to van Tonder (Derogatory reference to the average Afrikaans-speaking farmer.) in the Free State and tell him this. We believe we know what the problem is, and we will stick by our findings.

I want to go a little deeper in this discussion because it is time we killed this false political coalition between blacks and whites as long as it is set up on a wrong analysis of our situation. I want to kill it for another reason – namely that it forms at present the greatest stumbling block to our unity. It dangles before freedom-hungry blacks promises of a great future for which no one in these groups seems to be working particularly hard.

The basis problem in South Africa has been analysed by liberal whites as being apartheid. They argue that in order to oppose it we have to form non-racial groups. Between these two extremes, they claim, lies the land of milk and honey for which we are working. The *thesis*, the *anti-thesis* and the *synthesis* have been mentioned by some great philosophers as the cardinal points around which any social revolution revolves. For the *liberals*, the *thesis* is apartheid, the *anti-thesis* is non-racialism, but the *synthesis* is very feebly defined. They want to tell the blacks that they see integration as the ideal solution. Black Consciousness defines the situation differently. The *thesis* is in fact a strong white racism and therefore, the *anti-*thesis to this must, *ipso facto*, be a strong solidarity amongst the blacks on whom this white racism seeks to prey. Out of these two situations we can therefore hope to reach some kind of balance – a true humanity where power politics will have no place. This analysis spells out the difference between the old and the new approaches. The failure of the liberals is in the fact that their *anti-thesis* is already a watered-down version of the truth whose close proximity to the thesis will nullify the purported balance. This accounts for the failure of the Sprocas (Study Project on Authority in an Apartheid Society. Set up by S.A. Council of Churches and Christian Institute in 1968.) to make any real headway, for they are already looking for an 'alternative' acceptable to the white man. Everybody in the commissions knows what is right but all are looking for the most seemly way of dodging the responsibility of saying what is right.

It is much more important for blacks to see this difference than it is for whites. We must learn to accept that no group, however benevolent, can hand power to the vanquished on a plate. We must accept that the limits of tyrants are prescribed by the endurance of those whom they oppress. As long as we go to Whitey begging cap in hand for our own emancipation, we are giving him further sanction to continue with his racist and oppressive system. We must realize that our situation is not a mistake on the part of whites but a deliberate act, and that no amount of moral lecturing will persuade the white man to 'correct' the situation. The system concedes nothing without demand, for it formulates its very method of operation on the basis that the ignorant will learn to know, the child will grow into an adult and therefore demands will begin to be made. It gears itself to resist demands in whatever way it sees fit. When you refuse to make these demands and choose to come to a round table to beg for your deliverance, you are asking for the contempt of those who have power over you. This is why we must reject the beggar tactics that are being forced on us by those who wish to appease our cruel masters. This is where the S.A.S.O. message and cry '*Black man, you are on your own!*' becomes relevant.

The concept of integration, whose virtues are often extolled in white liberal circles, is full of unquestioned assumptions that embrace white values. It is a concept ling defined by whites and never examined by blacks. It is based on the assumption that all is well with the system apart from some degree of mismanagement by irrational conservatives at the top. Even the people who argue for integration often forget to veil it in its supposedly beautiful covering. They tell each other that, were it not for job reservation, there would be a beautiful market to exploit. They forget they are talking about people. They see blacks as additional levers to some complicated industrial machines. This is white man's integration – an integration based on exploitative values. It is an integration in which black will compete with black, using each other as rungs up a step ladder leading them to white values. It is an integration in which the black man will have to prove himself in terms of these values before meriting acceptance and ultimate assimilation, and in which the poor have always been black. We do not want to be reminded that it is we, the indigenous people, who are poor and exploited in the land of our birth. These are concepts which the Black Consciousness approach wishes to eradicate from the black man's mind before our society is driven to chaos by irresponsible people from Coca-cola and hamburger cultural backgrounds.

Black Consciousness is an attitude of mind and a way of life, the most positive call to emanate from the black world for a long time. Its essence is the realisation by the black man of the need to rally together with his brothers around the cause of their oppression – the blackness of their skin – and to operate as a group to rid themselves of the shackles that bind them to perpetual servitude. It is based on a self-examination which has ultimately led them to believe that by seeking to run away from themselves and emulate the white man, they are insulting the intelligence of whoever created them black. The philosophy of Black Consciousness therefore expresses group pride and the determination of the black to rise and attain the envisaged self. Freedom is the ability to define oneself with one's possibilities held back not by the power of other people over one but only one's relationship to God and to natural surroundings. On his own, therefore, the Black Man wishes to explore his surroundings and test his possibilities – in other words to make his freedom real by whatever means he deems fit. At the heart of this kind of thinking is the realisation by blacks that the most potent weapon in the hands of oppressors is the mind of the oppressed. If one is free at heart, no manmade chains can bind one to servitude but if one's mind is so manipulated and controlled by the oppressor as to make the oppressed believe that he is a liability to the white man, then there will be nothing the oppressed can do to scare his powerful masters. Hence thinking along lines of Black Consciousness makes the black man see himself as a being complete in himself. It makes him less dependent and more free to express his manhood.

In order that Black Consciousness can be used to advantage as a philosophy to apply to people in a position like ours, a number of points have to be observed. As people existing in a continuous struggle for truth, we have to examine and question old concepts, values and systems. Having found the right answers we shall then work for consciousness among all people to make it possible for us to proceed towards putting these answers into effect. In this process, we have to evolve our own schemes, forms and strategies to suit the need and situation, always keeping in mind our fundamental beliefs and values.

In all aspects of the black-white relationship, now and in the past, we see a constant tendency by whites to depict blacks as of inferior status. Our culture, our history and indeed all aspects of the black man's life have been battered nearly out of shape in the great collision between the indigenous values and the Anglo-Boer culture.

The first people to come and relate to blacks in a human way in South Africa were the missionaries. They were in the vanguard of the colonialisation movement to 'civilise and educate' the savages and introduce the Christian message to them. The religion they brought was quite foreign to the black indigenous people. African religion in its essence was not radically different from Christianity. We also believed in one God, we had our own community of saints through whom we related to our God, and we did not find it compatible with our way of life to worship God in isolation from the various aspects of our lives. Hence worship was not a specialised function that found expression once a week in a secluded building, but rather it featured in our wars, our beer-drinking, our dances and our customs in general. Whenever Africans drank they would first relate to God by giving a portion of their beer away as a token of thanks. When anything went wrong at home they would offer sacrifice to God to appease him and atone for their sins. There was no hell in our religion. We believed in the inherent goodness of man – hence we took it for granted that all people at death joined the community of saints and therefore merited our respect.

It was the missionaries who confused the people with their new religion. They scared our people with stories of hell. They painted their God as a demanding God who wanted worship 'or else.' People had to discard their clothes and their customs in order to be accepted in this new religion. Knowing how religious the African people were, the missionaries stepped up their terror campaign on the emotions of the people with their detailed accounts of eternal burning, tearing of hair and gnashing of teeth. By some strange and twisted logic, they argued that theirs was a scientific religion and ours a superstition – all this in spite of the biological discrepancy which is at the base of their religion. This cold and cruel religion was strange to the indigenous people and caused frequent strife between the converted and the 'pagans,' for the former, having imbibed the false values from the white society, were taught to ridicule and despise those who defended the truth of their indigenous religion. With the ultimate acceptance of the western religion down went our cultural values!

While I do not wish to question the basic truth at the heart of the Christian message, there is a strong case for a re-examination of Christianity. It has proved a very adaptable religion which does not seek to supplement existing orders but – like any universal truth – to find application within a particular

79

situation. More than anyone else, the missionaries knew that not all they did was essential to the spread of the message. But the basic intention went much further than merely spreading the word. Their arrogance and their monopoly on truth, beauty and moral judgment taught them to despise native customs and traditions and to seek to infuse their own new values into these societies.

Here then we have the case for Black Theology. While not wishing to discuss Black Theology at length, let it suffice to say that it seeks to relate God and Christ once more to the black man and his daily problems. It wants to describe Christ as a fighting god, not a passive god who allows a lie to rest unchallenged. It grapples with existential problems and does not claim to be a theology of absolutes. It seeks to bring back God to the black man and to the truth and reality of his situation. This is an important aspect of Black Consciousness, for quite a large proportion of black people in South Africa are Christians still swimming in a mire of confusion – the aftermath of the missionary approach. It is the duty therefore of all black priests and ministers of religion to save Christianity by adopting Black Theology's approach and thereby once more uniting the black man with hid God.

Along look should also be taken at the educational system for blacks. The same tense situation was found as long ago as the arrival of the missionaries. Children were taught, under the pretext of hygiene, good manners and other such vague concepts, to despise their mode of upbringing at home and to question the values and customs of their society. The result was the expected one – children and parents saw life differently and the former lost respect for the latter. Now in African society it is a cardinal sin for a child to lose respect for his parent. Yet how can one prevent the loss of respect between child and parent when the child is taught by his know-all white tutors to disregard his family teachings? Who can resist losing respect for his tradition when in school his whole cultural background is summed up in one word – barbarism?

Thus we can immediately see the logic of placing the missionaries in the forefront of the colonisation process. A man who succeeds in making a group of people accept a foreign concept in which he is expert makes them perpetual students whose progress in the particular field can only be evaluated by him; the student must constantly turn to him for guidance and promotion. In being forced to accept the Anglo-Boer culture, the blacks have allowed themselves to be at the mercy of the white man and to have him as their eternal supervisor. Only he can tell us how good our performance is and instinctively each of us is at pains to please this powerful, all-knowing master. This is what Black Consciousness seeks to eradicate.

As one black write says, colonialism is never satisfied with having the native in its grip but, by some strange logic, it must turn to his past and disfigure and distort it. Hence the history of the black man in this country is most disappointing to read. It is presented merely as a ling succession of defeats. The Xhosas were thieves who went to war for stolen property; the Boers never provoked the Xhosas but merely went on 'punitive expeditions' to teach the thieves a lesson. Heroes like Makana (Early nineteenth-century Xhosa prophet, sentenced to life imprisonment on Robben Island and drowned while escaping in a boat. Refusal by blacks to accept the truth of his death led to the mythical hope of his eventual return.) who were essentially revolutionaries are painted as superstitious trouble-makers who lied to the people about bullets turning into water. Great nation-builders like Shaka are cruel tyrants who frequently attacked smaller tribes for no reason but for some sadistic purpose. Not only is there no objectivity in the history taught us but there is frequently an appalling misrepresentation of facts that sicken even the uninformed student.

Thus a lot of attention has to be paid to our history if we as blacks want to aid each other in our coming into consciousness. We have to rewrite our history and produce in it the heroes that formed the core of our resistance to the white invaders. More has to be revealed, and stress has to be laid on the successful nation-building attempts of men such as Shaka, Moshoeshoe and Hintsa (Tswana.). These areas call for intense research to provide some sorely-needed missing links. We would be too naive to expect our conquerors to write unbiased histories about us but we have to destroy the myth that our history starts in 1652, the year Van Riebeeck landed at the Cape.

Our culture must be defined in concrete terms. We must relate the past to the present and demonstrate a historical evolution of the modern black man. There is a tendency to think of our culture as a static culture that was arrested in 1652 and has never developed since. The 'return to the bush' concept suggests that we have nothing to boast of except lions, sex and drink. We accept that when colonialisation sets in it devours the indigenous culture and leaves behind a bastard culture that may thrive at the pace allowed it by the dominant culture. But we also have to realise that the basic tenets of our culture have largely succeeded in withstanding the process of bastardisation and that even at this moment we can still demonstrate that we appreciate a man for himself. Ours is a true man-centred society whose sacred tradition is that of sharing. We must reject, as we have been doing, the individualistic cold approach to life that is the cornerstone of the Anglo-Boer culture. We must seek to restore to the black the great importance we used to give to human relations, the high regard for people and their property and for life in general; to reduce the triumph of technology over man and the materialistic element that is slowly creeping into our society.

These are essential features of our black culture to which we must cling. Black culture above all implies freedom on our part to innovate without recourse to white values. This innovation is part of the natural development of any culture. A culture is essentially the society's composite answer to the varied problems of life. We are experiencing new problems every day and whatever we do adds to the richness of our cultural heritage as long as it has man as its centre. The adoption of black theatre and drama is one such important innovation which we need to encourage and to develop. We know that our love of music and rhythm has relevance even in this day.

Being part of an exploitative society in which we are often the direct objects of exploitation, we need to evolve a strategy towards our economic situation. We are aware that the blacks are still colonised even within the borders of South Africa. Their cheap labour has helped to make South Africa what it is today. Our money from the townships takes a one-way journey to white shops and white banks, and all we do in our lives is pay the white man either with labour or in coin. Capitalistic exploitative tendencies, coupled with the overt arrogance of white racism, have conspired against us. Thus in South Africa now it is very expensive to be poor. It is the poor people who stay furthest from town and therefore have to spend more money on transport to come and work for white people; it is the poor people who use uneconomic and inconvenient fuel like paraffin and coal because of the refusal of the white man to install electricity in black areas; it is the poor people who are governed by money on fines for 'technical' offenses; it is the poor people who have no hospitals and are therefore exposed to exorbitant charges by private doctors; it is the poor people who use untarred roads, have to walk long distances, and therefore experience the greatest wear and tear on commodities like shoes; it is the poor people who have to pay for their children's books while whites get them free. It does not need to be said that it is the black people who are poor.

We therefore need to take another look at how best to use our economic power, little as it may seem to be. We must seriously examine the possibilities of establishing business co-operatives whose interests will be ploughed back into community development programmes. We should think along such lines as the 'but back' campaign once suggested in Johannesburg and establish our own banks for the benefit of the community. Organisational development amongst blacks has only been low because we have allowed it to be. Now that we know we are on our own, it is an absolute duty for us to fulfill these needs.

The last step in Black Consciousness is to broaden the base of our operation. One of the basic tenets of Black Consciousness is totality of involvement. This means that all blacks must sit as one big unit, and no fragmentation and distraction from the mainstream of events be allowed. Hence we must resist the attempts by protagonists of the Bantustan theory to fragment our approach. We are oppressed not as individuals, not as Zulus, Xhosas, Vendas or Indians. We are oppressed because we are black. We must use that very concept to unite ourselves and to respond as a cohesive group. We must cling to each other with a tenacity that will shock the perpetrators of evil.

Our preparedness to take upon ourselves the cudgels of the struggle will see us through. We must remove from our vocabulary completely the concept of fear. Truth must ultimately triumph over evil, and the white man has always nourished his greed on this basic fear that shows itself in the black community. Special Branch agents will not turn the lie into truth, and one must ignore them. In a true bid for change we have to take off our coats, be prepared to lose our comfort and security, our jobs and positions of prestige, and our families, for just as it is true that 'leadership and security are basically incompatible,' a struggle without casualties is no struggle. We must realise that prophetic cry of black students: 'Black man, you are on your own!'

Some will charge that we are racist but these people are using exactly the values we reject. We do not have the power to subjugate anyone. We are merely responding to provocation in the most realistic possible way. Racism does not only imply exclusion of one race by another – it always presupposes that the exclusion is for the purposes of subjugation. Blacks have had enough experience as objects of racism not to wish to turn the tables. While it may be relevant now to talk about black in relation to white, we must not make this our preoccupation, for it can be a negative exercise. As we proceed further towards the achievement of our goals let us talk more about ourselves and our struggle and less about whites.

We have set out on a quest for true humanity, and somewhere on the distant horizon we can see the glittering prize. Let us march forth with courage and determination, drawing strength from our common plight and our brotherhood. In time we shall be in a position to bestow upon South Africa the greatest gift possible – a more human face.

Chapter 8

The Meaning of a Minority in America

By Gwinyai H. Muzorewa

The concept of "a minority" is not only sociological, psychological, racial, economical, but it is also political. As the term is used, especially in the so-called First World, minority is not just a community that is smaller than others within society. Neither is it a numerical factor, because, if it were, the white community globally speaking, would be more qualified to be designated as minority. Caucasians would be the ones struggling with the current concerns of those presently designated as minority. Also, the rich (1%) of most countries would be the minority. Or, males rather than females, would be properly designated "minority", but such is not the case. In fact it is interesting to note that sometimes minority may in fact be describing the two-thirds of the world's population! Obviously, this signifies that there is more to it than just population or numbers. What is "a minority" in America?

A Definition of Minority

A definition of a minority group according to sociologists is people differentiated from others in the same society by race, nationality, religion, or language. Such a group thinks of itself as a differentiated people and is in fact differentiated with derogatory or negative connotations. The definition of "a minority group" is not complete without the dimension of power. As we have noted in this chapter, being minority has nothing to do with numbers (as in population) or age (as in a dependent youth). Rather, a minority group is generally subjected to certain exclusions, discriminations, and other differential treatment. Being a minority tends to be characterized by a set of attitudes and behaviors.

The term "minority" is not to be taken literally because its definition is socio-political. No group of people is a natural minority, or inevitably minority because cultures define them as minority even before any demographic considerations. If being minority were a question of population, minorities would have eventually disintegrated over generations through amalgamating and assimilating. If the group chose not to do either of these, it would still cease to be minority by simply not differing themselves. Thus, a set of attitudes must be in place in order to designate a group minority, or, as a condition for a group to differentiate itself as such.

We re-iterate, numbers are not definitionally crucial. For instance, what sense does it make to describe people of African descent as minority (as is done in the United States of America) when black people in the world are a clear majority compared to the so-called white race? Or, in the states of Mississippi, Alabama or South Carolina where blacks are a clear majority numerically, why would one continue to describe blacks as "minority?" The population of the United States of America is by far smaller than that of the continent of Africa (not including Caucasians!). Yet, an African Head of State visiting Washington is designated "minority" the moment he lands in Washington International Airport or JFK International Airport! Clearly then, what is at stake is a certain set of attitudes, which dates back to Europe, the cradle of ethnocentrism.

The Origin of the Term "Minorities"

The term minority can be traced back to Europe where it was applied to various national groups who were identified with particular territories by virtue of long residence, but had lost their sovereignty over these territories to other more numerous groups of a different nationality. The criterion was power. Note, the "minority" group did not have to live together. They could be dispersed all over the country of which they were now subjects. So, it made no difference whether they lived in clusters or in *Diaspora*, (if we may borrow the term), what mattered was the fact that there were dominant political and economic institutions which looked out for the benefit of the "majority", as well as enacted laws to regulate the political existence of the minorities. A good example would be that the minority groups might have to send their own community leaders to the national assembly rather than being able to participate in the general national electoral process. Such preferential treatment always goes with political oppression no matter how subtle. For instance, a representative elected under such "privileged conditions" is being told: "You really do not represent the nation. You were only chosen by a small group therefore your *vote* carries less weight than that of the regular representative.

If then this is the definition of minority, and since this is what white America understands to be the meaning of *minorities*, why have the people of African descent embraced (and, one might say) gladly such a designation? While no one should impose an answer on others, this author simply wishes to point out two things:

a) whereas minorities in America, including the Native American, Mexicans, Chicanos, etc., receive some material benefits (scholarships, business loans, window-dressing political positions, etc.) by accepting the designation minority;

b) whereas minorities generally and legally are entitled to preferential treatment in employment situations, housing subsidy, etc.

Therefore, it follows that they have accepted the guest status in their own land of nativity. They have yielded their right to this land. Along with that, they have

86

also lost their full status as full humanity. Worse still, they have disowned their original identity in favor of the transient and often elusive benefits which the dominant and deceptive culture is giving them. The message in this chapter (and the rest of the book) is: *Know Thyself.*

We could describe the meaning of minority in religious or linguistic terms, but time and space does not allow us here. However, it is fairly obvious that being oppressed because of one's race is more devastating than oppression based on religious conviction or linguistic pattern. These two are learned whereas race is God-given. No one can choose what race to be born in.

Generally, the term minority is used to describe people who have certain physical characteristics, which set them apart from the majority community. Of course, there are references to ethnicity, which may also be racially identifiable because of their peculiar characteristics, such as faith, language and tradition. They may also shape certain customs which make them peculiar to the society as a whole. When we say "peculiar" we are not to be misconstrued to connote negativity.

We note from the beginning that we subscribe to the theory of "different, but equal." It is erroneous if not evil to ill-treat a group of people just because they are different from the dominant group. In fact, human beings ought to respect each other precisely at the point of their "difference," as well as their commonality. Our differences in color, language, religion, or physique are a mark of the genius of the creator. For those who believe in and argue for various evolution theories, this contention is still valid namely, that the uncaused cause had the genius of creating matter which had the potential of "being different" but still the same! It was apparently a conscious decision to create variety. If "different, but equal" were to be adopted world wide one would predict that most of the notorious problems of the minority would be non-existent. For, why should "being different" by design be a problem, or the basis for ill treatment?

Differences may influence one's choice or preference, but need not license ethnocentrism. The problem arises when the self-acclaimed dominant group develops some preconceived ideas (stereotypes) about other communities, which are different (though equal) from themselves. If we are to analyze most stereotypical behavior, we readily discover that at the root of it all, is ignorance, insecurity and sheer vanity, all caused by a false sense of superiority. Stereotypical thinking is a manifestation of hidden insecurity, explicit arrogance, disguised hypocrisy and ignorance. In the age of post-enlightenment where scientific research methods play a significant role to collect useful data, one can readily assemble and identify stereotypical attitudes.

Characteristically, what is aroused by stereotypical behavior triggers "a stereotypical response" in the targeted community. Differently put, a group that is "stereotypically" branded, for instance, lazy or dishonest, will necessarily elicit behavior (perhaps, in their defense) which confirms that for which the group is falsely accused. Should one out of ten say steals, or acts in a lazy manner, such behavior is treated as "the norm" or "the rule," serving the purpose of confirming or substantiating a wrong hypothesis. People are made into a minority when their general behavior is different from the majority group. Apparently, the initial problem is with the dominant group, which conjures up a set of attitudes, which, in turn, creates a corresponding and necessary response in the thinking of the minority community. What develops is the age-old manifestation of phobia-phobia, (fear of fear), not even simply fear of the unknown. This phenomenon also indicates the emergence of evil. Sin was not created, rather it "comes into being" out of ignorance, which is often a negative force. Knowledge is power, and, in responsible hands, often has positive effects. Therefore, knowledge tends to empower a person, whereas, ignorance undermines one's sense of self-worth. The key is: KNOW THYSELF!

The problem of the minority is grave concern when these people are subjected to inhumane conditions due to "whatever aspect" their culture differs from that of the ethnocentric and dominant community. Once a feeling has been fostered, the rest of what follows can, in fact, become devastatingly tangible. What might have started as the community's "figment of its' imagination," takes on, not only tangible, but destructive proportions. As a consequence, when a minority group takes on an isolationist or separatist stance, which may be misinterpreted for being racism, the motive is to self-reaffirm, and consolidate what good they own, versus the vain negativity they sustain. This is why the question has lingered in some people's minds. Some people have actually dared to ask for an example: "Are black people in America not racists?" Those who raise this question at least are, crafty enough not to ask the ridiculous: "Are black people in America angry about how they are treated?" In addition to an affirmative answer to the latter question, one is advised that when a minority community clings to itself, that is not "being racist." In fact, the minority ought to prefer its own kind for the purpose of self-affirmation and preservation. Self-empowerment is not to be confused with being "racist." Race conscious and color conscious behavior need not be mistaken for bigotry. When the people of African descent express their wish to retain and reaffirm their identity, that is not the same as when a dominant group puts other groups at a socio-economic disadvantage on the grounds that "they are not like us." Or, "they are not as good as us." Or, plainly they are inferior to us," simply because they are different from us. Characteristic of the attitude of the dominant community, is the false assumption that "all other people are wrong."

> "The whole world should look up to us for rightness: right accent, ideology, right foods, right values, right religion, right family concepts, right everything."

Knowingly, or unconsciously, the dominant community puts social pressure on the "minority group" to conform, failing which the latter group is penalized in both subtle and obvious ways. There is a rather unfortunate coincidence that occurs. Members of a new group usually tend to strive to conform in order to be acceptable. At the same time, the ethnocentric group consciously or unconsciously puts pressures on the minority to conform and typically, this entails giving up one's culture, socio-religious values, and often times even one's dignity, replacing these with foreign value systems, meaning, less structures, and dehumanizing status.

Thus, the term "minority" as defined elsewhere in this chapter refers to any group that is "forced" to give up its values, folkways and mores in order to trade off with the values of the "ethnocentric" and dominant culture. It has everything to do with survival, not justice or equality. In rare instances, one could be a "minority" among people of one's own race if one is "held ransom" by the group. Another meaning of "minority" simply designates anyone depending on the socio-religious and economical circumstances prevalent at the time in question. The term "minority" cannot be applied at any time as an empowerment label. However, it may be used for the purpose of "recruiting" people in a similar condition, wanting to consolidate themselves for the purpose of self-affirmation. But there is a great danger in this practice once one permanently internalizes the concept. In the United States many college students "benefit" from answering to the oppressive name: minority because they need financial aid. Upon graduation, the same population is lured into internalizing "being minority" by corporations which advertise jobs "for minorities and women" to apply. Such minorities go through life answering to the name: minorities! But in this chapter we intend to conscientize people of African descent by asking ourselves: How long will we answer to a name that is other than who God created us to be? How long? To this rhetorical question, the answer is: As long as one does not know who he or she is.

Furthermore, it is evident that the society which used to label amenities (public toilets) as "For blacks only" or "For whites only" now has attempted to be subtle by posting signs: "For Minorities Only!" The main danger with this system of dehumanization (other systems include slavery) is that a whole race can completely lose its identity and destiny, not to mention achieving full humanity.

The Problems of the Minorities in General

The dilemma of any group of people labeled "minorities" stems largely from the "choices" that these groups are forced to make in order to survive. In the case of North America, many groups that choose to migrate to the United States of America find themselves having to make one more choice, this time a "forced choice." The racist American society greets the immigrant with a subtle, but clearly ethnocentric attitude. "You have to be like us, in order to be truly welcomed by all of us." Sometimes this concept is expressed in a variety of subtle ways. In the Church they may say: "Pray in your language", or "sing in your dialect." ... Thus, for one to be accepted into racist America, one has to "willingly" renounce one's cultural identity, values and languages just to mention the major items.

The sad part comes when, after the group has done all it can, the racist American society still will not accept it completely because, in the case of people with rich malign, their pigmentation can never be totally accepted by those deficient in malign. Whites are jealous and insecure because as some theorists argue, they are headed toward extinction. Or, one group has a particular ethnic background, which white America can never completely destroy. The Jewish tradition is a good example. Again, when this happens, the group realized it could only do so much. The only other line of action would be to "cling to themselves" after all, that is the best form of humanity they know and are familiar with. In sum, self-affirmation is the ultimate key to racial empowerment, and this is the gateway to true freedom.

Furthermore, as the new immigrant approaches the City of New York, or whatever port of entry, one is "warmly" greeted by the Statue of Liberty, a beacon of freedom. The statue represents the belief of the American people that "all men are created free and equal," that American's dedicate their country to guaranteed "unalienable right to life liberty, and the pursuit of happiness." But there is a gross discrepancy between this message and how most white Americans treat different groups of immigrants, which thereby puts freedom and justice to a test. For some, the message is a simple and straight forward as it reads. For others, specifically, people of color, what one reads is quite different from what one may experience. One encounters the socio-economic pinch of a grossly unjust society. The group without any reference to statistics experiences that feeling of injustice. One white American could make one million colored immigrants feel this injustice because the felling creates a chasm between "us" (the white American) and "them" (the colored immigrants). This is what creates the "minority complex" among those who are held hostage in "a free country."

The irony of the American situation is that when the Anglo-Saxon white Protestants came to North America in the 17th century, the native Americans welcomed them warmly, until the natives themselves were "held hostage" and are being gradually forced into extinction. White Americans' concept of false superiority and practice makes it difficult for them "to Learn" true hospitality from the native Americans be cause these are people of color. "What good can come out of colored people?" They ask themselves.

The Future of Minority Presence in the United States of America

Discussing the problems of the minorities in general tends to turn a painful existential reality into nothing more than an academic topic, unfortunately. Yet there are real people hundreds of millions of them who are made to suffer due to this phenomenon. Therefore, there is need to address specific issues in this discussion. Major groups involved in the category of the oppressed in the U.S.A. include the Asians, the Filipinos, the Chinese, the native Americans, and the African Americans, on whom I am going to focus. Note, these groups experience this "minority" complex whether they are American citizens or not, since we have established that "being minority" is not about census. Neither is it about legal status. It is mainly a question of who is "in" and who is "out." Assimilation is the watchword. Let us remember that the African Americans, even after the emancipation, and being citizens who have the right to vote, are still treated as "minorities in their own country and by their own constitution." This makes our argument more substantial. Oppression in the United States is

90

not only based on being foreign; rather, it is based on race. An African American may rise to the highest position in this society, but he or she will always be despised in the eyes of most white Americans who are representatives of their own stereotypical "world view." As it is true that not all white racists perceive "people of color" in exactly the same way, it is also the case that people of African descent in America have responded and reacted in different ways to the problem of oppression, due to racism in America.

Four distinct schools of thought (or tendencies) have developed over the decades of struggle for "full humanity" in America. Let me quickly point out that one hopes that these "schools of thought" do not represent division among the African Americans in their oppression because such a division would further weaken the African. Neither should it be interpreted to mean that some accept the status quo more than others do. Rather, these perspectives are to be viewed as representing perceived methods by which the oppressed African Americans believe they can overcome the persistent burden. Again, this can only happen if classism is not allowed to create economic cracks and crevices within the black community (or any of the oppressed minority victims). Most prominent leaders including Booker T. Washington, who was born during slavery in Virginia, W.E.B. Du Bois who was "born free" and was the first black to receive a Ph.D., a Jamaican born, Marcus Garvey and then several civil rights activists, all believe in unity in community, self-affirmation, and black empowerment. However, each represents a different school of thought ... different perspective and approach.

Booker T. Washington's approach to the problem of "being the minority" found an institution which would serve as a model of the vocational education he saw as the way for blacks to raise themselves and gain the respect and tolerance of whites (Karenga. 1992.152.). Karenga has summarized Washington's philosophy succinctly in his words:

Washington's thought and practice were molded and informed by four major factors:

1. His experience in slavery
2. His education at Hampton Institute
3. The tasks before him at Tuskegee; and,
4. His reading of the socio-historical setting in which he operated" (Karenga. 1993. 152.).

Washington had experienced the devastating effects and condition of slavery. He had known the brutality and immorality of the conscienceless Caucasians who raped African women and killed their men like non-human beings. Washington had been patronized so much by whites while he was at Hampton that he learned that to get what one wants from the whites, just pay them the homage they expect. Finally, Washington had rationalized that it was of no use to protest against the Southern whites because all that would be counterproductive. Washington's own philosophy is spelled out in his Atlanta Exposition Speech: 1968: 218-224.

In sum, Washington advocated black accommodation to racial inequality and disenfranchisement. He was willing to settle for less than his full share of the pie! Washington simply believed that blacks ought to be at the disposal of the whites, and blacks had better comply, occupying a subordinate role. He believed that blacks ought to be preoccupied with "material prosperity" even at the expense of equality and political rights. For him, economic progress was more crucial than political power and human rights combined. In addition to his accommodationist's philosophy, he also realized that the African American is entitled to the right to vote, equality and genuine freedom with responsibility, but believed that was asking for too much! Could it be that this is the type of people racist Americans would rather live with?

Another major voice for a significant black sector was W.E.B. Du Bois, a Harvard Ph.D. graduate, a historian and sociologist. Du Bois differed with Washington on several issues. According to Karenga, Du Bois rejected "Washington's demand that blacks give up political power, insistence on civil rights and higher education." However, using different methods and strategies, Du Bois and Washington always opposed "racism and oppression." But, on matters of "injustice, the caste system and higher education" the two men did not see "eye to eye." Du Bois argued for the "talented tenth" that would lead black people to freedom and a higher level of human life (Karenga. 1993. 156.). Du Bois also advocated a cultural nationalism and pluralism emphasizing black pride and heritage. However, Du Bois, unlike the advocates of the "back-to-Africa" movement, believed that blacks fully belonged to the United States. Blacks have contributed too much to the development of the American economy.

As full members of this American society, Du Bois believed in "confrontational activities in the struggle for social, political and economic right and gains" (Karenga. 1999. 156.). He advocated concepts of self-determination and racial solidarity. Along with this, Du Bois was among the first to promote Pan-Africanism -- actually, he chaired four of the six Pan-African congresses held between 1919 and 1945. As if to commemorate his commitment to the motherland, Du Bois spent last days on earth in Ghana, where he died, and was buried at the age of 95. His socialism was clearly outweighed by his nationalism, implying that for him, human dignity, justice, freedom and power had preceded over other matters.

Marcus Garvey, an ardent Pan-Africanist, dedicated to the liberation of all people of African descent, has been known by many as the father of modern Black Nationalism. Garvey's nationalism was more like Washington's than Du Bois' in that Garvey did not see much hope in blacks fighting for political power in the U.S.A. He believed the most viable proposition was for blacks to find their freedom in their own continent of Africa hence the back-to-Africa movement. Racial pride was the most crucial quality.

But, more than Washington, Garvey believed that industrial opportunities were as important and desirable as political power. Another major point of

92

difference was on the issue of integration. Du Bois advocated integration, while Garvey believed in the purity of the race, pride of the African race, and to achieve this "separate but equal" was the solution. Clearly, Garvey did not want to compromise African identity, pride, freedom, and full potential.

Since the NAACP was obviously white dominated, Garvey accused Du Bois of being controlled by the whites on that board. Garvey's Universal Negro Improvement Association where himself was the founder, was obviously "a black people's organization." It was this and other examples, which Garvey used to demonstrate to Du Bois that he was not only realistic but also practical, whereas Du Bois was merely a theorist and abstract academician. Furthermore, Garvey advocated statehood and power at the state level self-governing while Du Bois emphasized political participation in the context of the U.S. political machinery. In short, many scholars agree that Garvey set up a model for a classic Black Nationalism, which many have been imitating ever since fully belonged to the United States. In short, many scholars agree that Garvey set up a model for a classic Black Nationalism, which many have been imitating ever since fully belonged to the United States. Blacks have contributed too much to the development of the U.S.A. economy.

Several theories emerge from our brief discussion of various African philosophical and political perspectives of our African American ancestors. A brief comment on each of them should point us to future prospects.

Booker T. Washington's accommodationist philosophy has been successful and practical for people of African descent and who are satisfied with less than their full share of the pie. The question is who are these people? They are those who are so tolerant that they answer to names given to them by the racist oppressors; they are those who will accept second place when they are entitled to first place. Like everybody else; they are those who will accept second place when they are entitled to first place. Like everybody else; they are those who are busy trying to hide their identity; they are those who are busy trying to be who they are not (and will never be!). Those who settle for accomodationism refuse to be "bona fide" citizens of the United States of America, yet they are native to this land. Finally, there are those who seriously need to be awakened to the reality of racism, and how people of the African descent must claim their proper place in society.

Chapter 9

Black Economics

By Maulana Karenga

Introduction

Economics is generally defined as the study and process of producing, distributing (or exchanging) and consuming goods and services. Such a definition, however, in part hides the fact of how economics penetrates every aspect of social life. Whether one talks of poverty, income, jobs, housing, class, racial discrimination, education, religion, the arts or social status, all at one level imply and necessitate a concern with economics. Even the major ideologies and social systems of today which compete for the minds of people i.e., capitalism, socialism, nationalism, etc., have been shaped in significant part by important economists of the past, i.e., Adam Smith, Karl Marx, and John Maynard Keynes, etc. (Heilbroner, 1972; Fusfield, 1977).

Moreover, it would be relatively impossible and certainly unwise and irregular for national leaders to make political decisions without economic considerations. In fact, politics and economics are unavoidably linked on several levels. First, wealth and power are mutually engendered and supportive. The possession of one implies and leads to the possession of the other. Likewise, the lack of one implies the lack of the other. Secondly, those with wealth and power tend to strive to monopolize both. Thirdly, those with wealth and power tend to shape society in their own image and interests at the expense of those without it, especially Blacks and other Third world peoples whose relative possession of both wealth and power are at low levels. It is thus difficult to imagine corporations not having political power, i.e., significant and greater control and influence over public policy, especially as it relates to their own interests. Finally, the struggle for distributive justice or an egalitarian distribution of social wealth is both an economic and a political struggle. In fact, the decision of who gets what and how much is both an economic and political decision, made by those whose wealth and political power enable them to control directly or indirectly the decision-making process.

It is this interrelatedness of politics and economics which prompts some Black and radical economists to insist that the science of economics is best categorized as *political economy*. As the staff of the *Review of Black Political Economy* explained in their inaugural issue (Spring/Summer, 1970), the term seems a more accurate one. For it "includes within its scope the political realities of economic relations" and thus describes "the necessary focus of Black economic development." Moreover, given the political dimension of economics, "for Black people to affect any significant alteration in their economic position, they will first be obliged to develop a sound political strategy."

Political Economic Status

The ghettoization of the African American community is both an economic and political reality as argued in Chapter IV. Even allowing for class differences, the general state of political and economic subordination is obvious and unarguable. The only question is the character and process of the subordination. The race and class character and process of the exploitation and oppression of the Black community has been summed up by many as domestic colonialism. As early as 1962, in an article reprinted in a later book, Harold Cruse (1968) used the category "domestic colonialism" to discuss Black-white relations in the U.S. society. He (1968:77) argued that "from the beginning (the African American) has existed as a colonial being... The only fact which differentiates the (African American's) status from that of a pure colonial status is that his position is maintained in the "home country" in close proximity to the dominant racial group." Kenneth Clark (1964) argued the colony analogy two years later using the political, economic and social structure of Harlem to demonstrate it. Although, he (1965) did not pursue the analogy in *Dark Ghetto*, he used the category and most of his analysis pointed to the same conclusion.

Two years later, Stokely Carmichael and Charles Hamilton (1967:6ff) advanced the internal colony analogy in their book on Black power. Admitting that "the analogy is not perfect," they argued that regardless of the difference between the classical colony and the ghetto, there are still enough significant similarities to justify calling the ghetto an internal colony. Among these similarities were: 1) economic exploitation of the colony as a cheap supply of labor and a captive market; 2) external control of the colony by the ruling country, usually by indirect rule through political puppets; 3) the socio-psychological results of racist humiliation and assignment of Blacks to "subordinate, inferior status in society." Robert Allen (1970) also discussed the Black community in terms of the internal colony analogy. He (1970:7ff) maintained that "Black communities are victims of white imperialism and colonial exploitation." Colonialism, he suggested, can be defined as direct and overall subordination, administration, economic exploitation and cultural destruction of a nation, people or country by another whose power is enshrined in law and backed by coercive bodies, i.e., armies and police. Thus, he concludes, the status of the Black population in the United States shows a striking similarity to this colonial situation.

Allowing for limitation of the analogy, one still is unavoidably struck by the political oppression and economic exploitation of the Black community which stand at the heart of any form of colonialism. The ghetto economy stands out at the center of urban poverty. Its unemployment is so high that if it occurred in the overall economy, it would be defined as symptomatic of a depression. Its labor is superexploited in both racial and class terms, being employed mainly in the low-wage sector of the economy and with unequal power in unions in spite of proportional representation (Harris, 1982).

Moreover, the ghetto economy is marked by a continuous drain of financial, physical and human resources. The savings are placed in financial institutions whose loans are primarily made to enterprises outside the inner city. The approximately $287 billion annual purchasing power is spent mainly outside the ghetto. Andrew Brimmer (1982:30) had noted that Black firms are continuously losing ground in growing competition by white firms for Black consumer dollars. "In 1969 receipts of Black firms were equal to 13.5 percent of total Black income. By 1980 the share was down to .9 percent, and his projection for 1990 was a decline to 7 percent. Furthermore, products sold in the ghetto and outside it are made outside the ghetto, most of the businessmen live outside the ghetto, and the enterprises which service the retail business, i.e., wholesale, shipping, advertising, etc., also are located outside the ghetto (Browne, 1971).

Finally, there is a lower level of repairs and renewal of physical plants in the ghetto, and better educated Blacks with higher salaries tend to move out, thus depriving the ghetto of persons whose education, income, and initiatives would be valuable to its revitalization and organized efforts to free itself. It is in such context of oppression, exploitation and relative powerlessness, that the colonial analogy seems to be the definitive one (Tabb, 1970; Fusfield, 1970; Browning, Marshall and Tabb, 1984).

Data of Economic Disadvantage

Summing up this situation, David Swinton (1990, 1991, 1992) has argued that the African American community is above all marked by *economic disadvantage* in varied and essential ways. In his reports to the National Urban League on the economic *State of Black America*, Swinton (1992:61) states that "in comparison to Americans of European descent, African Americans experience substantially lower economic status throughout the income distribution." Moreover, he continues," (as) we have noted on several occasions, relatively well-off Blacks are much less well off than well-off whites, and relatively poor Blacks are much poorer than poor whites." He concludes saying "all standard measures of central tendency have consistently revealed the relatively low economic status of the population as a whole."

Income Inequality. Swinton (1992:74) shows a clear pattern of inequality between Blacks and whites. As he notes, "African American per capita income in 1990 was $9,017 compared to $15,265 for whites." This translates as Blacks' having "only 59.1 percent as much income per capita as whites had during 1990." Moreover, data show the Black male median income to be $12,868 for 1990 compared to white male income of $21,170. This equals only 60.8 of white male median income. The Black female median income of 1990 was $8,328 compared to $10,317 of the white female's median income or 85 percent.

Poverty Rates. Swinton (1992:88) also states that "income disadvantages for Blacks lead directly to higher rates of poverty. In 1990, 31.9 percent of Blacks were in poverty as compared to 10.7 percent of whites. This means that "for Blacks 9.8 million persons were in poverty, up by 500 thousand over 1989." This picture is made bleaker by the fact that the rate of poverty among Black children was 44.8 percent compared to 15.9 percent for white children. Thus over 44 out of every 100 Black children are in poverty compared to 16 of every 100 white children. This picture of child poverty is explained in part and at the same time made more severe by the fact that over 50 percent of all persons living in female-headed Black families (6,005,000) live in poverty compared to 30 percent of persons in white female-headed households. Female-headed Black families are 45 percent of all Black families compared to 12 percent of white families. Swinton (1992:91) concludes that "the problem of female-headed poverty is of much larger magnitude for Blacks." Finally, Swinton (1992:95) states that 13 percent of the African American community received public assistance (6.5 percent) or supplemental security income (5.3 percent) compared to 33.3 percent of the white population.

Employment Status. The economic disadvantage of African American community appears also in employment data and labor market trends. Employment for Blacks fluctuates between 54.1 and 55.7 percent. This low employment rate, however, is higher than the historical average and "is primarily due to the increasing participation and employment of Black women" (Swinton, 1992:97ff). The "employment rates for Black women have risen from mid-40 percent range to 54 percent of the (African American community) over the past two decades." Overall unemployment fluctuates also and ranges between 11.8 and 13.1 percent for the Black community as a whole. For the first three quarters of 1991, the unemployment rate average was 12.4. The past two decades have yielded data of high unemployment among Black men, Black women and Black teenagers. "Adult Black men have had unemployment rates above 10 percent for every year since 1980 and adult Black women have had unemployment rates above 10 percent in every year except 1989 and 1990 when their employment rate was 9.8 percent" (Swinton, (1992:102). Moreover, "the lowest unemployment rate experienced by Black teenagers since 1980 was 31.1 percent in 1990." The unemployment rate of Black teenagers, however, fluctuates between 30 and 50 percent and there is the likelihood it will rise higher given the fact they will "comprise an increasing proportion of the youth population; and probably will continue to be concentrated in areas of limited job opportunities" (Anderson, 1982:5). Furthermore, Black youth unemployment will be more difficult to reduce due to increased competition for jobs and the problems of preparation (Freeman and Holzer, 1986).

There are several reasons offered for Black unemployment: low educational levels and lack of job skills, the recurring recession, unwillingness to take menial jobs; displacement, the move of industry from the central city; shutdowns in industries where Blacks are in heavy numbers; lack of viable social networks and above all, continuing discrimination (Wilson, 1987; Jaynes

98

and Williams, 1989:315-324). In his analysis of racism, Alexis (1980) challenges Becker's (1957) often quoted study on discrimination for its focus on personal rather than collective discrimination and the problem this poses for employment. He (11980:338) argues that Becker's focus on personal discrimination fails to see that "discrimination is against Blacks as a group, not as individuals" and that hiring or not hiring is a political decision as well as an economic one. In what he calls the "malice-envy approach," the economic discriminator (employer, employee, government or consumer) interprets the relative well-being of Blacks as a decrease in his/her own welfare. Blacks are thus viewed as opponents and under such competitive conditions, the white employer "might be willing to reduce (his/her) own welfare, if by doing so, (he/she) could reduce the welfare of (his/her) competitor by more." Given this political aspect of economic discrimination, Alexis maintains that the "remedy to the economic plight of Blacks is not to be found in economic activity alone." Thus, "until and unless Blacks achieve some degree of effective power, (i.e., command over institutions – public and private – that establish the rules of the game and determine the payoffs) they will continue to suffer from second-class economic citizenship."

The problem of preparation indeed remains a problem of employment. Brimmer (1982:32) predicted correctly in the 80's that science and technology with heavy reliance on computers would be the area of the fastest growing occupations. Thus, he stated, "if Blacks are to get a fair share of the new jobs, they will have to accelerate and upgrade their basic preparation in mathematics and communication skills." Secondly, Brimmer argued that the private sector will expand more rapidly than the public sector. He also projected that this decline will cost Blacks jobs given their large share of public jobs.

Not only will most of the jobs be in the private sector, he predicted correctly, but they will demand a high degree of skill. In fact, corporate requirements for entry and promotion are the typical skills needed, as Brimmer suggested they would be. For many of these professional and managerial positions are in production, marketing, distribution and financial controls (i.e. accounting). Clearly, Black preparation is necessary to be eligible for these positions. But whether they will get them depends not only on their availability, but also the willingness of firms to hire Blacks. Without a concern for the problems of the economy and the problems of discrimination in it, job possibilities are not a realistic assumption.

Nevertheless, as Margaret C. Simms of the Joint Center for Political and Economic Studies argues, "the key to creating a productive work force is quality education and training" (McCoy, 1992:202). For "increased real incomes are closely related to education." She maintains that for Blacks, especially higher educational levels are associated with greater employment. As other African American economists, she advocates a comprehensive strategy for improving the productivity of the U.S. workforce which will, of necessity, include African Americans. She notes that such a comprehensive strategy "will provide: adequate preparation of new entrants to the labor force; the upgrading of low-skilled workers; and the retraining of adult workers for new jobs and improved technology."

Occupational Distribution. Swinton (1991:62) reports that African Americans are further disadvantaged by unfavorable occupation distribution. "Employed Black males (are) only about half as likely as white males to be employed in managerial, sales or professional occupations, and only about three-quarters as likely to be employed as technicians or craft workers." These occupational categories are the top-paying ones for males and, of course, Blacks are restricted in these areas and highly represented in the lowest paying occupational categories. Similarly, Black women were less likely to be employed in the top paying jobs. "In 1990 40.8 percent of white women and only 28.1 percent pf Black women were employed in these good jobs" (Swinton, 1992:106). On the other hand, "37.3 percent of Black women compared to 22.9 percent of white women were more likely to be employed in household or other service, laborer and operative occupations."

Finally, although education is noted as central to the possibility of better paying jobs, Swinton (1992:114) argues that in general "racial inequality does not decline with education." For both males and females, racial inequality in wages are about the same across educational levels. "For females, racial inequality increased slightly with education up to a college degree (whereas) females with four years of college have equal wages."

Darity and Myers (1992:136-137) list several factors for earning inequality: 1) increase in female-headed families who earn less; 2) "the continued decline in the relative earnings and educational prospects of young Black males;" 3) the unevenness of educational gains within the Black community; and 4) a continuing gap between Blacks and whites in higher education. For example, "in 1990 46 percent of whites had some college education compared to only 37 percent of Blacks."

Problems of Race and Class

The race and class question serves as a problem for Black economics on two levels. First, both race and class are the bases of Black exploitation and oppression. And secondly, the development of sharp class divisions among Blacks tend to impede an overall solution to the problem of Black economic development (Turner, 1976). In fact, the interpretation of the source of and solution to the problem of Black oppression can in fact end up as a class focused interpretation rather than an overall Black one.

For example, one could take the interpretations of Thomas Sowell (1975, 1981a, 1981b). Sowell essentially argues that race is not as important a factor as often suggested and that the attitudes and skills of Blacks may be as important to social achievement and social status as racism. Moreover, he maintains that demographics rather than racism explain differences in income among ethnic groups. Thus, the source of Blacks' differential income can be found for example in the fact of age, i.e., they are disproportionately younger and still climbing the income ladder, and in the fact of residence, i.e., they live more often in the South where wages are usually lower. He also rejects affirmative action as insulting treatment and gratuitous government intervention in an admittedly flawed though essentially workable system. Finally, Sowell argues that racism, where it exists, can be explained by economic motivations and interests and that once racism becomes economically unprofitable, racists will no longer practice it. Therefore, he argues that market forces are much more effective mediators of racial inequalities than non-market forces like the collective Black struggle and government intervention.

Much of the criticism of Sowell has been ad hominem and unworthy of repetition. But his argument tends to support and dovetail William Wilson's ideas which will be covered below. Thus, criticism of Wilson's contentions will for the most part answer Sowell's. However, it is important to note that Sowell, like Wilson, tends to blame the victim, overlook or minimize the active force and result of racism, and while blaming Blacks for defective attitudes and habits, seems reluctant to indict racist attitudes and practices of whites. Moreover, his contention that racism ends when it is no longer profitable is not always true. Reich (1981:311-312) discovered that although "racism works against most whites' economic interest, it is being reinforced today" by a series of social, cultural and personal factors. Also, Malveaux (1992; 1987) has shown that both racial and gender discrimination are deep-rooted persistent problems for African Americans in their quest for economic justice and parity.

Certainly, one of the most provocative works in recent sociological literature is William Wilson's (1978) *The Declining Significance of Race*. Wilson's work, while attempting to de-emphasize the significance of race, also points to the problem of uneven development among African Americans and the accompanying class divisions. Essentially, Wilson argues that race has declined in significance and been replaced by class as the key determinant affecting life-chances and institutional access in U.S. society. He contends that this shift on the basis of social stratification is due to government intervention and support, the current predominance of service industries (transportation, government and social service, public utilities, finance, social welfare, etc.) over productive industries (manufacturing, mining, etc.), and the substitution of class characteristics for racial ones as criteria for employment. Moreover, he maintains that this declining significance of race has created a new middle class insensitive to "lower" class Black needs and is increasingly used by whites to control Blacks in the working class and underclass. Furthermore, he (1978:152) argues that "the traditional struggles for power and privilege have shifted away from the economic sector and are now concentrated in the sociopolitical order."

The arguments against Wilson's thesis are numerous and cogent and Wilson, himself, found it necessary to clarify further his ideas in a more recent work (Willie, 1979; Pinkney, 1984; Wilson, 1987). First, Wilson's use of the advancing middle class as an index of the declining significance of race is impoverished data, showing not that race has declined, but suggesting that racism against the middle class has declined. Furthermore, Black and white middle class income are still not the same and evidence of "catching up" does not eliminate the fact that significant differences still exist. Also, there are not enough African Americans in these new positions or significant power positions to claim such a momentous event as the decline of the significance of race. They are not in ownership positions or significantly represented in high level management. And even when they arrive, they continue to suffer severe discrimination (Benjamin, 1991). Finally, it could be argued that allowing certain sectors of the Black middle class access to new status is also based on race and a political calculation. For it tends to legitimize and reinforce the system and win it new Black allies which, even Wilson admits, can and may be used against the interests of the Black masses.

Secondly, Wilson concentrated only on the narrow data of income increase to prove his thesis, as if income discrimination were an inclusive category of the various forms of racism. A modicum of acquaintance with the various open and covert expressions of racism tends to disprove such a contention. Thirdly, he commits a gross conceptual error by attempting to separate the economic arena from the socio-political one. A holistic conception of society shows that all areas of society interact, and policies in one area tend to affect and often determine conditions and behavior in others. Affirmative action legislation had impact on the economic and educational spheres. And the Supreme Court decision outlawing segregation, *Brown vs. Board of Education*, affected virtually every area of social life (Kluger, 1977).

Fourthly, Wilson's contention that the discrimination against the Black poor is only because of their low level of education and few marketable skills, overlooks the fact that it is racism which imposed this condition on them and continues to exclude them (Harris, 1982; Cotton, 1988). Thus, a system which is responsible for inadequate acquisition of education and skills by African Americans and other Third World peoples cannot escape the charge of racism simply by saying that their lack of qualifications is the reason for their occupational rejection. Finally, Wilson's position suggests that now Blacks are responsible for their non-access and non-achievement, as if wealth and power were equitably distributed and equally available. This personalization of blame for social evils could be and perhaps already is being used as a justification for an end to public and private policies and programs designed to end racist and socio-economic inequities in U.S. society.

Regardless of Wilson's flawed interpretation of the declining significance of race, his charge of increasing class division and middle class insensitivity to the interests of the Black masses requires discussion. For if he and others are correct, then rather than being a resource for Black liberation and economic development, the Black middle class will serve the opposite function of retarding development and the social struggle for a higher level of social life (Wilson, 1987).

The Middle Class

The problem of the middle class was first raised extensively by E. Franklin Frazier (1962) in his classic work, *Black Bourgeoisie*. In it, he posed the middle class as essentially living in a world characterized by make-believe, self-hate, conspicuous consumption, rejection of the Black masses and fruitless and frustrating quest for white status and acceptance.

Nathan Hare (1965), a student of Frazier, reinforced Frazier's view of the middle class in his book, *Black Anglo-Saxons*, which posed "aping of the white man as their overriding concern." Cruse (1967:312) in his seminal work on the African American intellectual also reinforced Frazier's stress on the theme of personal self-interest of the middle class, arguing that "No matter how you view it, the integration movement is run by the middle class who, even when they are militant and sometimes radical, twist the meaning of integration to suit their own aspirations." If these assessments are correct, then the problem of class division and distance become not simply a problem of economics, but also a problem of politics. For if middle class interests are pushed at the expense of the masses of Blacks, then, rather than being a resource in terms of capital and leadership for economic development, the middle class will become an obstacle in both the political and economic sense.

The above claims do not go without challenge. There is evidence to suggest that the claims of a growing middle class are exaggerated and must be seen in the light of several related facts. First, although "professionals and managers" is the standard census category for middle class, it also includes modest status jobs as dental technicians and night managers, along with doctors, lawyers and other traditional professions. Moreover, growth in the professional occupations is concentrated at the lower end of the income scale with technicians, counselors and health technologists. Secondly, Anderson (1982:7) notes that many of these occupational gains were in the public sector in social welfare. This public sector concentration makes the Black middle class highly vulnerable to a reduction-in-force policy which calls for heavy layoffs at the social service agencies which employ large numbers of Blacks as was the case during the Reagan Administration.

In addition, Robert Hill (1978) argues that the advocates of the new middle class are confusing "middle income" with "middle class." "income only indicates how much money a person has, while class helps determine how that money is spent." In a word, a class is not simply defined by income but by wealth, status, "styles of life, living standards, values, beliefs." Also Hill (1980:40) contends that although middle class classifications usually include all persons holding white collar jobs or moving into higher status jobs, movement into higher status jobs does not necessarily mean higher paying jobs. In fact, he (1980:37) states, "only a small minority of Black white collar workers have middle class incomes." He concludes that instead if a spectacular growth of the Black middle class, one has statistics that show 25% of Blacks belong to the middle class as compared to 50% of whites.

Finally, in terms of middle class insensitivity, the argument can be made that the leadership of the civil rights movement and their constant struggle to maintain gains of the 60"s contradict the insensitivity and selfishness suggested by Frazier and reinforced by those after him (Morris, 1984). Moreover, it can be argued that a distinction must be made between the radical or socially conscious and active segment of the middle class and the "tomish" sector. The former, it can be said, led the struggle, and the latter served the traditional role of buffer between the masses and the rulers of society. The radical, Cabral (1969:110) argues, has committed "class suicide" and identified with the aspirations of the masses whereas the toms have thrown their lot in with society's rulers. The problem, then, becomes one of how to initiate and sustain the process which radicalizes a significant sector og the middle class and causes them to assume the "Talented Tenth" role of leadership Dubois (1969) and others posed for them. Working for this community consciousness is, of course, the fact that in spite of middle-class advancement, racism still restricts their movement and reminds them of their limitations in a racist society (Benjamin, 1991; Landry, 1987).

The Underclass

The problem of class also figures in the ongoing discourse around the question to the *underclass*. Douglas Glasgow (1981:3,5) offered one of the earliest studies of this group and defined underclass as "a permanently entrapped population of poor persons, used and unwanted... unemployed, welfare dependent and without sufficient income to secure a decent quality of life." Such an entrapped sector of the population, Glasgow maintains, not only poses a threat to the broader social order, but more importantly to the safety, survival and development of the African American community. For such a state of things creates not only the potential and reality of violence turned inward and crime, but also diminishes the life chances of those so trapped.

More recently, William J. Wilson (1987) has also contributed an important study of this class which he calls "the truly disadvantaged." He (1987:8) defines the underclass as "...the most disadvantaged segments of the Black urban community, that heterogeneous grouping of families and individuals who are outside the mainstream of the American occupations system." Defining this class more extensively, he goes on to say that "included in this group are individuals who lack training and skills and either experience long term spells of poverty and/or welfare dependency."

Wilson sees the evolution of this class as being shaped by both internal and external factors in a context of both historic and contemporary discrimination. These factors include: 1) the flow of migrants which created a large concentration of the disadvantaged; 2) the increasing number of young people among inner city residents which is associated with major problems, i.e., out-of-wedlock births, crime, female-headed households and welfare dependency; 3) structural changes in the economy "such as the shift from goods-producing to service-producing industries, the increasing polarization of the labor market into low-wage and high-wage sectors; technological innovations and the relocation of manufacturing industries out of the central cities" to the suburbs and low-wage foreign countries (Wilson, 1987:45); and 4) concentration of poverty in the inner city which as a result of middle class exodus creates both extreme social isolation and an institutional inability to effectively intervene in community problems or build on role models of possibility and achievement.

Moreover, Wilson argues that key to the solution of the problem of the underclass is to first concede its existence and problematic character and then develop a comprehensive public policy to solve it. He (1987:163) concludes that this comprehensive program must be one "that combines employment policies with social welfare policies and that features universal as opposed to race- or group-specific strategies." This would include stress on generation of a tight labor market, industrial competitiveness, increased skills for the labor force and social welfare policies of child support, family allowance and child care. His stress on the universal programs rather than race-specific ones is called a "hidden agenda" which will appeal to the larger public while simultaneously solving specific problems of the disadvantaged in a general framework.

There are arguments against both the identification of an underclass and Wilson's "hidden agenda" strategy to solve problems of the underclass. First, the term underclass is rejected as stigmatizing and indicting ghetto residents. It is argued that not only does such conceptualization of problems give racist categories with which to indict ghetto residents, but it also tends to blame the victims of the system rather than the system itself (Katz, 1986). A second problem with the term is its tendency toward imprecision, lumping together different peoples with different problems for different reasons and with differing capacities to solve them. Thirdly, such a formulation can easily deny or diminish the importance of racism in the very factors Wilson cites as shaping the formation of the underclass.

Fourthly, it is argued that underclass arguments are uncomfortably close to the culture-of-poverty arguments which stress the interconnection between cultural traditions, family history and individual character and values (Auletta, 1982: Chapter 2). The conservatives who argue these points tend to see the situation of the underclass as self-perpetuating and a reflection of the pathological character of both the subculture and the persons who compose it (Murray, 1984; Gilder, 1981). Although Wilson clearly rejects this stress on cultural tradition, family history and individual values and instead stresses structural factors which shape the formation and maintenance of the class, it is argued that focus on the problems of the group rather than society's oppressive character still leave open the door for racist manipulation.

Finally, Wilson's approach to solving the problems associated with the underclass has been questioned. The issue revolves around his "hidden agenda" strategy which suggests that one must disguise the real and greater needs of the poor and vulnerable and offer advantaged groups a public policy proposal which is universal and caters to their moral insensitivity to the truly disadvantaged. As I (Karenga, 1992:70) have argued, "the question is: do we cater to the advantaged group's insensitivity to issues involving the poor and vulnerable by disguising or hiding our real agenda and offering them similar benefits or do we challenge them to grow morally and recognize and respond positively to the priority of the poor and the vulnerable?" To search for common ground in public policy, as Wilson suggests, is imperative, but to find or fashion it at the expense of the disadvantaged is both morally untenable and politically counter-productive.

The Problem of Business

The problem of economic development is also tied to the problems of Black business. Although Frazier's (1862) contention that Black business was a "social myth" was extremely harsh, one cannot disagree that it has certainly found itself fragile and marginal to the larger economy (Swinton, 1992; Coles, 1975; Tabb, 1970). In fact, African Americans, "own 424,000 business firms out of a total of 17.5 million for the entire country (Swinton, 1992:65). First, among the problems of Blacks businesses is undercapitalization which insures smallness and inefficiency, prevents acquisition of managerial competence and often leads to failure. It is estimated that Black firms in 1987 generated receipts of 22.8 billion or one-tenth of one percent of the total U.S. 11,4 trillion dollars generated (Swinton, 1992:67).

Secondly, African American businesses in spite of some diversification are essentially concentrated in personal services as in the past. *Black Enterprise's 1992 Top 100 Black Businesses* report (June, 1992) reaffirms this. Thus, the essential process of production escapes them and is not a fundamental part of government or private proposals for Black economic development. Thirdly, as mentioned above, Black businesses are losing in the grossly unequal competition for Black consumer dollars. Fourthly, low-level of managerial competence continues to plague Black businesses. Most are self-owned and too small to hire any other employee, let alone skilled managers which insure correct business decisions. Hacker (1992:108) reports that "only 70,000 of the 425,000 (Black businesses) have any paid employees. In other words, almost 85 percent are one person enterprises or family-run firms."

Fifthly, Black businesses essentially operate in a restricted market which is marked by small savings, high debt, low income, high unemployment and an environment shunned by possible large investors although the top 100 Black firms do not have these problems to the same degree (McCoy, 1992). Finally, the shift in the politics and economics of the country to the right with a focus on the rich at the expense of the poor and stress on less government assistance to the Black community in general and Black businesses in particular had an ill effect on Black business. For government assistance had been an important source not only of loans but also of support for affirmative action contracts for The *Black Enterprise's* assessment of Black businesses' future in the 90's links it to a variety of continuing practices. In order to sustain growth and avoid falling on the fatality list, Black businesses will have to, among other things: 1)

106

acquire increased amounts of capital from other sources than the government; 2) diversify and work to get a greater share of the approximately $265 billion income of Blacks; 3) locate in industries such as telecommunications, cable, high technology and manufacturing; 4) engage in collective community planning; and 5) participate in building political bases among Blacks through service, donation and investment which come back in higher levels of Black support as consumers, investors, and partners in political and economic development of the Black community (McCoy, 1992).

Solutions

Introduction Given the severity of the political-economic problems of the inner city, the question of what is to be done and who is to do it are necessarily raised. Three basic resource structure are identified as fundamental to reversing the tendency and fact of ghettoization: 1) government; 2) the private sector; and 3) the Black community itself (Barnett and Hefner, 1976; Williams, 1982; Karenga, 1980; Jaynes and Williams, 1989; Swinton, 1990, 1991, 1992). Governmental intervention and assistance are proposed for four basic reasons (Franklin and Norton, 1987). First, the problems are of dimensions beyond the means of any one or combination of community structures. Secondly, the problems are socially rooted and the result of racist discrimination and the government is obliged to assist in providing necessary correctives for these problems. Thirdly, Blacks helped create the social wealth of America and deserve an equitable share of it, not in the sense of sympathetic welfare, but in the sense of *distributive justice*, i.e., that share which is rightly theirs by their contribution and by just reasoning. Finally, it is objectively in the interest of the whole society to solve these problems, for as long as they remain unsolved, their negative effect will impact on the larger society also. For example, acquisition crime, generational poverty, socially incompetent members of society, and violently aggressive alienation all merit societal attention.

Secondly, the private sector is proposed because 1) there is a sense that businesses, especially larger corporations, have drained and exploited the community and thus, we owe it support in its revitalization efforts; 2) that business will benefit in tax credits, public relations, and even make a profit on their investment in the ghetto; and 3) they too should be concerned about the negative impact of unsolved ghetto problems on the larger society.

Undoubtedly the most important resource structure, however, in solving Black problems is the Black community itself. Regardless of external goodwill, a people must initiate and lead the struggle for its own liberation. However, this necessitates the structural capacity – an institutional and organizational network – to wage such a struggle. As noted above, one of the greatest, if not the greatest, problems Blacks face is structural incapacity to define, defend and develop their interests. This, therefore, must be a priority. Each year in its *State of Black America*, the National Urban League gives recommendations for the struggle for Black freedom, justice and equality, placing heavy emphasis on governmental intervention and assistance. However, the tasks proposed and the struggle to be waged presuppose and necessitates a self-conscious organized people to execute them. After all, one cannot expect the government to respond simply because recommendations are published or verbally proposed yearly. The government is a political structure, organized around the holding, using and respect of power. Thus, African Americans must politically educate and organize themselves and become a self-conscious social power with which to reckon.

Often, it is pointed out that the problems of the ghetto are too large and deep-rooted for Blacks to solve and that talk of community self-help is utopian. There are several things wrong with this "reasoning" which are immediately observable. First, no one offers such a position to Jewish or Gentile communities or any other Third World communities except the African American community. Secondly, as noted above, resources from the government or others still require organization, knowledge of policy, collective strategy and the power to have an impact on policy. Thirdly, given Black structural incapacity, the government and the private sector are not likely to run to the rescue with the immediate necessary resources, as history has shown. Moreover, given the shift to the right in and out of government, the unlikelihood of this is even greater. Fourthly, given the above reality, it would seem sensible and contributive to survival and development if Blacks developed structures which, even on a limited scale, helped improve conditions of the ghetto.

Finally, Blacks have already built structures to deal with their deprivations imposed by discrimination; the point then would be how to expand and strengthen them. And here again, the Sixties provide a model, as I have argued in Chapter II. For not only were structures built to provide services, politically educate and organize the community, pressure was also put on the system to produce legislation, judicial decisions and programs which improved conditions in a significant way. The problem often faced is the one of dismissing Black strategies that do not produce the maximum goals or result and making alternative suggestions that theoretically produce maximum gains, but practically are less than effective or realistic. It is obvious that without a *structural base* of its own, the Black community will not only be unable to effectively demand from government and the private sector what is rightfully theirs, but will also be unable to provide for itself what is possible in the meantime. Black history is full of examples of Black self-help and struggle to win their rightful share of social wealth and social space. Not to honor this history by continuing it, seems not only an avoidable loss, but also an irrational and self-defeating position.

In terms of proposals for each resource structure, several recommendations for government and the private sector (businesses) are most often quoted (Barnett and Hefner, 1976; Williams, 1982; Franklin and Norton, 1987; Simms, 1989). Recommendations for the state and federal governments to assist in economic development are: 1) continued and reinforced employment training programs; 2) more federal government revenue for domestic programs and less for an inflated defense budget; 3) less layoffs of government workers which

108

affect Blacks, other Third World people and women disproportionately; 4) perception of federal Third World business programs as economic programs rather than social welfare programs and improvement of delivery services to them; 5) encouragement of majority-owned and operated business to assist and use services of Third World businesses; 6) encouragement of employment and training of Blacks by private industry and small and medium business through tax incentives, wage subsidies, work study, etc.; 7) rejection of altered minimum wage for youth; 8) serious efforts toward full employment; 9) a reduction of budget cuts which affect monies and services vital to Blacks, other Third World peoples and the poor; and 10) continued application and support of Affirmative Action. Recommendations for the private sector are: 1) location of plants in the inner city; 2) job training and employment for Blacks; 3) use of Black business services and products; 4) provision of resources to insure expansion of alternative educational programs.

Politically, government, especially federal, is asked to : 1) resume and reinforce its traditional defense of civil rights; 2) monitor white terrorist and racist organization like the Klan and neo-nazi groups; 3) appoint qualified Blacks in the government structure; 4) support the Voting Rights Act; and 5) oppose reapportionment schemes that dilute Black voting power or dissolve districts represented by Blacks. Educationally, government should: 1) oppose the voucher education system which is detrimental to public education; 2) increase support for historically Black colleges; 3) continue federal resources for quality education for the disadvantaged; and 4) insist that post-secondary institutions receiving federal monies maintain effective affirmative action programs for faculty and students.

In terms of the Black community, is clear as stated above, that their primary focus must be on building the *structural* capacity to define, defend and develop their interests. This essentially means building an organizational, institutional and enterprise network that not only provides social services, but politically organizes and educates the community to its interests and possibilities. This requires strengthening existing structures and building new ones, building economic enterprises on the individual and cooperative level, alternative educational institutions, Black united fronts for collective planning and actions, and eventually, a Black political party which is dedicated exclusively to organizing Blacks for political power and effectively participating in the exercise of state power.

Broad Strategies   There are obviously several eclectic approaches to Black economic development which are initiated and controlled by Blacks (Coles, 1975; Cash and Oliver, 1975; Browne, 1976; America, 1977; Woodson, 1987; Wilson, 1987; Simms, 1989). Approaches can also be defined by their rootedness in or advocacy of three broad developmental strategies, advocates of each usually tend to praise one and condemn or severely question the others. However, cooperative economic and socialist strategies are often linked and capitalist advocates have been known to tolerate parallel cooperative strategies.

The discussion below seeks to give the basic contentions of each of these strategies with explanatory comments where warranted.

Black Capitalism   Black capitalism which gained popularity as a strategy during the Nixon Administration attempted to reduce the "perceived cycle of Black dependency" on governmental intervention.   The alternative was to expand Black ownership which would stress private efforts, profit pursuit and free marketism for Blacks using the model of capitalism on a societal level (Cross, 1969).

First, it argues that increase in Black private ownership and control will enhance Black independence and pride, employ Blacks and help ease unemployment, increase the availability of services for the community and expand the wealth in the community.   Secondly, Black capitalism argues for market protectionism that would shield Black enterprises from competition with larger more competitive outside enterprises.   Thirdly, it advocates Black self-help and solidarity which would support Black business and benefit from its expansion.   Fourthly, Black capitalism demands subsidization from the dominant society, i.e., government and the private sector.   Subsidization may take the form of loans, grants, property equipment or training and is seen as a contribution to capital formation as well as a moral and economic debt U.S. society owes African Americans for long-term discrimination and deprivation.

Criticism of Black capitalism is severe and from many quarters.   First, Boggs (1970) argues that it is an irrational strategy which poses itself as a collective strategy, but is in fact a class strategy to further enrich a few at the expense of the many.   Secondly, Allen (1970) and Zweig (1972) argue that the political economy of subsidization is negative to Black self-determination and will mean creation of a manipulated class still dependent on outside sources. Thirdly, Ofari (1970) calls attention to the fact that the strategy is overweighed toward service rather than *production*, the key process in economics.   And, finally, Brimmer and Terrell (1971), as well as Ofari, point to its nonviability given the small amount of capital available to Black enterprises, their low expansion possibility, low efficiency, marginal existence, high mortality rate, and restricted and problematic market, i.e., the ghetto economy.

Socialism   Black advocates of socialism see Black capitalism as a myth and hindrance to serious Black economic development and political emancipation (Ofari, 1970; Allen, 1970).   Their focus is essentially on Black labor rather than Black capital.   As Harris (1978:14) argues, "Blacks cannot be adequately understood except as an integral part of the capital labor relation as a whole in U.S. capitalism."   Given the fact that the Black working class is approximately 90% of the Black population, a strategy which does not focus on problems and possibilities of Black labor is both deficient and self-deluding.

Secondly, Black socialists argue that regardless of the temporary and partial measures that Blacks institute for economic betterment, a real and full solution depends on the transformation of society from capitalism to socialism.   Given this reality, Black socialists argue for greater stress on the political dimensions

110

of the economic process, and stress the need for organizing Black workers and Black community into a self-conscious political force which challenges and transforms the established order (Alkalimat and Johnson, 1974).

Fourthly, the Black socialist strategy involves seizure of power and institution of: 1) collective ownership and control of the productive apparatus; 2) an egalitarian distribution of wealth; 3) a planned economy; 4) a political and economic democracy; and 5) an end to class, race and sexual alienation (Karenga, 1980:61-61). Essentially this is seen as a long-range strategy, and the organization of the Black workers (and the Black community) as a fighting force for democratic rights, higher wages, better work and living conditions and greater participation in political and economic decision-making are posed as immediate goals.

The stress on the working class, especially by orthodox Marxists, however, often poses a problem for a specifically Black solution. For not only does it tend to play down racism as a simple function of capitalism (Harris, 1978), but it also ends up with no ethnic-specific program for African Americans – only for workers in general. Thus, as Browne (1976:153) contends, given Marx's and Lenin's failure to "directly address the unique situation in which American Blacks find themselves... there are very real limits on the extent to which that analysis speaks to our racial situation, irrespective of how eloquently it may dissect our economic dilemma." Moreover, the failure of communism to establish humanist societies and the recent collapse of the Soviet Union and communism in Eastern Europe have made both communists and socialists reevaluate the problematics and possibilities of socialist society, especially in a multicultural context (Davis, et al, 1987).

Cooperative Economics   As Ofari (1970:89) states, the theory and practice of cooperative economics has an early history in the mutual aid societies in northern Black communities which pooled resources and dedicated themselves to social service and community development. Stewart (1984) has also written concerning the challenge of building a cooperative economy and the lessons which evolve from the Black experience in this ongoing historical project. The idea of cooperative economics among African Americans, however, was eventually submerged with the emergence of a Black elite which developed a capitalist merchant class orientation (Harris, 1936). But in 1940, DuBois (1968) had proposed a comprehensive theoretical framework and rationale for cooperative economics as a viable and necessary alternative to capitalism.

He (1968:216-219) stressed the need for a communal, Black-focused solution which would emphasize and establish: 1) social ownership; 2) strong family and group ties; 3) consumer unions; 4) economic planning; 5) socialized medicine; 6) cooperative organization of Black professionals for social service; 7) the elimination of private profit; 8) a Black controlled educational system; and 9) the essentiality of collective self-reliance. This solution he called "a cooperative commonwealth," a communal social system which built new relations among African Americans and gave them the internal strength to resist the corrupting influence of capitalism and collective values necessary for cooperative community development.

Although DuBois' program was never implemented, it did yield an important model and since the 60's cooperatives have been posed as an important mode of Black economic development, especially in the South (Marshall and Godwin, 1971). Over one hundred were formed during the 60's in the South and ninety of those were organized in the Federation of Southern Cooperatives. Although they have been resisted by hostile forces, they nevertheless have provided food, jobs, and capital otherwise unobtainable and Ofari (1970:89), though a socialist, admits that in spite of its problems, the Black cooperative proposal is "by far the most positive proposal that has been offered." Likewise, Allen (1970) who is also socialist, concedes the limitations of cooperative economics, but maintains that given the distance of the socialist revolution and the problems of integrating into capitalist economy, a transitional program of cooperative economics is necessary." Led by an independent Black party, this transitional program, he (1870:278) states, should involve "a struggle to create an all encompassing, planned communal social system on a national scale and with strong international ties."

Finally, as I (1980:62-64) argued elsewhere, cooperative economics proves its validity in that it: 1) aids in increasing capital capacity, necessary for economic development; 2) increases the beneficiaries, unlike Black capitalism; 3) teaches the value for shared social wealth, egalitarianism, collective work and decision-making, the priority of the person over profit and the centrality of the community; and 4) establishes cooperative thought and practice which can be transferred to other areas, i.e., political struggle and social construction. Again, then, it is clear that politics and economics are unavoidably linked and any strategy for one must have as a major focus concern for the other.

SELECTED REFERENCES

Alexis, Marcus. (1999) "The Economics of Racism," *Review of Black Political Economy*, 26, 3 (Winter) 51-76.

Alkalimar, Abdul H. and Nelson Johnson. (!974) *"Toward the Ideological Unity of the African Liberation Support Committee,"* a position paper, South Carolina (June-July).

America, Richard. (1977) *Developing the Afro-American Economy*, Lexington, MA: Lexington Books.

- - - . (1995/1996) "Reparations and the Combative Advantage of Inner Cities," *Review of Black Political Economy*, 24, 2/3 (Fall/Winter) 193-206.

- - - . (1999) "Reparations and Public Policy," *Review of Balck Political Economy*, 26, 3 (Winter) 77-83.

Anderson, Bernard C. (1982) "Economic Patterns in Black America," in James D. Williams, (ed.) *The State of Black America*, 1982, New York: National Urban League, pp. 1-31.

Andrews, Marcellus. (1999) *The Political Economy of Hope and Fear: Capitalism and the Black Condition in America*, New York: New York University Press.

Banner-Haley, Charles P. (1994) *The Fruits of Integration: Black Middle Class Ideology and Culture*, Jackson: University of Mississippi Press.

Becker, Gary. (1957) *The Economics of Discrimination*, Chicago: University of Chicago Press.

Boston, Thomas D. (1998) *Affirmative Action and Black Entrepreneurship*, New York: Routledge.

- - - . (1996) *a different Vision: African American Thought*, New York: Routledge.

Brimmer, Andrew, and Henry S. Terrell. (1971) "The Economic Potential of Black Capitalism," *Black Politician*, 2, 4 (April) 19-23, 78-88.

Browne, Robert S. (1971) "Cash Flow in a Ghetto Economy, " *Review of Black Political Economy*, (Winter/Spring).

Coles, Flournoy A. (1975) *Black Economic Development*, Chicago: Nelson Hall.

Conley, Dalton. (1999) *Being Black, Living in the Red: Race, Wealth and Social Policy in America*, Berkeley: University of California Press.

Cruse, Harold. (1967) *The Crisis of the Negro Intellectual*, New York: William Morrow & Co.

DuBois, W.E.B. (1969) "The Talented Tenth," in Ulysses Lee, (ed.), *The Negro Problem*, New York: Arno Press and The New York Times, pp. 31-76.

Feagin, Joe. (1994) *Living With Racism: The Black Middle-Class Experience*, Boston: Beacon Press.

Frazier, E. Franklin. (1962) *Black Bourgeoisie*, New York: Collier Books.

Hogan, Lloyd. (1984) *Principles of Black Political Economy*, London: Routledge and Kegan Paul.

Karenga, Maulana. (1980) *Kawaida Theory: An Introductory Outline*, Inglewood, CA: Kawaida Publications.

Kikazi, Kikolo. (1997) *African American Economic Development and Small Business Ownership*, New York: Garland Publishing.

Kluger, Richard. (1977) *Simple Justice*, New York: Vintage Books.

Mandle, Jay R. (1992) *Not Slave, Not Free: The African American Economic Experience Since the Civil War*, Durham: Duke University.

Morris, Aldon. (1984) *The Origins of the Civil Rights Movement: Black Communities Organizing for Social Change*, New York: The Free Press.

Ofari, Earl. (1970) *The Myth of Black Capitalism*, New York: Monthly Review Press.

Reed, Adolph, (ed.) (1999) *Without Justice for All: The New Liberalism and Our Retreat from Racial Equality*, Boulder, CO: Westview Press.

Simms, Margaret C. (1989) *Black Economic Progress: An Agenda for the 1990's*, Washington, DC: Joint Center for Political Studies.

Tabb, William K. (1970) *The Political Economy of the Black Ghetto*, New York: W.W. Norton and Company.

Williams, James D. (ed.) (1982) *The State of Black America, 1982*, New York: National Urban League, Inc.

Williams, Rhonda M. (1999) "Unfinished Business: African American Political Economy During the Age of 'Color-Blind' Politics," *The State of Black America*, New York: National Urban League.

Wilson, William J. (1978) *The Declining Significance of Race*, Chicago: University of Chicago Press.

Woodson, Robert. (ed.) (1987) *On the Road to Economic Freedom*, Washington, DC: Regency Gateway.

Zweig, Michael. (1972) "The Dialectics of Black Capitalism," *Review of Black Political Economy*, 2 (Spring) 25-37.

113

Chapter 10

Black Religion-Based Politics, Cultural Popularization and Youth Allegiance

By R. Drew Smith

Scholarship on Afro-American religion documents the existence of three ideological variants amongst its more politicized expressions – cultural nationalism, direct-action racial protest, and electoral participation. Viewed by their respective practitioners as vital forms of political resistance, each of the three have periodically fueled mass-based political responses to Black social urgencies. However, these strategies have often been at odds with each other, diverging fundamentally over the importance placed on participating in mainstream social institutions and procedures within the United States. Civil rights and electoral activists have been committed to channeling Blacks unto the American mainstream while cultural nationalists have been known to reject movement in this direction. Efforts to effect a broad-based political incorporation of African-Americans have been plagued by this division, among others, throughout the twentieth century.

Currently, all three strategies are jockeying for ideological advantage amongst the Black populace, with popular support for the positions often divided along generational and class lines. Integrationist civil rights and electoral strategies continue to hold the allegiance of most Blacks in the middle to upper age and income ranges. On the other hand, the rejectionist orientation of cultural nationalism remains strongly attractive to Blacks in the lower age and income ranges.

It also appears that these class and generational antagonisms are mounting within the African-American community. First of all, Black class disparities have become more pronounced as a result of an economic and social policy climate that has dramatically increased the quantitative and qualitative dimensions of Black poverty.[1] However, while Blacks in higher age and income brackets have been fairly reticent on class issues (preoccupied as they have been with consolidating institutional gains) younger, poorer Blacks have been far more vocal, thanks to a growing industry centered around commercial outlets for the popular expression and cultural articulation of Black youths. Given in mounting social despair of younger Blacks, and the availability of highly conspicuous channels for expressing it. Black urban youths have become the axis around which any politics of resistance necessarily revolves.

Alert to this, cultural nationalists, such as Nation of Islam and related groups, have artfully cast themselves as the religion of oppressed Black urban youths. However, popular gains by cultural nationalists are as attributable to their successes at tapping into growing Black disaffection as they are to the failure of Black mainstream groups to do likewise. Within cultural nationalism, not only the message, but the forms of communication are defiant and grass-roots. The forms range from rap recordings and music videos, to hand-distributed newspapers and pamphlets, to types of apparel that symbolically or concretely convey cultural nationalist messages.

On the other hand, Black civil rights and electoral leaders make obvious that their discourse and activities are targeted primarily at mainstream audiences rather than lower-income and younger-generation Blacks. First, their political activities (rightly concerned with accessing power-wielding institutions and procedures) increasingly associate them with the American establishment. Secondly, the venues and methods through which their agendas are conveyed seem more concerned with reflecting their higher social attainments than reflecting identification with the grass-roots. The venues are formal social, educational, religious and political contexts where lower-strata Blacks, particularly urban youth, are not represented in significant numbers. The methods of communication are formal oratory and writings, neither of which possess particular popular appeal amongst younger, poorer Blacks conditioned to be only minimally responsive to such stimuli.

Greater level of political cooperation across these generational and class divisions cannot be achieved without improved communication between mainstream and counter-mainstream Blacks. The following discussion will explore barriers to communication between the two groups, reflecting more on stylistic than ideological differences between them and speculating on the extent to which these differences appear negotiable.

*****

Efforts to politicize the Black rank-and-file have often been frustrated from without and within and, consequently, the emergence of any instance of collective Black political action has been greeted as a triumph of Black perseverance. In instances where significant African-American political action has occurred, religion has frequently played an important role in its development.

First of all, religion often provided Blacks with the only ideological and institutional terrain permitting freedom of operation. In addition, the ideological substance of their religion proved politically potent in important respects, particularly in its tendency to diminish the sovereignty of existing political authorities. Black Protestantism has supplied the ideological and institutional basis for a great deal of this religion-based resistance, although innovations on the doctrinal substance and ecclesiastical practices of Islam have also factored significantly in African-American resistance activities over the last fifty years.

On one level, this religion-based resistance has moved in a nationalistic direction, emphasizing territorial independence. Occasionally, this has embraced actual land-appropriating, nation-building intentions, such as in

116

Alexander Crummell's Edward Blydon's and Marcus Garvey's nineteenth and twentieth century emigrationist yearnings for African Christian nationhood. More often, territorial independence has had an institutional focus, beginning with 18th and 19th century Black Protestant breaks with White religious authority and extending through their subsequent social and economic institution-building initiatives.[2] However, as Black Protestantism evolved from being an institutional protest against mainstream Protestantism to becoming, to a large degree, part of the mainstream itself, nationalistic ferment flourished mostly in non-Christian Black religious contexts.[3]

Perhaps the most radical and enduring formulation of oppositional nationalism has persisted in the quasi-Islamic domain of the Nation of Islam. The Nation of Islam was founded on the belief that an enigmatic Black man, W. D. Fard, who surfaced in Detroit in 1930, was divine. Fard's main teaching was that Blacks were of noble, Islamic origins, and that they could reclaim their spiritual and social centering only by hearkening back to their Islamic roots. Elijah Muhammad, one of Fard's first followers and his designated messenger, became the sole leader when Fard disappeared four years after his mysterious appearance. Elijah Muhammad embellished upon Fard's themes, teaching his quickly growing following that Blacks were the original people of the Earth, that Whites were devils, and that the socio-political agenda of Blacks should be based in the anticipation of divine retribution against Whites.[4]

These teachings were component parts of the Nation of Islam's overarching social doctrine of Black self sufficiency through separatism. The Nation believed in the necessity of Black social formation in an environment free of the distortions that come through interactions with Whites, and it pursued this aim with some success in its institution-building initiatives. With a membership during its peak years – 1950 to 1964 – of between fifty and one hundred thousand (spread across twenty-seven states),[5] the Nation built a financial empire valued at about $25 million. This included "15,000 acres of farmland ... several aircraft, a fish import business, restaurants, bakeries and supermarkets."[6] Combined with its holdings of properties used for teaching and worship purposes, these material, as well as human resources amassed by the Nation, provided compelling affirmation of the vitality of self-sufficiency and separatist themes within the Black community.

However, an even greater symbol of the Nation of Islam's vitality during the reign of Elijah Muhammad, was the emergence of its gifted spokesman, Malcolm X. Malcolm, who faithfully followed Elijah Muhammad until breaking with him in 1964 over questions of ethics and politics, played a critical role in popularizing the Nation across space and across time. Nonetheless, Malcolm's 1965 assassination started a precipitous decline in the Nation's fortunes, finally concluding in the total fragmentation of the Nation after the 1975 death of Elijah Muhammad.

More recently, Louis Farrakhan, who was originally introduced to the Nation of Islam by Malcolm X, has successfully regrouped an estimated 20,000 current members around the Nation's legacy. Through his national, and occasionally, international speaking tours and his widely circulated newspaper,

The Final Call, Farrakhan has promoted Elijah Muhammad's original teachings to audiences extending beyond the Nation of Islam's active membership and beyond the institutional context of its mostly northeastern and midwestern urban mosques.

However, Farrakhan's popularity has also been aided (in a way that Malcolm's and Elijah Muhammad's never were during their careers), by a recently found access to electronic media via surrogates who have either actively or sympathetically related to his movement. As Adolph Reed, Jr. Points out, this media access is an outgrowth of the discovery by a broad range of profiteers within the commercial sector that Black cultural nationalism sells.[7] And as the entrepreneurs have experienced financial success, Farrakhan and his Nation of Islam have benefitted from the high-profile, sympathetic exposure they have received. The result is that Elijah Muhammad, Malcolm, and Farrakhan have become sacrosanct figures for a growing number of Black urban youths who take their cues from popular media forms.

One of the primary high-tech venues servicing Farrakhan's cause has been rap music recordings and music videos. One rap music group that has symbolized the political edge of the rap phenomenon for some time, and in doing so has maintained a decidedly pro-Nation of Islam disposition, has been "Public Enemy." Centered around primary rapper "Chuck D," the group consists of a complementary rapper, "Flavor Flav," a public relations-oriented "Minister of Information," and a small militia-like force called the Security Force of the First World (S1W). By way of its repertoire of rap lyrics, music video images and its frequent interviews, Public Enemy has been consistent in its celebration of Nation leaders Elijah Muhammad. Malcolm and Farrakhan. For example, in a taped interview, the S1W's commented:

> [we do what we do] out of our love for the Minister [Farrakhan] and our love for the work that he's doing from the teachings of Elijah Muhammad.

They went on to say that "the Nation at this point is at the forefront of the Black struggle and in order to be a part of the Black struggle you have to be a part of the Nation."[8] Briefer homages to the Nation are interspersed throughout Public Enemy's lyrics, while the symbolism in which the group cloaks itself (from its Malcolm X emblazoned apparel, to its S1W – replication of the Nation's Fruit of Islam) pays tribute to the Nation on other levels.

More important that the associative images between Public Enemy and the Nation is Public Enemy's advocacy of the Nation's racial, economic and political doctrines. Public Enemy has led the way amongst rap artists in promoting a Black nationalism rooted in the separatism and racial essentialism characteristic of the Nation. As Gene Santoro states, Public Enemy:

> self-consciously voice[s] Malcolm's] contentions that black Americans must elevate their own values, build their own economic bases and understand that worldwide political and social movements against ruling powers are inextricably linked because they all confront Eurocentric racism.[9]

Although Public Enemy is among the more well known of the Nation's rap surrogates, an even broader based, rap-driven offshoot of Elijah Muhammad's original Nation of Islam is a loose-knit "movement" of younger generation urban Blacks calling themselves the Five-Percent Nation. This "movement," currently evolving symbolically alongside Farrakhan's Nation, is centered primarily, but not exclusively, in the Northeast and is sufficiently concentrated in places like Brooklyn and northern New Jersey that Five-Percenters refer to the former as "Medina" (after one of Islam's holy cities) and the latter as "New Jerusalem."[10] Among its proponents are highly visible rap artists such as "Poor Righteous Teachers," "Brand Nubian," "X-Klan" and "King Sun." Five-Percenters are extremely cryptic, from their coded language, to their lack of visible organizational structure, to their core proposition that practitioners represent an enlightened remnant ("gods") who possess privileged knowledge about the "Black planet." A Five-Percent "lesson" illustrates this clearly where it states:

> Who are the Five-Percent of this planet earth? They are the poor righteous teachers, people who are all wise and know who the true living god is, who teach that the almighty true and living god is the black.

It could be said that the overall thrust of Five-Percenter teachings is directed toward various notions of race duality, political conspiracy, and retributionist wars against White oppressors, drawing on similar themes from the Nation of Islam.

These counter-cultural variants of religion-based resistance have clearly achieved substantial popular momentum. Nevertheless, most religiously-minded, politically-active Blacks continue to be wedded to forms of resistance with decidedly more mainstream intentions. Characterized by an insistence on laying claim to the power and resources of American society, this stream of resistance has challenged the political establishment from the outside through protest or from the inside electorally.[12] The direct-action protest variant gained inspiration from the religion-based political action of slavery resisters Nat Turner, Gabriel Prosser and Denmark Vesey but attained heights of mass involvement and its specifically non-violent character in the civil protest activities of the 1950s and 1960s. However, as direct-action protest gave way by the 1970s to unprecedented Black electoral opportunities, religiously-minded Blacks adjusted their mass-resistance instincts more than ever to the tactical demands of the electoral arena. They did so with some success as evidenced by dozens of Black clergy achieving elective office over the last twenty years and the routine and often strategic clerical marshaling of theological, material and human resources on behalf of electoral candidates and causes.[13]

A middle-income, middle-age, sector of Black Protestants almost singularly constitute this legacy's current vanguard. However, it is increasingly clear that if this legacy is to prevail, or even endure, it must be carried beyond its existing ranks far more systematically and effectively than it has been. In the first place, the new generation of resistance defining itself amongst the burgeoning ranks of lower-strata urban Blacks over the last two decades, has been largely uncoupled from the mainstream, institutional agendas of middle-class Blacks and increasingly antagonistic toward their institutional terrain. Therefore, the points of contact across the class-based and generational divide have been few, and where they have existed they have not been sufficiently compelling to counter younger-generation cynicism toward the institutional and ideological enthusiasms of civil rights and electoral oriented Blacks. The extent of this cynicism is captured in remarks by Chuck D in the music video version of Public Enemy's extremely popular song "Fight the Power." He states: "that march in 1963 was a bit of nonsense; we ain't rolling like that no more."[14]

Not only have mainstream Blacks failed to convincingly spell out why resistance-oriented Blacks on the other side of the divide should share their enthusiasms, but they have also not been very attentive to the problem of how to take their case (once suitably developed) to their less-than-conventional counterparts. That is, if they are going to address their waning influence amongst younger, poorer Blacks, mainstream Blacks will need to pay much greater attention, not just to matters of substance, but also to matters of style.

What is most lacking in the style of mainstream religious resistance is a level of defiance appropriate to the level of social despair existing amongst large portions of the Black populace. While counter-mainstream resistance conveys a noticeable level of defiance in the images they project and the actions they promote, mainstream resistance has become increasingly conventional throughout this century. There was, in certain respects, a brief hiatus from this trend during the Civil Rights movement. Nonetheless, as mainstream religious activists shifted from the protest of the 1950s and 1960s to the electioneering of subsequent years, and as their image evolved from one of dissatisfied outsiders to one of comfortable insiders, marginalized, disaffected Blacks could find less and less to identify with politically within mainstream Black religion.

A more direct *cultural* barrier to lower-strata identification with mainstream religion is that the politically active sector of Black Protestantism has tended to come from its more middle-class ranks, resulting in a Black church-based political activism that has been traditionally tied to a cultural agenda reflective of middle-class tastes. The church activism of the Civil Rights movement drew heavily on cultural styles and symbolism associated with more formal dimensions of Black church culture, from the "literary-style" sermons of Martin Luther King, Jr. To Black "heritage" traditions of sacred music, including classical oriented anthems and Negro spirituals. Likewise, the sermonic and musical styles characteristic of churches comprising the current wing of Black church activism tend to share an emphasis on educated preaching and "heritage" music, with the latter expanded to include Black Gospel music more than was true during the Civil Rights movement.

On the other hand, the musical and artistic expansions of the counter-culture, from the angry poetry and renegade rock and jazz music of the 1950s and 1960s, to rap music during the 1980s and 1990s, has been largely excluded from the cultural arsenal of mainstream activist churches. Where stylistic dimensions of the prevailing counter-culture have been appropriated by

120

mainstream Black Protestants, it has usually been within Protestantism's more evangelical wing. In such instances, Christian artists have embraced a stylistic identification with the counter-culture of the time, but in a way that has denuded it of its more direct political content, favoring more conventional theological concerns instead.

In view of the urgency of bridging the communication gap between politics of the religious mainstream and the counter-mainstream, the negligence of activist churches in enlisting Christian rappers in this cause (or the jazz-rock gospel innovators which preceded them) is a major strategic error. This costly negligence has its roots in the instinctive cultural conservatism of mainstream Black Protestantism – a paradoxical feature, given its political progressivism. Nevertheless, the truth is that on very few occasions since the Black church independency days of the 19th century has both the cultural style and the political content of Black Christianity departed radically from its mainstream ecclesia and social surroundings.

Exceptions to this would include Marcus Garvey's African Orthodox Church and, more recently, a new generation of cultural nationalist Protestant churches. This new-style Protestant "cultural nationalism" (or "Afrocentrism," as it goes by now) has renewed the call for alternative Black religious terrain, contending that Black group-progress within the U.S. can be assured only through appropriating uniquely African outlooks. Expressed most often in efforts to revise ecclesiastical culture, this cause has been zealously pursued by Black clergy such as Albert Cleague (Detroit) and Jeremiah Wright (Chicago) of the United Church of Christ, Frank Reid, III of Bethel A.M.E. church in Baltimore, Calvin Butts of Abyssinian Baptist church in Harlem, and former Roman Catholic priest George Stallings (Washington),[15] to name a few. Most Protestant Afrocentrists believe that Afrocentric perspectivism represents a crucial popular challenge to elite cultures.

However, while Protestant Afrocentrism may pose significant challenge to White elite cultures, it merely builds on existing cultural "heritage" commitments of Black elite cultures. Perhaps it is due to the cultural safeness of this agenda, intra-racially speaking, the activist churches have embraced it (more than they have counter-cultural music) as a method for reaching out to younger, poorer Blacks. They have employed this method as outreach usually by way of "rites of passage" programs, designed to engage young males from both church and community in educational and service activities that generate self-esteem and racial pride. Despite their inherently middle-class cultural dimensions, these Afrocentric youth programs currently stand among the more credible initiatives taken by mainstream churches in the direction of forging political linkages with counter-cultural Blacks.

But just as there is a dispositional exclusivity to the cultural domain of mainstream churches, the same could be said of the domain of counter-cultural Blacks. Access to and inclusion in either domain is determined, to a significant degree, by one's disposition toward mainstream educational legacies and pursuits. A favorable disposition is a requirement for cultural membership in mainstream Black religion while the reverse is true with respect to counter-cultural Black religion. The latter eschews association with these mainstream legacies and pursuits, and distrusts, if not rejects, even those persons sympathetic to their agenda who have not sufficiently severed their existing links to such legacies and pursuits.

This is tellingly illustrated in the controversy that greeted Black film-maker, Spike Lee's involvement in a long-awaited motion picture about the life of Malcolm X. An array of Black cultural nationalists decried placing Malcolm's legacy in Spike Lee's custody (despite the fact that Lee is a great admirer of Malcolm) charging that Lee's cultural and ideological bearings were too middle-class for him to produce an authentic representation of Malcolm's life and legacy. One of Lee's main critics, poet Amiri Baraka, expressed a common sentiment among protestors when he stated: "We will not let Malcolm X's life be trashed to make middle-class Negroes sleep easier."[16] Clearly, class divisions effectively exclude access in both direction.

Without a doubt, the restricted cultural flow across age and class barriers amongst religiously-minded Blacks remains one of the major obstacles to the development of a broader religion-based political culture. In any event, the onus would seem to lie with mainstream religious groups to take the leadership initiative, given their institutional and ideological prevalence. However, even if they do consent to grab the initiative, it will remain to be seen whether greater appeal by these churches to the more renegade popular styles and forums of the counter-culture can close the gap between the political culture of the two camps. Nevertheless, to the extent that mainstream Blacks are not more attentive to contemporizing their style, they deny their message a fair and adequate hearing amongst a growing population of Blacks currently opting in a counter-cultural direction. On the other side of the equation, if counter-cultural Blacks are not willing to back away from their own forms of exclusivism, no mainstream concessions along stylistic or any other lines will be of any consequence. Short of both sides taking steps in these respective stylistic directions, prospects can only fade further for overcoming the significant communication impairments (and, thereby, the more vexing ideological antagonisms) currently undermining consolidation of broad-based Black resistance.

NOTES

1. Recent figures show that "the percentage of high-income Black families more than doubled from 1967 to 19990. . . (while) the population of black families at the lowest income level grew by 50%" (New York Times, September 25, 1992).

2. See Gayraud Wilmore, Black Religion and Black Radicalism: An Interpretation of the Religious History of Afro-American People (Maryknoll, NY: Orbis Books, 1983) and E. Franklin Frazier, The Negro Church in America(Liverpool: Univ. of Liverpool, 1963).

122

3. See Wilmore, op. cit., especially Chapter 7.
4. See C. Eric Lincoln, The Black Muslims in America (Boston: Beacon Press, 1973) and E. U. Essien-Udom, Black Nationalism (Chicago: Univ. of Chicago Press, 1962).
5. Lincoln, op. cit., 4.
6. Steven Barboza, :A Divided Legacy," Emerge magazine, Volume 3, #6 April 1992: 27.
7. Adolph Reed, Jr., "The Allure of Malcolm X and the Changing Character of Black Politics," in Joe Woods (ed.), Malcolm X: In Our Own Image (New York: St. Martin's Press, 1992).
8. Video, Rap's Most Wanted (New York: Luke Records, 1991).
9. Gene Santoro, "Public Enemy," The Nation, June 25, 1990; 903.
10. Charlie Ahern, "The Five-Percent Solution," in Spin Magazine, Vol. 6, #11, 1991.
11. Cited in Ahern, op. cit., 56.
12. See Adolph Reed, Jr., The Jesse Jackson Phenomenon: The Crisis of Purpose in Afro-American Politics (New Haven: Yale Univ. Press, 1986); Chapter 1.
13. C. Eric Lincoln and Lawrence Mamiya, The Black Church in the African American Experience (Durham: Duke Univ. Press, 1990); Chapter 8.
14. Included within Rap's Most Wanted, video, op. cit.
15. By refusing to submit to the authority of the Catholic church, Stalling is technically no longer a Catholic, and could, ecclesiastically speaking, be considered a Protestant at this point.
16. New York Times, August 9, 1991.

Chapter 11

Afrocentrism in the 21st Century

By W. Edward Reed, Erma J. Lawson, and Tyson Gibbs

Afrocentricity is a mood or philosophy that has largely erupted and or emerged in the past 15 years in response to integration or perhaps more precisely, to the failure of integration.
Gerald Early *from Understanding Afrocentrism*

As a movement, Afrocentrism is another of the clever but essentially simple-minded hustles that have come over the last 25 years.
Stanley Crouch from *The Afrocentric Hustle*

Afrocentricity is the centerpiece of the human regeneration.
Molefi Kete Asante from *Afrocentricity*

Introduction

The lives of many African-Americans have changed drastically following the Civil Rights Movement (Hacker, 1992; Pinkney, 1981; Staples, 1985; Wilkinson & King, 1987). Such changes are especially obvious in the sports and entertainment arenas. Reportedly, one of the highest-earning individuals in America is Bill Cosby, estimated to have earned nearly $100 million in the late 1980's (Farley & Allen, 1987). Mr. Cosby then moved to the number two position, replaced by Michael Jackson in the number one position. The two-year combined earnings of the top ten African-American entertainers and athletes is nearly a billion dollars (Farley & Allen, 1987).

On the other hand, African-American men constitute only 6% of the United States population, but represent over 50% of male prisoners in local, state, and federal jails (Jones, 1996). Jerome G. Miller's (1996) study by the California State Assemblies Commission on the status of African-American males revealed that one-sixth (104,000) of California's 625,000 Black men 16 and older are arrested each year. Specifically, the study findings suggested that "ninety-two percent of the Black men arrested by police on drug charges were subsequently released for lack of evidence or inadmissible evidence. Black men who made up only three percent of California's population accounted for forty percent of those entering state prisons." Approximately forty-six percent of African-American men between the ages of 16 and 62 are not in the labor force, and thirty-two percent of working African-American men have incomes almost ten thousand dollars less than White males (Dickson, 1993; McAdoo, 1997; Pinkney, 1993; Staples, 1985). Indeed, African-Americans remain the lowest, least integrated underclass in a nation of immigrants, albeit African-Americans were forced into immigration and slavery (Franklin, 1980; Genovese, 1976; Lawson & Thompson, 1995; Miles, 1992).

One of the ironic consequences and contradictions in American Society is the fact that African-Americans can become the number one entertainer in America, or they can become number one on the "10 Most Wanted List." Such irony reveals both the success of integration and its failure. While the majority of Americans have become comfortable accepting African-Americans who entertain and make large sums of money, there remains the staunch reluctance to concede an equitable sharing of power with African-Americans in other arenas.

Critics might argue that African-Americans in the political arena have wielded power through the many major cities, currently and in the past, which have had African-American mayors. However, those same critics would have to concede that most of the cities over which these mayors have presided had, and still have, decaying infrastructures, low level tax bases, and poor economic growth potential in the near future. Political power has not led to economic power.

Moreover, the paradox of race and skin color in America is that the common destiny of African-Americans is more pronounced when economic divisions within the African-American culture are scrutinized. Many social scientists believe that the social and economic divisions among African-Americans are growing deeper and that there is a younger generation of African-Americans estranged from the African-American mainstream. They place less value on life, believing they have nothing to lose including life itself.

One presumable consequence of the classic dilemma (on the one hand, struggling with the reality of being Black in America; and, on the other hand attempting to understand the many racial contradictions in American society) is the emergence of a series of thoughts and actions which have been termed as "Afrocentric." According to Gerald Early (1996). Afrocentrism is an intellectual movement, a political view, an historical evolution, and a religious orthodoxy. It stresses the culture and achievements of Africans. Molefi Kete Asante (1988) believes that Afrocentricity is "a transformation of attitudes, beliefs, values, and behavior results." He also suggests, "It is the first and only reality for African people, it is simply rediscovery."

However, despite the impressive growth of attempts to capture the actions of African-Americans in the concept of Afrocentrism, there is an absence of articles examining whether Afrocentrism, as currently defined, adequately explains the multiplicity of survival tactics employed by African-Americans in post-industrial, post-modern American culture. As in the times of W.E.B. Du Bois, and later in the times of Martin Luther King, Jr., it is important to reexamine African-American subsistence strategies to understand the deep multilayered events which direct ideology and behavior.

The purpose of this article is to extend the conversation and discussion of what some scholars believe is a controversial and impractical philosophy. W.E.B. Du Bois (1903) asserted that the problem of the twentieth century is the

126

"problem of the colorline." Du Bois' observation almost one hundred years ago is still apropos as we move into the twenty-first century. Many African-Americans are still in a quandary about what it means to be an American of African descent (Early, 1993). This article draws from three different authors' schools of thought regarding Afrocentricity as a philosophical movement: Gerald Early, Stanley Crouch, Molefi Asante. Generally, we look at drastic material, legal, social, and psychological changes in African-American lives since the early 1960's (pre-Civil Rights era), and the reality of African-American life in the United States in the 1990s (post-Civil Rights era). We discuss whether or not Afrocentrism is the answer to the dilemmas, conditions, challenges, and paradoxes of being African-American in the United States. Thus, the question remains: Can Afrocentrism establish a framework for individuals and groups interested in coalition/progressive politics and/or gauging the viability of multiculturalism and diversity in the twenty-first century? A second question is: Can the Afrocentric movement capture the myriad of issues afflicting the African-American community nationwide in the twenty-first century?

The Expectations of the Afrocentrists

Afrocentricity is based on the premise that there is somewhere in the universe a collective African Consciousness. Many scholars contend that there is not a unity of thought across the continent of Africa; there is not a single derived African Consciousness in the Americas. There has never been a collective African Spirit or thought or action despite the efforts of the pan-Africanism movement at the turn of the century and the Negritude movement of the 1930s, 1940s, and 1950s. The premise is, therefore, questionable regardless of its promise of bringing clarity of mind, unity of purpose, and collectivity of spirit. However, many Blacks buy into this philosophy. Specifically, many Blacks who have succeeded in the White world tend to be more Afrocentric because of their experiences in the workplace and social environment (Early, 1996).

According to Early, young Blacks tend to buy three effective lines of entry that draw on Afrocentric impulse, mood, and/or philosophy: (1) Islam is the true religion of Black people. (2) Black people need business enterprises in their community in order to liberate themselves from "oppressive Whites." (3) Jews of European descent are not to be trusted. All three positions have remarkable support within the Black middle class. Many middle class Blacks have money, respectability, and organizational know-how (Dyson, 1995; Early, 1996; West, 1993).

Historically, the human race tends to coalesce around religious myths or ethnic group ideology or national character issues. African-Americans, with their blood tainted from the admixture of multiple ethnicities in the United States, cannot coalesce around religion, ethnicity, or ideology exclusively.

Specifically, African-Americans have created memberships for multiple religions, developed dislike for differences in skin tones, participated in acknowledging class differences, and accepted the ideology of money as important to self and family. This is not a new conceptual idea in identity formation. Nathan Hare (1965) discussed the issues and problems facing what he described as the "Black Anglo-Saxons." Frantz Fanon (1967) dealt eloquently with this conceptual idea in his book, *Black Skin, White Masks*.

To have unity of spirit, one must see the commonality in the cultural aspects of life. African-Americans do not share these cultural aspects of life. In reality, African-Americans cannot and will not, en masse, embrace a philosophy which shadows back to a people whom many African-Americans see as negative aspects of their past. In many African-American communities around the United States, it is considered an insult to call one "an African." Many Black children use the term "African" as a way of making one another feel "bad." In these small transactions across the United States, the first seeds of hate are planted for the word "African," and the first steps toward self-hate are initiated.

For the protagonist, the idea of self-hate brings to mind the "brainwashing by the White man." The reality beyond the metaphor of brainwashing is that African-Americans are not unified along any cultural aspects; and, while the cries of "self-hate" will be heard loud and clear from the Afrocentrists, the reality which remains is that unity of spirit can only be achieved through unity of perceived "self-collectivity" by African-Americans in the United States. Such collectivity is not found in the United States or on the African continent. Such collectivity cannot be found in the other places where the descendants of Black Africans reside elsewhere in the World – South America, West Indies and Caribbean Basin, or the Australian Continent. However, there are isolated enclaves of solidarity and collectivity all over the world.

Indeed, the blood which flows through the veins of former slaves, Blacks who live in the Americas and Sub-Sahara Africa, have forged a history whose allegiance lies with those whose soil they now call home. The mixture of European blood and the blood of other ethnic groups has created seeds which have borne the fruit of "others," called by such names as Guyanans, Jamaicans, Brazilians, Nigerians, Kenyans, Puerto Ricans, Panamanians, for hundreds of years. Unity of spirit, thought, and actions, which are the calls of the Afrocentrists, fall on muffled ears of those whose struggles lay with their place called "home."

There is no singular tongue to which these dark-skinned people can listen. Even in the United States, there is the separation of language dialects between African-Americans in the upper, middle, and lower classes. There is not the sense of "our struggle" which unifies the mixed African minds peopling the world as we know it. There is not the availability of an ideology which crosses these many boundaries of ethnicity, class, skin tone, language, and social habits. However, many Afrocentrists are seeking an ordered reality in this diversity and monolithic sea of "Blackness" (Asante, 1993).

There is little question about the need for a commonality of spirit and politic among the African-Americans in the United States. People of African descent, including those on the Continent of Africa, suffer from the exploitation of others. There is little to argue about the historical acts which changed the mind focus of these people forced out of Africa hundreds of years ago. There is no argument that years of false truths have made "mish-mush" of the Black folks' brains. Afrocentrism, as articulated by its advocates, is an ideological vehicle to correct the "mish-mush."

But, the rallying cry for unity through Afrocentrism is asking for the impossible that is seldom achieved world-wide throughout all cultures. To achieve the unity of spirit requested by Afrocentrism is not a realistic goal. The contamination of former African continent residents by the admixture of blood and mind has created between African-Americans in the United States the idea of "US" and "THEM" within Black culture. Within African-American culture, Blacks are asking themselves: "Who is my friend?" and "Who is my enemy?" "Is the Black person of light skin complexion than me, my friend or my enemy?" "What about the guy who makes more money than me?" "What about the Black person who has married a White person: are they my friend or enemy?" "Is the Black lesbian or gay person my friend or my enemy?" "The Mulim Black, the Catholic Black, the Baptist Black, the Methodist Black: where do they all stand on the question of Black unity and/or Afrocentricity?"

Common condemnation and recrimination of those whose philosophies do not embrace Afrocentrism does little to promote the concept of unity and spirituality. The reality lies in the facts. The Africans on the continent of Africa are not of one common line of descent or mind. There should be little expectation that this will change in the twenty-first century. Many believe that Africans will become more nationalistic.

Types of Afrocentrists

Adherence to Afrocentrism falls into three basic types – race distancing elitists, race-embracing rebels, and race-for-profit. The first type are dominant at the more exclusive universities and colleges. They often view themselves as the "talented tenth" who have a near monopoly o the sophisticated and cultural gaze of Afrocentrism. The "talented tenth" harkens back to the ideas discussed in *The Souls of Black Folk* (1903) by W. E. B. DuBois. They revel in severe denigration of many Africa-Americans who fail to be enlightened by Afrocentrism, yet posit little potential or possibility of African-Americans. At times, they denigrate others who do not wear African clothes or wear braids. They distance themselves from other African-Americans by ironically calling attention to their own marginality.

The second type of Afrocentrism behavior is the race-embracing rebels, who often view themselves in the tradition of Malcolm X. That is, race-embracing Afrocentric rebels express their resentment of Whites, but reproduce similar hierarchies based on class and gender within a Black context. They rebel against the insularity and snobbishness of Whites, yet their rebellion excludes other African-Americans with doubled marginality such as gays, lesbians, and those in the under and lower-class. They tend to be self-invested in advancement and hunger for status. Hence, rhetoric on the glorious African past becomes a substitute for analysis. Stimulatory rapping on the merits of Africa becomes a replacement for serious analysis and reading of the predicament of African-Americans.

The for-profit Afrocentric is usually self-taught in Egyptian history and African Continent histories. They expose a cultural style and a moral stance of capitalism. They are usually committed to convincing African-Americans to consume African goods, including clothes from the "motherland." This kind of behavior is not only symptomatic of the alienation of African-Americans and desperation – it also reinforces the fragmentation of African-Americans as symbols of African clothing and dress becoming the essence of an "African-American identity." In this way, Afrocentrics often inadvertently contribute to the very impasse they are trying to overcome. Moreover, it contributes to cynicism among African-Americans; it encourages the ideas that we can not really make a difference in changing our society without consumer symbols of Africa which in many cases, the average African-American cannot afford.

According to Bell Hooks (1994), "Learning from the past, we need to remain critically vigilant, willing to interrogate our work as well as our habits of being to ensure that we are not perpetuating internalized racism."

Afrocentrism in the Context of American Society

Much of the Afrocentrism theoretical framework reflect an inability to comprehend the reality of existence for White America, and its effects on African-Americans. For example, Afrocentrism links the psychological redemption of African-Americans with their reacquaintance to Africa rather than questioning the type of America which could foster the type of human being capable of setting a Black man on fire because of his race. In 1993, Christopher Wilson stood soaked with gasoline in a dusty field while he heard clocks of matches, then a lighter, and then was set on fire simply because he was Black. Wilson said, "I never did anything to anybody, Why are you doing this to me?" when he was set on fire.

Gretchen Wright, 16, was shot in the head while standing near Sixth and Bryant streets, in Washington, D.C. A.30-caliber bullet entered the right side of her brain. The assailant was arrested and charged. He simply said that he was "nigger hunting." Indeed, the United States Department of Justice, Civil Rights division, has reported an increase in hate crimes. Hate crime, an offense motivated by the victim's race, religion, ethnic origins, or sexual orientation, has doubled in the past five years. Every year, the division investigates about 450 reported violations of federal racial violence statutes. Indeed, the recent burning

130

of Black churches and the incidents of people burning crosses or painting racial slurs on homes has doubled.

Where Should Afrocentrists Focus Their Energies?

According to Afrocentric proponents, Afrocentrism is the ideological glue to bring African-Americans together as the expression of a cultural and spiritual level which transcends class and geographical lines; and African-American solidarity is viewed as critical since there is extensive internalized oppression among African-Americans. Because slave holders deliberately dehumanized African-Americans during slavery, it is important to recognize that African-Americans share a common history and suffered a common disaster.

The rhetoric has led to an increases appeal of the Afrocentric ideology to younger Blacks and converting middle class African-Americans that yearn for an idealized group. The paradox of this aspect of Afrocentrism is that it fails to address the issue of class, retrograde views on Black women, gay men, and lesbians. To engage in a serious discussion of Afrocentrism among African-Americans, one must begin with the problems of White America. However, there is a need to look in the mirror and ascertain the magnitude and depth of self-hatred, homophobia, and a host of other problems. Ultimately, the goal is to engage in human wellness and appreciation of all the diverse cultures of the world.

Early (1996) says, "It would be easy, on one level, to dismiss Afrocentrism as an expression, in White workplaces and White colleges, of intimidated Black folk who are desperately trying to find a space for themselves in what they feel to be alien, unsympathetic environments." He argues that there is something to Afrocentrism because "the greatest psychic burden of the African-American is that he must not only think constantly about being different, but about what his or her differences means. And it might be suggested that Afrocentrism does not solve this problem but merely reflects it in a different mirror." He notes that Afrocentrism is an attempt to wed knowledge and ideology. Early says that currently Afrocentrism is not a mature political movement but rather a cultural style and a moral stance. He concludes his article by stating that "what Blacks desire during these turbulent times is exactly what Whites want: the security of a golden past that never existed."

Post-1965

According to many sociologists, African-Americans might be an exception to the general tendency toward ethnic assimilation because of the special power of color prejudice among White Americans (Early, 1993; Hacker, 1992; Pinkney, 1993; Staples, 1985; West, 1993; Wilkinson & King, 1987). Although surveys from the thirties through the fifties and sixties noted there was a consistent decline in racial prejudice and stereotypic thinking, the post-civil rights that appeared, on the surface, to be moving toward equality.

Consequently, Afrocentrism is intense because Whites are in a special period of social development and the United States is experiencing an enormous transition. The ambivalence and increased racial tension demands that Afrocentrism address the shattered civil, market-driven American society. Moreover, it is important for Afrocentrists to expand their acknowledgement that although of African ancestry and blood, African-Americans have tried to live together as equals with their ex-slave masters for more than three hundred years.

1990s

Why does Afrocentrism have such an appeal to a diverse lot of African-Americans at the dawn of the twenty-first century? Offered are several reasons for the appeal, which includes the ideas offered by Early (1996) in which he discusses why Blacks dream of a world without Whites.

Early intimates that one reason is that Afrocentrism is a mood that has largely erupted in the past ten to fifteen years in response to integration, or, perhaps, to the failure of integration. Many African-Americans emerged from the post-Civil Rights era shattered because of the death of Martin Luther King, Jr., and the Civil Rights movement. Furthermore, Early notes that the bourgeois "midcult" element of Afrocentrism is very strong. Specifically, he shows that "integrated" middle class Blacks see it as a demonstration of their race loyalty and solidarity with their brothers and sisters throughout the world, whether in American cities or on African farms. Early argues that the Black middle class has given Afrocentrism its force as a consumer ideology. We would agree with Early and add that Afrocentrism is meant to be an ideological glue to bring Black people together, not just on the basis of color, but as the expression of cultural and spiritual will that crosses class and geographical lines.

A second reason is the appeal of Afrocentrism to African-American college professors. Many use it as a mechanism to call attention to "differences" and to buffer themselves and their colleagues against racism. African-American college students seeking an identity on Black and White college campuses are attracted to Afrocentrism. Why? Some use it to justify their petty bourgeois and middle class backgrounds. A number of students feel guilty for not being poor. Therefore, Afrocentrism presents an ideological glue or bonding across class lines.

One of the authors was questioned once by a male African-American student on an upstate New York campus: "Are you Afrocentric?" He was totally befuddled and confused. His terse response was related to his upbringing in Southern society. He reminded the student that he came from Black Mississippi, a.k.a. "Sugar ditch."

132

A third reason is that African-American prisoners are attracted to the ideology and philosophy of Afrocentrism. Reed found in his work experience in four state prisons, that many African-American brothers, and others, are in search of identification with Blackness and the symbols of Blackness. Many incarcerated individuals are relating to the "struggle" or symbols of the revolution for the first time in their lives. Why? Many have dropped out of high school/life and have been running after the almighty dollar and drugs, sex, and rap, and have been captured. A few try to focus on Black history month and Afrocentrism to look good to the parole board and to attract ladies who come to the county jail or state penitentiary.

A fourth reason proposed is that Afrocentrism has widespread commercial appeal during the summer months at African/American-African world festivals nationwide in big venues, e.g., New York City, Detroit, Chicago, Gary, Chicago, Los Angeles, Cleveland, Seattle, etc. Many "high profile" rap stars, singers, dancers, and professional athletes wear the garb and relate to the symbolism of Afrocentrism philosophy. Many seem to be genuinely interested in sharing and living the values of the ideology.

Finally, many Blacks find that Afrocentrism provides an emotional as well as psychological appeal. This aspect is evident by Blacks naming their children African names, i.e., upper, middle, and lower class, and is also evident by the numerous trips taken to Africa by upper middle class Blacks.

Early (1996) makes the point that affirmative action, which promotes group identification and group differences, tends to intensify Black self-consciousness. Early surmises, "Blacks, through no fault of their own, are afflicted with a debilitation of self-consciousness when around Whites. When Whites are in the rare situation of being a minority in a sea of Blacks, they often exhibit an abject self-consciousness as well, but the source of that self-consciousness is quite different." Early notes that the White person is used to traveling anywhere in the world and having his cultural inclinations accommodated. However, the Black person is neither used to having his needs met nor does he realistically expect it to happen. Afrocentricity is an attempt to wed knowledge and ideology and enhance the Black person's self-esteem and identity.

Stanley Crouch – The Critic

One of the major critics of the Afrocentric philosophical movement is Stanley Crouch. He contends that it is a simple-minded hustle with no substance that has come about over the last twenty-five years, descended from what was once called the "professional Negro" (Winter 1995/1996). He said:

> At its core, though Afrocentrism has little to offer any intellectual substance, it benefits in spades from the decline of faith so basic to how intellectuals have fumbled the heroic demands of our time. ... For all its pretensions to expanding our vision, the Afrocentric movement is not propelled by a desire to bring about

any significant enrichment of our American culture. What Afrocentrists almost always want is power.

However, Crouch needs to look closely at Studs Terkel's article, *Under Our Skin* (May/June 1992). The author reminds us that Americans are obsessed about race and race reasoning. He worked on his book, *RACE: How Blacks and Whites Think and Feel About the American Obsession* (1992), for over 30 years and reached the conclusion that most Americans are obsessed with racial issues and racism. As long as racism exists, many individuals, Black and White and others, will resort to race reasoning to explain their status and lot in America. Afrocentric thinking will find a place in the 21st century because of our society's uneasy perceptions and values and because of our inequality in wealth and social standing in our nation.

We contend that Afrocentrism has its problems; however, it has a deeper meaning for middle-class Black students seeking to find themselves on all-White campuses. For instance, Nicholas Lemann (1993) interviewed African-American students on two college campuses, University of Pennsylvania and Temple University. He found that the students at Temple were more likely to find work in municipal bureaucracies, e.g., school systems, welfare departments, whereas Penn students were likely to be headed for professions which are overwhelmingly White. What was noteworthy from the interviews conducted by Lemann with the predominantly Afrocentric/Nationalist students was that remaining within Black American communities and careers was the "right thing" to do and integration was the wrong thing to do. Many of the students expressed the choice of working for social change and pursuing business careers.

The Dilemma Facing African-Americans

The dilemma, now crisis, among African-Americans is the presentation of these three types of Afrocentrism (discussed earlier) as one mode of thinking. Such a dilemma can be remedied only by candidly confronting the existence of the degree of Americanization in the African-American Community. There is a need to critically interrogate our values of "conspicuous consumption," lack of support for the family unit, limited support for little boys and little girls, and most of all, the seduction of Black criminality that impacts everyone. Dyson (1995) reminds us that in turning the corner, we must be alert and "come to grips with how we do each other in." We need local and national forums to reflect, discuss, and plan how best to respond to major social changes in the twenty-first century. It is not a matter of a new Martin Luther King, Jr., emerging or starting another new organization. Rather, it is a matter of grasping the positive and negatives of Afrocentrism and understanding the need for nurturing a collective critical consciousness, and moral commitment for the future.

134

Cornel West (1993) indicates, "Blackness is a political and ethical construct. Appeals to Black authenticity ignore this fact; such appeals hide and conceal the political and ethical dimension of Blackness." Specifically, the authors concur with West when he argues that claims to racial authenticity trump political and ethical argument and racial reasoning discourages moral reasoning.

As we move into the twenty-first century, there is a need for serious strategic and tactical thinking about how to create new models that include Afrocentrism and to forge the kind of leadership to realize these models. These models must question the silent assumptions about Afrocentrism, but also force one to question color discrimination, sexism, homophobia, and most of all, the anger, rage, and despair directed toward African-American citizens by other African-Americans. We can no longer afford to ignore the ethical dimension of Blackness.

REFERENCES

Asante, Molefi Kete. (1987). *The Afrocentric Idea*. Philadelphia: Temple University Press.
Asante, Molefi Kete. (1988). *Afrocentric*. Trenton, NJ: Africa World Press, Inc.
Asante, Molefi Kete. (1993). "Racism, Consciousness, and Afrocentricity." In Gerald Early (ed.), *Lure and Loathing* (pp. 127-143). New York: The Penguin Group.
Crouch, Stanley. Winter (1995/1996). "The Afrocentric Hustle." *The Journal of Blacks in Higher Education*. pp. 77-82.
Dickson, L. (1993). "The Future of Marriage and Family in Black America." *Journal of Black Studies*. 23, 472-491.
DuBois, W.E.B. (1903). *The Souls of Black Folk*. Chicago: A.C. McClurg & Company.
Dyson, Michael Eric. (1995). *Making Malcolm: The Myth and Meaning of Malcolm X*. New York: Oxford University Press.
Early, Gerald (Ed.). (1993). *Lure and Loathing*. New York: The Penguin Group.
Early, Gerald. (1996). "Understanding Afrocentrism: Whay Blacks Dream of a World Without Whites." In Geoffrey C. Ward (ed.), *The Best American Essays 1996* (pp. 115-135). New York: Houghton Mifflin Company.
Edley, Christopher. September/October (1996). "Affirmative Action Angst: Contemplating Campus Policy After Hopwood v. Texas." *Change*. pp. 13-15.
Fanon, Frantz. (1967). *Black Skin, White Masks*. New York: Grove Press, Inc.
Farley, R., & Allen, W.R. (1987). *The Color Line and the Quality of Life in America*. New York: Russell Sage Foundation.
Franklin, C.W. (1980). "White Racism as a Cause of Black Male/Female Conflict: A Critique." *Western Journal of Black Studies*. 4. 42-49.
Genovese, Eugene. (1976). *Roll Jordan Roll: The World the Slaves Made*. New York: Random.
Hacker, A. (1992). *Two Nations: Black and White, Separate, Hostile, Unequal*. New York: Charles Scribner's Sons.
Hare, Nathan. (1965). *The Balck Anglo-Saxons*. Nw York: The MacMillan Company.

Hooks, Bell. (1994). Outlaw culture: Resistance Representations. New York: Routledge.

Jones, Gene A. (1996). *The Seduction of Black Criminality: A Psychopolitical Analysis of Black Crime in America*. Fort Worth, TX: CGS Communications.

Lawson, Erma Jean, & Thompson, Aaron. April (1995). "Black Men Make Sense of Marital Distress and Divorce: An Exploratory Study." *Family Relations*. 44, 211-218.

Lemann, Nicholas. January (1993). "Black Nationalism on Campus." *The Atlantic*, 271 (1). pp. 31-47.

McAdoo, Harriette Pipes (ed.). (1997). *Black Families* (Third Edition). Thousand Oaks, California: SAGE Publications.

Miles, Jack. October (1992). "Blacks vs. Browns." *The Atlantic Monthly*, 270 (4), pp. 41-68.

Miller, Jerome G. (1996). *Search and Destroy*. New York: Cambridge University Press.

Pinkney, A. (1993). *Black Americans* (4th ed.). Englewood Cliffs, NJ: Prentice-Hall.

Staples, R. (1985). "Changes in Black Family Structure: The Conflict Between Family Ideology and Structural Conditions." *Journal of Marriage and Family*, 53, 221-230.

Terkel, Studs. May/June (1992). "Under Our Skin." *Mother Jones*, 17 (3), 36-45.

West, Cornel. (1993). *Race Matters*. New York: Vintage Books.

Wilkinson, D., & King, G. (1987). "Conceptual and Methodological Issues in the Use of Race as a Variable: Policy Implications." *The Milbank Quarter*, 66: 56-70.

Chapter 12

Affirmative Action:
The Future of Race Based Preferences in Hiring

By Le Von E. Wilson

Justice John M. Harlan perhaps said it best in his now famous resounding dissenting opinion which was expressed in *Plessy v. Ferguson*. [1] He argued that a governmentally enforced system of "separate but equal" racial segregation was inconsistent with the letter and spirit of the Fourteenth Amendment's equal protection guarantees. He said:

> In respect of civil rights, common to all citizens, the Constitution of the United States does not, I think, permit any public authority to know the race of those entitled to be protected in the enjoyment of such rights. Every true man has pride of race, and under appropriate circumstances, when the rights of others, his equals before the law, are not affected, it is his privilege to express such pride and to take such action based upon it as to him seems proper. But I deny that any legislative body or judicial tribunal may have regard to the race of citizens when the civil rights of those citizens are involved. [2]

While recognizing the perceived position of the White race, Justice Harlan went on to state what now constitutes the most famous lines of his dissent:

> ... The white race deems itself to be the dominant race in this country. And so it is, in prestige, in achievements, in education, in wealth, and in power. So I doubt not it will continue to be for all time, if it remains true to its great heritage, and holds fast to the principles of constitutional liberty. But in view of the Constitution, in the eye of the law, there is in this country no superior, dominant, ruling class of citizens. There is no caste here. Our Constitution is colorblind, and neither knows nor tolerates classes among citizens. In respect of civil rights, all citizens are equal before the law. The humblest is the peer of the most powerful. The law regards man as man, and takes no account of his surroundings or of his color when his civil rights as guaranteed by the supreme law of the land are involved. [3]

Aftermath of Brown

Justice Harlan predicted that the court's majority opinion in *Plessy* would in time prove to be a pernicious one. Fortunately his prediction came true in later cases such as *Brown v. Board of Education of Topeka*,[4] *Sweatt v. Painter*,[5] *Bolling v. Sharpe*[6] and others wherein the question of equal protection was raised. Obviously, the most noteworthy of the cases was *Brown*. Probably no decision in the history of the Court has directly concerned so many individuals. At the time of the *Brown* case, segregation in the schools was required by law in seventeen states and the District of Columbia. In this area there were over 8 million White and 2.5 million Black school children enrolled in approximately 35,000 White schools and 15,000 Black schools.[7] The intrinsically difficult problems of implementing the *Brown* decision were intensified by salvos of defiance by political leaders and by vigorous defensive action in the legislatures of some states.

In another much celebrated case, *Swann v. Charlotte Mecklenburg Board of Education*,[8] the United States Supreme Court, largely in reliance on its previous decision in *Green v. County School Board*,[9] which required the creation of a unitary school system, suggested that the District Court has the powers to fashion a remedy which will so far as possible eliminate the present effects of past discrimination as well as bar like discrimination in the future.[10] Although courts have broad equity powers in fashioning an effective remedy in an effort to eradicate discriminatory practices, the power to provide an effective remedy affords no basis for depriving others of a constitutionally protected right. If one is to assume the obvious, one must realize that a court cannot order governmental officials to take any action which would itself be unconstitutional.

In the early cases following *Brown* the courts engaged in a careful and systematic review of the problems involved in the utilization of benign racial classifications. The cases were judged by a permissive rather than a strict standard of review when a court was convinced that the purpose of the measure using a racial classification was truly benign; that is, the measure represented an effort to use the classification as part of a program designed to achieve an equal position in society for all races.

The United States Code[11] and the Fourteenth Amendment, by their plain and unambiguous language, accord equal rights to all persons regardless of race. Those provisions proscribe any discrimination in employment based on race whether the discrimination be against Whites or Blacks. This view is supported by *Griggs v. Duke Power Company*[12] where it was held:

> Congress did not intend by Title VII, however, to guarantee a job to every person regardless of qualifications. In short, the Act does not command that any person be hired simply because he was formerly the subject of discrimination, or because he is a member of a minority group. Discriminatory preference for any group, minority or majority is precisely and only what Congress has proscribed. What is required by Congress is the removal of artificial, arbitrary and unnecessary barriers to employment when barriers operate invidiously to discriminate on the basis of racial or other impermissible classification.[13]

Benign Discrimination

The issues raised in *Griggs* have again and again been litigated where the results of the administration of an employment examination have a disparate impact on minorities. Under most of the early minority preference provisions, a White person who, in a subsequently conducted examination fairly conducted and free of racial discrimination, obtained a higher rating than a minority person may have been denied employment solely because he was White. Is the fact that some unnamed and unknown White person in the distant past may, by reason of past racial discrimination in which the present applicant in no way participated, have received preference over some unidentified minority person with higher qualifications, in any way justification for discriminating against the present better qualified applicant upon the basis of race?

The school integration cases such as Swann are clearly different. Because Whites have no constitutional right to insist upon segregated schools, no constitutional rights violations can be alleged in decrees ordering school integration. However, in employment situations, an absolute preference ordered by the court can operate as a present infringement on those non-minority group persons who are equally or superiorly qualified for the job in question. While a court may acknowledge the legitimacy of erasing the effects of past racially discriminatory practices, does a court have the power to implement one constitutional guarantee by the outright denial of another? This question creates a present-day dilemma.

America is faced with the crucial question of whether giving absolute preference to a racial minority who meets the qualification tests and standards infringes upon the constitutional rights of White applicants whose qualifications are established in a particular instance to be superior. In an effort to accommodate these conflicting considerations, the courts were willing to entertain some reasonable ratio for hiring carefully constructed qualification standards that were imposed for a limited period of time, or until there was a fair approximation of minority representation consistent with the population mix in the area. Although such procedures were viewed generally as a quota system, the courts did not consider them as such because as soon as the trial court's order was fully implemented, all hearings would be on racially non-discriminatory basis, and it could well be that many more minority persons or fewer, as compared to the population at large, over a long period of time would apply and qualify for the positions. As a method of presently eliminating the effects of past racial discriminatory practices and in making meaningful in the immediate future the constitutional guarantees against racial discrimination, the courts required more than a token representation. As a result the courts were permitted to use mathematical ratios as a starting point in the process of shaping a remedy. The United States Supreme Court found the practice to be constitutional and "within the equitable remedial discretion of the District Court."[14] It is obvious that fashioning a remedy in these cases was a practical question which differed substantially from case to case, depending on the circumstances. Affirmative Action had thus moved beyond the infancy stage.

A full-scale attack on the early use of racial classifications in an effort to aid underprivileged groups is contained in Alexander and Alexander, "The New Racism: Analysis of the Use of Racial and Ethnic Criteria in Decision-Making."[15] The authors concluded:

> We do indeed have an obligation to aid the unjustly disadvantaged and to oppose prejudice and discrimination, but we have an equal obligation to do so without resorting to the use of irrelevant group membership criteria such as race. The moral and legal basis for our attacks on disadvantagement and discrimination are the same principles of liberty and justice (embodied in the Constitution as due process and equal protection) which require that we do not take irrelevant group membership into consideration. There could be no greater catastrophe for this nation than abandonment of these principles of individual equality for the spurious justice of equality among arbitrarily chosen groups.

The Impact of Croson

In *Albermarle Paper Co. V. Moody*[16] the United States Supreme Court ruled that nondiscriminatory alternatives to testing can be used by private companies in an effort to bring Blacks into the work force. In the now famous and often cited case of *Regents of the University of California v. Bakke*[17] the Supreme Court held that while race can be taken into account as one factor in determining admission policies at a state university, the actual setting aside of a specific number of positions for minorities, thus amounting to a quota, is unconstitutional. One year following the *Bakke* decision the Court decided *Kaiser Aluminum Co. And Steelworkers of America v. Weber*.[18] In that case, the Court upheld a voluntary affirmative action program which had been the result of negotiations between a labor organization and a private company even though the program favored minorities over Whites who may have had more seniority. The purpose of the program was to increase minority representation in certain jobs where they had been effectively excluded. The goal of the program was to raise the level of minority participation in those jobs to a percentage which was equal to that of the community at large. In *Fullilove v. Kluznick*[19] the Supreme Court held that narrowly tailored remedies for past societal and systematic discrimination may be appropriate in limited circumstances. In deciding the case the Court upheld a ten percent (10%) minority set-aside program which was established by Congress. In *Wygant v. Jackson Board of Education*[20] the Court ruled that race conscious relief would be permissible in the context of hiring, but there must be convincing evidence of past discrimination. In perhaps the most celebrated case of the 1988-89 term, the Supreme Court ruled in *City of Richmond v. Croson*[21] that the Constitution limits the power of states and local governments to reserve a percentage of their business for minority contractors if they are not correcting well documented past cases of discrimination.

140

In *Croson*, The City of Richmond, Virginia argued that the Supreme Court's decision in *Fullilove* should be controlling, and that as a result the city enjoys sweeping legislative power to define and attack the efforts of prior discrimination in its local construction industry. In *Fullilove*, the Court upheld the minority set aside contained in Section 103 of the Public Works Employment Act of 1977[22] against a challenge based on the equal protection component of the Due Process Clause. The Act authorized a four billion dollar approbation for federal grants to state and local governments for use in public works projects. The primary purpose of the Act was to give the national economy a quick boost in a recessionary period. The Act also contained the following requirements: "Except to the extent the Secretary determines otherwise, no grant shall be made under this Act ... unless the applicant gives satisfactory assurance to the Secretary that at least 10 percent of the amount of each grant shall be expanded for minority business enterprises."[23] Minority business enterprises (MBE's) were defined as businesses effectively controlled by "citizens of the United States who are Negroes, Spanish-speaking, Orientals, Indians, Eskimos, and Aleuts."[24]

The Court's strict scrutiny standard as applied in *Croson* would suggest that the Court is willing to accept only a *remedial* purpose as sufficiently compelling governmental action. The Court reasons that unless racial classifications are strictly reserved for remedial settings it may prove to promote motions of racial inferiority and perhaps lead to racial hostility. In order to use racial preferences, there must be adequate evidence of remedial necessity. The Principal opinion in *Fullilove* did not employ "strict scrutiny" or any other traditional standard of equal protection review. Chief Justice Warren E. Burger, who wrote the opinion, noted that although racial classifications call for close examination, the Court was at the same time, "bound to approach [its] task with appropriate deference to Congress, a co-equal branch charged by the Constitution with the power to 'provide for the general welfare of the United States' and 'to enforce by appropriate legislation,' the equal protection guarantees of the Fourteenth Amendment."[25] The principal opinion in *Fullilove* asked two questions: first, were the objectives of the legislation within the power of Congress? Second, was the limited use of racial or ethnic criteria a permissible means for Congress to carry out its objectives within the constraints of the Due Process Clause?

On the issue of congressional power, the Chief Justice found that Congress' commerce power was sufficiently broad to allow it to reach the practices of prime contractors on federally funded local construction projects.[26] He further suggested that Congress could mandate state and local government compliance with the set-aside program under its Section 5 power to enforce the Fourteenth Amendment.[27] Next, he addressed the issue of the constraints on Congress' power to use race-conscious remedial relief. In upholding the MBE set-aside program, he stressed two factors. First was what he described as the unique remedial powers of Congress under Section 5 to enforce the Fourteenth Amendment:

> Here we deal ... not with the limited remedial powers of a federal court, for example, but with the broad remedial powers of Congress. It is fundamental that no organ of government, state or federal, does there repose a more comprehensive remedial power than in the Congress, expressly charged by the Constitution with competence and authority to enforce equal protection guarantees.[28]

Because of these unique powers, the Chief Justice concluded that "Congress not only may induce voluntary action to assure compliance with existing federal statutory or constitutional antidiscrimination provisions, but also, where Congress has authority to declare certain conduct unlawful, it may, as here, authorize and induce state action to avoid such conduct."[29]

The second factor emphasized by the principal opinion in *Fullilove* was the flexible nature of the 10 percent set-aside. Two "congressional assumptions" underlay the MBE program: first, that the effects of past discrimination had impaired the competitive position of minority businesses, and second, that "adjustment for the effects of past discrimination" would assure that at least 10 percent of the funds from the federal grant program would flow to minority businesses. The Chief Justice noted that both of these "assumptions" could be "rebutted" by a grantee seeking a waiver of the 10 percent requirement.[30] Thus, a waiver could be obtained where minority businesses were not available to fill the 10 percent requirement or, more importantly, where an MBE attempted to "exploit the remedial aspects of the program by charging an unreasonable price, i.e., a price not attributable to the present effects of prior discrimination."[31] The Chief Justice further indicated that without this fine tuning to remedial purpose, the statute would not have "pass[ed] muster."[32]

In viewing *Croson* in light of its decision in *Fullilove*, the Supreme Court stated that because Congress may identify and redress the effects of society-wide discrimination does not mean that, a fortiori, the states and their political subdivisions are free to decide that such remedies are appropriate. The Court further stated that Section 1 of the Fourteenth Amendment is an explicit constraint on state power, and the states must undertake any remedial efforts in accordance with the provision. To hold otherwise, the Court said, would be to concede control over the content of the Equal Protection Clause to the 50 state legislatures and their myriad political subdivisions. The mere recitation of a benign or compensatory purpose for the use of a racial classification would essentially entitle the state to exercise the full power of Congress under Section 5 of the Fourteenth Amendment and insulate any racial classification from judicial scrutiny under Section 1.[33]

The Strict Scrutiny Standard

In *Wygant*, four members of the Court applied heightened scrutiny to a race-based system of employee layoffs. Justice Lewis F. Powell, writing for the plurality, again drew the distinction between "societal discrimination" which he suggested was an inadequate basis for race-conscious classifications, and the type of identified discrimination that can support and define the scope of race-based relief. The challenged classification in that case tied the layoff of minority teachers to the percentage of minority students enrolled in the school district. The lower courts had upheld the scheme based on the theory that minority students were in need of "role models" to alleviate the effects of prior discrimination in society. The Supreme Court reviewed, with a plurality of four justices reiterating the view expressed by Justice Powell in *Bakke* that "[s]ocietal discrimination, without more, is too amorphous a basis for imposing a racially classified remedy."[34]

In applying the stricter test in *Croson*, the Court went on to say that absent searching judicial inquiry into the justification for such race-based measures, there is simply no way of determining what classifications are in fact motivated by illegitimate notions of racial inferiority or simple racial politics. The purpose, said the Court, of strict scrutiny is to "smoke out" illegitimate uses of race by assuring that the legislative body is pursuing a goal important enough to warrant use of a highly suspect tool. The Court further suggested that the test also ensures that the means chosen "fit" this compelling goal so closely that there is little or no possibility that the motive for the classification was illegitimate racial prejudice or stereotype.[35]

Although the decision by the Court in *Croson* did not entirely close the door on the official use of some form of narrowly defined racial preference in "extreme" circumstances, it nevertheless greatly restricted their use by state and local governments. The Court went on record to suggest that all racial classifications are subject to the strict scrutiny standard of review and that such classifications will be upheld only if it is justified by a compelling state interest and is narrowly defined to serve that purpose.

The Supreme Court made it clear that it was not totally stripping the state or local subdivision (if delegated the authority by the state) of the authority to eradicate the effects of private discrimination within its own legislative jurisdiction. In the original panel opinion, the Court of Appeals held that under Virginia law the city had the legal authority to enact the set-aside program.[36] That determination was not disturbed by the Court's subsequent holding that the Plan violated the Equal Protection Clause. This authority, said the Court, must be exercised within the affirmative program in order to qualify for certain government contracts; or 2) courts may order an employer that has intentionally discriminated against minorities to institute an affirmative program. Affirmative action programs have been upheld by the United States Supreme Court in both situations.

The executive branch of the federal government has undertaken direct responsibility in the area of affirmative action programs since the beginning of these programs in Executive Order 11264, [39] signed by President Johnson in 1965.

An employer with a federal contract[40] is required to analyze its workforce in order to determine whether minorities and women are underrepresented in relation to their availability in the local work force.

Courts have occasionally imposed an affirmative action plan on an employer that has intentionally discriminated. They have ordered quotas for hiring and promotion.[41] Some employers have voluntarily instituted affirmative action plans in an attempt to rectify past or present discrimination. This has promoted some White males to assert that Title VII protects' them from race and sex discrimination as well.[42] They have raised the issue of reverse discrimination.[43]

The term "affirmative action" has changed in meaning since it was first introduced. Initially, the term referred primarily to special efforts to ensure that equal opportunities were available for members of groups that had been subject to discrimination. Those special efforts included public advertising for positions to be filled, active recruitment of qualified applicants from the formerly excluded groups, as well as special training programs designed to help meet the standards for admission or appointment.

More recently, the term has come to refer to the necessity of providing some degree of definite preference for members of these groups in determining access to positions from which they were formerly excluded. Such preferences have been permitted to influence decisions between candidates who are otherwise equally qualified. Indeed, quite often such preferences have involved the selection of women or minority members over other candidates who are better qualified for the position.

The *Croson* majority seems to have expressed a discomfort with the ever-increasing use of race as a criterion for distributing public resources and opportunities. The decision in *Croson* strongly suggests that the Court is becoming less tolerant to government-sponsored racial preferences. The decision, however, will not prevent courts from remedying past discrimination where discrimination is found to be the cause of racial imbalances. In those cases, the Court has left open the availability of affirmative action remedies. It appears that mere racial imbalances based on past societal discrimination or even past discrimination in a particular industry, without any showing of actual discrimination, will no longer be the basis of a broad sweeping affirmative action quota program. A review of the basic goal of affirmative action programs reveals that most were designed and implemented for the purpose of providing a present solution to problems caused by past societal discrimination.

The *Croson* Court has not totally eliminated affirmative action but rather limited its scope. The concern of the Court is that racial preferences not become a commonplace and continuing part of the American society.

It is believed by many that companies will feel freer to discriminate, especially those which do not have a genuine commitment to a diversified work force. Some believe that these companies will use the recent Supreme Court decision as a basis for "going back to the good old days." Some believe that the Court is

144

moving faster than society. And still others hold the view that affirmative action should be a permanent solution.

The conservative majority of the Court appears poised to insist on proof that affirmative action plans will remedy proven bias and not just compensate for lingering past problems.

The Court is signaling a gradual end to such preferences.[44] The Court perhaps envisions a society which is color-blind, a society in which there are no classes of individuals based on race or color. Such a vision is mythical, indeed.

NOTES

1. 163 U.S. 537 (1896).
2. Id.
3. Id.
4. 347 U.S. 483 (1954).
5. 339 U.S. 629.
6. 347 U.S. 497 (1954).
7. *New York Times*, May 18, 1954, p. 18.
8. 402 U.S. 1 (1971).
9. 391 U.S. 430 (1968).
10. See also *Louisiana v. United States*, 380 U.S. 145.
11. 42 U.S.C. 1981.
12. 401 U.S. 424 (1971).
13. Id., at 430-431.
14. 402 U.S. 1, at 25.
15. 9 San Diego L. Rev. 190 (1972).
16. 422 U.S. 405 (1975).
17. 438 U.S. 265 (1978).
18. 443 U.S. 193 (1979).
19. 448 U.S. 448 (1980).
20. 476 U.S. 267 (1986) See 478 U.S. 1016 (1986).
21. 109 S.Ct. 706, 57 L.W. 4132 (1989).
22. Pub. L. 95-28, 91 Stat. 116, 42 U.S.C. 6701 et. Seq.
23. 448 U.S., at 454 [quoting 91 Stat. 116, 42 U.S.C. 6705(f)(2)].
24. Id.
25. 448 U.S., at 472.
26. Id., at 475-476.
27. Id., at 476 (citing *Katzenbach v. Morgan*, 384 U.S. 641, 651 (1966).
28. 448 U.S., at 483.
29. Id., at 483-484.
30. Id., at 487-488.
31. Id., at 488.
32. Id., at 487.
33. 109 S.Ct. 706. 57 L.W. 4132, at 4138.
34. 476 U.S., at 276 (plurality opinion).
35. 109 U.S., 706, 57 L.W. 4132, at 4139.

36. *J.A. Crosson Co. v. Richmond*, 770 F. 2d 181, 184-186 (4th Cir. 1985).
37. 476 U.S., at 274.
38. 109 S.Ct. 706, 57 L.W. 4132, at 4138.
   39. The key provision of the Executive Order is Section 202, which prohibits employment discrimination by government contractors.
   The Contractor will not discriminate against any employer or applicant for employment because of race, creed, color, or natural origin. The Contractor will take affirmative action to ensure that applicants are employed, and that employees are treated during employment without regard to their race, creed, color, or national origin. Such action shall include, but not be limited to, the following: employment, upgrading, demotion, or transfer, recruitment or recruitment advertising; layoff or termination; rates of pay or other forms of compensation; and selection for training, including apprenticeship.
   On October 13, 1967, the President issued Executive Order 11375, adding sex to the categories for which nondiscrimination and affirmative action are mandated by government contractors.
   Executive Order 112624 provides the basis for the federal government contract compliance program. Under the Executive Order, as amended, firms doing business with the federal government must agree not to discriminate in employment on the basis of race, color, religion, natural origin, or sex. The contract compliance program is administered by the Secretary of Labor through the Office of Federal Contract Compliance Program (OFCCP).
40. The regulations provide that all forms having contracts or subcontracts exceeding $10,000 with the federal government must agree to include a no-discrimination clause in the contract. In addition to requiring the no-discrimination clause, the OFCCP regulations may require that a contracting firm develop a written plan regarding its employees. Firms with contracts of service or supply for over $50,000 and having fifty or more employees are required to maintain formal written affirmative action plans for the utilization of women and minorities in their workplace.
41. In *United States v. Paradise*, 480 U.S. 149 (1987), the Alabama Department of Public Safety had been found guilty by a federal district court of "pervasive, systematic, and obstimatic" discrimination in the hiring and promotion of Blacks as state troopers. The court ordered 50 percent Black promotions until each rank was 25 percent Black, but only if there were qualified Black candidates, if a particular rank was less than 25% Black, and if the Department had not developed and implemented a promotion plan that did not have an adverse impact on Blacks. The U.S. Supreme Court held, in a 5 to 4 decision, that the order did not violate the equal protection clause of the Fourteenth Amendment: there is compelling governmental interest in eradicating stubborn discrimination against Blacks, and the one-for-one promotion requirement was sufficiently narrowly tailored to withstand even strict scrutiny analysis.
   Specifically, the plan was temporary in nature, it did not require gratuitous promotions, it could be (and had been) waived by the constitution if there were no qualified Black candidates, the numerical relief ordered bore a proper relationship to the percentage of nonwhites in the relevant labor force, and it did not impose an unacceptable burden on innocent White candidates for promotion.
   The court noted that the plan did not bar the advancement of Whites, but only postponed their promotion, and concluded that the plan represented as informal

146

attempt to balance the rights and interests of the plaintiffs, the Department, and White state troopers.

See also, *Sheet Metal Workers v. EEOC* 478 U.S. 421 (1986).

42. For the application of Title VII to White males see generally, *McDonald v. Santa Fe Trail Transportation Co.*, 427 U.S. 273 (1976).

43. The decision in *Martin v. Wilks*, 109S.Ct. 2180 (1989) permits court-approved affirmative action settlements to be reopened in nonminority (White male) employees allege reverse discrimonation.

It shouls be further noted that in *Wards Cove Packing Co. v. Antonio*, 109 S.Ct. 2155 (1989) the Court held that a racial imbalance in the makeup of an employer's work force is not itself proof of racial discrimination in hiring.

44. For a better understanding of the Court's current position on race based preferences, see *Metro Broadcasting, Inc. v. FCC*, 110 S.Ct. 2997 (1990).

Chapter 13

Liberation Ideologies of Select Black Intellectuals

By Gwinyai P. Muzorewa

Introduction

The inconsistencies of America's claims to liberty and freedom for all were apparent in the nation's maintenance and even advancement of the institution of slavery. Slave codes were introduced which essentially reaffirmed the ideology that Blacks were inferior beings and that they had no rights which Whites were bound to respect. Furthermore, the slave codes also introduced more rigorous measures which were designed to restrict the African American from rebelling against slavery, and escape to freedom. While the south experienced armed revolts and other more subtle acts of rebellion, the northern Blacks along with White abolitionists strengthened their resolve and intensified the cause of the abolition of slavery. In this chapter the intent is to identify the ideology which guided and enlightened the leading militant Blacks.

Rev. Henry Highland Garnet

Reverend Henry Highland Garnet was a clergy abolitionist as well as political activist. He eventually adopted the emigrationist ideology. In the 1840s he advocated publicly that the enslaved of America should take arms and rebel against their oppressors. Garnet adopted this position as all other tactics applied to that end had failed.

A former slave in Maryland, Garnet was well acquainted with the day to day effects of slavery. It is therefore not surprising that he, as well as a virtual corps of Black clergymen, was a major actor in the drama of the abolition of slavery in the north. Clergymen like Lemuel Haynes and Samuel Ringgold Ward, along with scores of supporters and fellow advocators of Black freedom in America[1], believed in armed struggle. Although many of that era were not clergy, they were affiliated with the church and were effective speakers in their stance against slavery, including the personalities of Frederick Douglass, Sojourner Truth (Isabella Baumfree), William Wells Brown, and Alexander Crummell among others. Garnet believed in God and was a Christian who was highly active in securing safe passage for runaway slaves as stations in the underground rail road. We agree with Charles Eric Lincoln and Lawrence H. Mamiya who posit the following regarding the activities of the Black Church, "...black churches and clergy have also been continually involved in a broad range of political activities, both reformist and radical. These reformist and radical activities stemmed from the liberation tradition of the heritage of Black churches...(1990, 202)."

Garnet's belief in God was of use in articulating his theological views of the evils of slavery and that all men are equal and should therefore be justly treated. Views of multiple other clergy and theologians "...were based on their own interpretations of Old Testament stories, prophetic pronouncements and New Testament apocalypse" (202). The liberation theology of which Garnet ascribed to, manifested itself in various ways, ranging from the three largest slave rebellions in American history which were led by Christian preachers[i], to speaking before European audiences with the objectives of informing attitudes of the equality of men, and the evils of slavery.

Garnet's initial activities in his fight for overcoming slavery included speaking engagements and publications including editing the pre-Civil war paper: *The National Watchmen*. It was believed that influencing White audiences would achieve the goal of politically over turning slavery. Also sought were international audiences such as those in Germany, England, Scotland and France, in the hopes that their influence might be used towards the same end[i]. Furthermore, it was believed that domestic and international speaking engagements would allow the White public to hear of the atrocities of slavery while also giving them the opportunity to observe the eloquence of the Black speakers. Support of sympathizers against slavery would be garnered and premises of the racial inferiority of Black people would be disproved. Garnet, as did Frederick Douglass, moved to disprove racist notions of Black intellectual inferiority by presenting as evidence to the contrary, the historical achievements of Africans[i].

This ideology culminated in the free African American people use of the political means to achieve goals set forward by the needs of the Black population of America, North and South[i]. In the late 1830s, following Pennsylvania's Bucks developments and successive waves of defeated petitions, Garnet, along with Charles Reason and others, would galvanize efforts and implement a universal manhood suffrage campaign. This involved repeatedly petitioning the New York State legislator for the right to vote[i]. Garnet showed discord with merely attempting to reason with the oppressive slaveholders. Also, deterred from political representation, Garnet turned to more drastic methods.

Armed Struggle and Liberation Theology

The most extreme note sounded by the Black Abolitionists of Garnet's caliber was "a call to self-defense by any means necessary" (Shortell, Spring 2004. Social Science History). Garnet believed in armed rebellion as a means of achieving emancipation for the enslaved Southern Blacks. Necessitated by preceding failures through the tactics of reasoning, intellectual presentation of information and asserting the equality of men, Garnet suggested more drastic

150

measures to an audience of abolitionists, White and Black, who tendered mixed reactions to his statements regarding armed resistance to the institution of enslavement. At that 1843 Buffalo Convention, he called support of the church and other abolitionists to support armed revolt in the south[i]. Apparently, Garnet went through an ideological shift, from being a gradualist to being a militant revolutionary.

Garnet was not alone in his religious beliefs beyond the Garrisonian approach. The stance of militancy and armed resistance is espoused by C. Eric Lincoln and Lawrence H. Mamiya who state "The liberation tradition of the Black Church also included radical revolutionary activity that, in certain instances, even supported the use of violence to achieve freedom and justice. American historians of slavery often tend to overlook the fact that the three largest slave revolts in American history were led by slave preachers who used their status as religious leaders to mobilize thousands of African slaves" (203).

Christian principles based on the religion's liberating message, helped to modify Garnet's idea of change and how to go about it bringing an end to the oppression of Blacks. Almost twenty years prior to the Civil war, Garnet used biblical references to validate that the reversal of the oppressed situation would not occur without armed struggle on the part of those who were oppressed[i]. Garnet's use of biblical references in support of armed resistance include an address to slaves cited by James H. Cone: "Your condition does not absolve you from your moral obligation. The diabolical injustice by which your liberties are cloven down, neither God, nor angels, or just men command you to suffer a single moment. Therefore, it is your solemn and imperative duty to use means, both moral, intellectual and physical that promise success" (1975, 154).

In April of 1861 the attack on Fort Sumter initiated the Civil War. At this time Frederick Douglass along with Garnet advocated for the masses of Black free and enslaved to join the war. Though this was deterred by Northern Whites who declared America their own to defend, sentiments changed as casualties mounted[i] and, with the passage of the Emancipation proclamation and other measures, Blacks were eventually allowed to enter the war.

Citizenship and Emigration

The ideology of emigration was highly contentious on both sides of the debate across color lines. For instance wealthy Blacks did not support the "Back to Africa movement," as such because they felt that such a move would diminish their relative affluence and wealth[i]. Boards such as the American Colonization Society (ACS) founded by Thomas Jefferson were distrusted by Blacks who suspected that forced emigration acts would follow. Garnet would also weigh in against emigration to Africa. This initial response to the question of the "Back to Africa movement" as first actualized by Paul Cuffee in 1815, would be supported by a 1848 declaration Garnet made.

I love every inch of soil which my feet pressed in my youth, and I mourn because the accursed shade of slavery rests upon it. I love my country's flag, and I hope that soon it will be cleansed of its stains, and be hailed by all nations as the emblem of freedom and independence (pg. 399).

This would however change. Garnet adopted the emigrationist ideology when he came to the conclusion that White America would not accept Black people as equals under the law with the full protection and benefits thereof. He was right. Berry Blassingame states, "By 1849, even Garnet had abandoned his patriotic stance and asserted that he was 'in favor of colonization...wherever it promises freedom and enfranchisement. In a word, we ought to go anywhere where we can better our condition'" (1982, 400). Such an ideology borders on pragmatism.

To summarize therefore, one could characterize Garnet's ideology as pragmatism. Garnet would pursue any methods which led to his people's liberation. He would not let any system - - be it theological, economic, political or cultural - - hinder progress toward true freedom and full humanity. Apparently Garnet eventually upheld the ethical stance that says the end justifies the means. Granted, this ethic can be controversial.

WEB Du Bois

William Edward Burghardt Du Bois asserts that the focal point for both the Diasporic and continental African should be Africa. With regards to the world war and social ills which plagued Black America until the first Pan African Conference of 1919, Du Bois reports that, "Particularly today most men assume that Africa is far afield from the center of our burning social problems and especially from our problem of world war" (Du Bois Darkwater 43). Now, it should be noted that Du Bois is intellectually engaged in the methodical arrangement of factors that would positively influence the continent of Africa. The Du Boisian stance in terms of the colonial question indicates concerted progress from African liberation and Western development, to African liberation and development based on the African. From a distant vantage point, his commitment appears also to be to the elevation of the Black politic in both America and Africa. In Darkwater, Du Bois espouses the education of the lower classes of the public (termed the "Lower Tenth"), in order for their voting and political activity to be best informed and utilized. In the same chapter "Of the Ruling of Men", education of the masses is essential, as is the autonomy of the African people. The Du Boisian stance in terms of the colonial question seems then to be geared fully towards the liberation of African people. The tools he sees fit to achieve this objective are located in education.

Among these suggestions are well-planned and orchestrated initiatives. Keeping this in mind, we also observe in the essay entitled *"Being Ashamed of One's Self: An Essay on Race Pride"* need for engaging intellectual discourse in

152

African interests by calling for "farsighted planning" (Huggins. et. al., Du Bois Writings, 1986, pg. 1022).

Du Boisian Mode of Instruction

In considering education as a tool to be used for the purposes of goal attainment, Du Bois labors to define his vision of those who should wield such tools. Du Bois calls them the "Talented Tenth" and depicts them in his writings. In Howard Brotz's work African-American Social and Political Thought 1850-1920, Du Bois posited such information in a 1903 statement entitled "The Talented Tenth."

Du Bois's first description is that these vanguards are the exception, by calling them exceptional. "The Negro race, like all races, is going to be saved by its exceptional men" (Brotz, et al. pg. 518). Then he stipulates that education of these people is to be more than the tools of a trade, but liberal arts that would allow the "Tenth" to be the leading and driving force of society. Furthermore, we cite Du Bois' Talented Tenth as those who have a greater vision than their immediate needs. These elites are to resign themselves to be such as to have the sites and motivations set righteously as the protectors of the people as opposed to profiting from their position. Du Bois goes further to depict the desired position of these people in society, as well as implicitly indicating their effect when he states, " ...but unless he has political rights and righteously guarded civic status, he will remain the poverty-stricken and ignorant plaything of rascals, that he now is"(Brotz, et. al. pg. 521).

Moral conviction and selfless leadership are to reside with these rising individuals. This is implicit in espousing the need to instruct pupils of the nuances of character. This is a wholistic approach to the education that Du Bois postulates as necessary. Du Bois forwards this in stating:

> A system of education is not one thing, nor does it have a single definite object, nor is it a mere matter of schools. Education is what that whole system of human training within and without the school house walls, which molds and develops men. If then we start out to train an ignorant and unskilled people with a heritage of bad habits, our system of training must set before itself two great aims- the one dealing with knowledge and character, and the other part seeking to give the child the technical knowledge necessary for him to earn a living under the present circumstances. (Brotz, et. al., pg. 527)

Perhaps most importantly is that point Du Bois makes concerning the instruction of these "Talented Tenth." He states, "We will not quarrel as to just what the university of the Negro should teach or how it should teach it – I willingly admit that each soul and each race-soul needs its own peculiar curriculum" (Brotz, et. al. pg. 523). Part of that curriculum is technically oriented. In this way the liberally trained Talented Tenth are productive members of society.

Du Bois points out the need for these skills in his statement concerning the education of such vanguards, which are to instruct their constituents. He states, "...The first is to give the group and community in which he works, liberally trained teachers and leaders to teach him and his family what life means; the second is to give him sufficient intelligence and technical skill to make him an efficient workman;" (Brotz, et. al. pg. 529). Du Bois further engages the need for technical training as a means for informing the masses of which the "Talented Tenth" are the educators. In this the melding of technical knowledge and liberal training are inclusive in the desired pedagogy of the ignorant, which would rise.

In summation, we may ascertain the following concerning the "Talented Tenth":

1. An exceptional people,
2. A people not tied down by the immediate work of survival while still being productive members of their society,
3. A people who enjoy a protected status within society,
4. A people who have a relevant liberal educational discourse in order to meet the needs of their people,
5. A people who are worthy of teaching character as part of the learning process. Presumably, having moral conviction and character themselves.

The Scope of the Vision

The Du Boisian assumption about the non-white world is that the aspirations thereof are grounded in freedom. This is seen in his assertion that, "Manifestly, you would want freedom for your people, -- freedom from insult, from segregation, from poverty, from physical slavery" (Du Bois, Darkwater, 1919, pg. 46). The attainment of freedom is therefore central in this piece of Du Boisian thought. In other words, the notion that *Freedom* is the desire of *Every* man is fundamental to the various ideologies of Du Bois.

The period of before, including and after 1919 is of significance to the understanding of Du Bois as he is at a crucial impasse. The moment is characterized by the extensive possibilities as the world comes to a peace conference that would reshape the world economic, political, and social scenery. The League of Nations would form here, the First Pan-African congress would meet, the precursors for the human rights initiatives of the 1940s would launch in this moment. The term critical would be insufficient to capture this moment.

In this moment, we are able to hear clear Du Boisian ideology as it is tested and under duress. In thought as per written word via his book Darkwater, Du Bois sets a weighty tone in Pan-African discourse. Darkwater was written in 1919, and therefore further examination of Du Boisian concepts of freedom at this moment in time is prudent. The Du Boisian mode of activity may not have changed forms, as he was an intellectual and scholar until his death in Ghana. Du Bois also consistently demonstrated an activist mode of operation in that he did more then simply produce written works in order to fill libraries, Du Bois engaged political and social issues that would be socially responsive. His position in 1919 conference would be amended, in response to the yearnings of his community, intellectual or otherwise.

Without descending into the arguments of Du Bois and Garvey, we will observe the following per actions of Du Boisian praxis. Du Bois is not immutable. His ideology concerning the liberation of African men and women was fundamental. This is the case while the tactic has transformed, superficially if nothing else. We may extrapolate this notion in considering Brenda Gayle Plummer's work *Rising Wind Black Americans and U.S. Foreign Affairs, 1935-1960*. In which she states:

> Large numbers of black people world wide found Garvey's logic more compelling than that of pan-Africanists, who eventually had to come to terms, even if obliquely and reluctantly, with UNIA success... Even as Du Bois denounced Garvey and refused to invite him to the pan –African congress, the UNIA's nationalist ideas crept into resolutions passed at the congresses of 1921, 1923, and 1927 (Plummer, 1996, pg. 21).

The movement and impact of Du Boisian ideology is captured by Plummer alone. In his essay, *"On Being Ashamed of Oneself: an essay on Race Pride,"* Du Bois himself questioned the direction of his former Pan-African stance, and was willing to posit questions that would not only undermine but shake the foundations that he had laid. This "conversion" to nationalism is demonstrated in *The Crisis* in September of 1933 when he states:

> What are we really aiming at? The building of a new nation or the integration of a new group into an old nation? The latter has long been our ideal. Must it be changed? Should it be changed? If we seek new group loyalty, new pride of race, new racial integrity- how, where, and by what method shall these things be attained? A new plan must be built up. It cannot be the mere rodomontade and fatuous propaganda on which Garveyism was based. It has got to be far-sighted planning. It will involve increased segregation and perhaps migration. It will be pounced upon and aided and encouraged by every "nigger-hater" in the land (Huggins & Du Bois, 1986, pg. 1022).

Without ever flinching at the face of hypocrisy in the re-evaluation of ideas, Du Bois was bold enough to transplant the tactical approach, to the strategic objective. This he did with integrity. One could argue that essentially the strategy changed. I would posit that even with a return to the 1919 mode of thought the goals of liberation of African people, was not aborted rather it was more intensely scrutinized and thus reevaluated. It is my opinion that this further demonstrated Du Bois' use of education as a tool for the people's liberation.

The stages for the presentation of such ideas included the Pan-African congresses, NAACP periodicals, United Nations forums, *The Amsterdam,* to mention a few. Instead of following each stage of Du Bois' life that each contains variations and complexities for consideration, we turn our attention to the foundational principles that inform the modality of activity. Darkwater is a possible source that may allow the student access to such principles. Barring the complexities and various plausible interpretations of this moment of Du Boisian thought, we seek the paradigm of which Du Bois posits as the guide by which governance and morality are informed.

Chapter six, *Of the Ruling of Men* lays the foundational elements of Du Boisian thought. The chapter begins with Du Bois's interpretation of the function of a ruler: "The ruling of men is the effort to direct the individual actions of many persons toward some end. This end theoretically should be the greatest good of all... " (Du Bois, 1919, pg. 105). This statement is also inclusive of the limitation of that theoretical position. Du Bois continues, "... but no human group has ever reached this ideal because of ignorance and selfishness" (Du Bois, 1919, pg. 105).

Barring the opinion of attainability or the absence thereof, we proceed to investigate the criterion of those who are to share in the ruling class, as well as Du Boisian interpretations of those who are to be subjected to the rulers' hegemony. According to Du Bois, the Talented Tenth are intellectually equipped to deal with and defeat such enemies of society as selfishness and ignorance.

Du Bois' Value of the Human Being

Du Bois displayed a value system that was devoid of monetary attainment. This was economic perception that would be problematic in his life as a politician, activist and intellectual. Du Boisian biographer David Levering Lewis depicts his financial arrangements as tentative at best. Though he was prepared to solve the Pan-African economic situation, his own was a series of borrowing and repayment though he did so when it was due.

In Black Reconstruction in America 1860-1880, Du Bois perhaps summarizes the effect of the prospect of economic attainment on society. In this book, Du Bois expresses his view that people are the measure by which the economy is based and vice versa. The human being should never be defined in terms of what property he or she owns. Du Boisian economic interest also locates the evaluation of the economy by White people. He does so in stating, "Birth began to count for less and less and America became to the world a land of opportunity" (Du Bois, 1935, 17). A correlation may be identified that in time of economic opportunity births were devalued.

The unwavering stances of which Du Bois never faltered were grounded in the well being of the politic in which Du Bois identified. Be it the Talented Tenth or the Philadelphia Negro, the scope of humanity to which Du Bois adhered, was unquestionably the location of which Du Bois would be engaged even at the expense of his freedom and economic attainment. In fact, one could not doubt the extent to which Du Bois would go in order to attain for those greater in number to himself, the advancement if not complete liberation of humanity, starting with his people. To summarize, it is instructive to note that Du Bois' concept of human worth is consistent with his anti-slavery ideology. Put differently, while the slave-holders and those who traded in human cargo believed that wealth is more important than human beings (especially the Black man), unless humans are defined as part of the means of production, Du Bois believed that wealth or money should serve human needs.

Malcolm X; El-Hajj Malik El-Shabazz; Omowale

Malcolm X adhered to Black Nationalism which found expression through the Nation of Islam. This Nationalism was based on the Qur'an and Elijah Muhammad's doctrines of Black divinity, a teaching juxtaposed to the tenet that White people are less than human. The Black man is the authentic being. Malcolm emphasized the pride in being Black and asserted that the inability of White people to be Black led them to hate that which was Black and socialized Black people to hate blackness as well. This brand of Black Nationalism also maintained that the conditions to which Black people were subject such as poverty, fatherless homes, prostitution, gambling, pimping and other social crimes, were the effect of White people's negative influence in the Black community. Malcolm investigated the righteousness of the Black man and woman, juxtaposed by the injustice imposed by White men and women. He had several examples in his life experience from which to draw upon. The ideals set before him by the Nation of Islam made sense in the context of Malcolm's own life. He became increasingly aware of and vocal about the injustices suffered by people of African. Malcolm emphasized the racist and destructive manner in which White people interacted with other races, especially Black people.

The message of the demonic nature of White people was contrasted by the message of the divinity of Black people. Racial equity was not asserted by the Nation of Islam at this time. Instead the racial supremacy of Black people as well as the need to separate was advocated[i]. These tenets were familiar to Malcolm as his parents practiced and organized the tenets of self sufficiency and racial pride under the auspices of the Universal Negro Improvement Association (UNIA). Of Malcolm, Michael Eric Dyson states, "Malcolm's ideas of black nationalism were shaped virtually from the womb by the example of his parents, Earl and Louise Little, both members of Marcus Garvey's Universal Negro Improvement Association (UNIA)" (1995, 3-4). The Nation of Islam's ideology of separatism was characterized by the organization's devotion to starting businesses and stores which would cater to the economic needs of Black people. For Malcolm, supporting Black business is not only good business but an expression of racial pride and consciousness. Numerous Mosques, schools, grocery stores and restaurants were also started by the Nation in order to further the goal of a separation of the races within America.

Malcolm's nationalism as experienced in the Nation of Islam was consistently geared towards the advancement of the interests of Black people in the United States even after he had been ousted from the Nation[i].

This mode of self sufficiency was fueled by the perception of Black people ending their tentative and subjected dependence on White people's industries and economic ethics which were said to be exploitative. The repressive conditions Black people endured in this era were also addressed by the Nation of Islam's Fruit of Islam (FOI), a branch charged with the defense of the members of the Nation of Islam. Thus they embodied the tenet of self-defense, of which Malcolm was a staunch supporter. Incidentally, it was on this point that Malcolm X and Dr. Martin Luther King, Jr. did not see eye to eye.

Strict discipline was another tenet the members of the National of Islam were expected to observe. Decorum included no smoking, no adultery, abstention from eating pork and drug abuse. Furthermore, every man was required to provide for the household. The religious based message was divergent from what Malcolm refers to as true Islam, but was based on the same text, the Qur'an. The restrictions of the Qur'an were observed and they dictated even the appropriateness of the spouse a man was allowed to choose.

Changes in the ideology of Malcolm took place after a series of events which include the rumors of the Honorable Elijah Muhammad contravening the ordnances he set forward in his teachings. Rifts between Malcolm and the Nation also included Malcolm being silenced within the Nation of Islam due to the comments he made concerning the assassination of President John F. Kennedy. Everything reached the acme when Malcolm made his pilgrimage to Mecca (Hajj), the holy city of the Muslim faith, which is required of all Muslims who are able to afford it. It was there that he experienced the Islam religion as inclusive. People from a variety of ethnicities, including white people actually embraced him as a brother in the faith. This opened Malcolm's spiritual eyes as well as intellectual awareness of what Islam was really about.

Further, Malcolm recognized that the differences in languages and customs were superficial with regards to the Islamic faith. Regarding the ethnic pluralistic experience, Malcolm states in his autobiography as told to Alex Haley, " I remember one night in Muzdalifa with nothing but the sky overhead, I lay awake amid sleeping Muslim brothers and I learned that pilgrims from every land –every color, and class, and rank; high officials and beggar alike all snored in the same language" (350). True Islam as practiced in the Middle East and in most of the world, was therefore pluralistic and did not exclude or include on the basis of race. This must have been a major doctrinal blow on Malcolm's theology, although it did not adversely affect his African ideology. Malcolm's travels would also lead him to Ghana and other African countries[i].

While in Africa Malcolm was exposed to the Organization of African Unity (OAU), now renamed African Unity. Upon gaining audiences with African heads of state and other groups social and intellectual the ideology Malcolm

158

observed in the United States was furthered to an international prospective[i]. He returned to Harlem with the vision of creating an organization with tenets and objects similar to the OAU. The Organization of African American Unity (OAAU) would be formed in order to advance the premise of unity among Africans and people of differing ethnicities and faith but all focusing on freedom. To this end, Malcolm is quoted as stating:

> I don't think that it serves any purpose for the leaders of our people to waste their time fighting each other needlessly. I think that we can accomplish more when we sit down in private and iron out whatever differences that may exist and try and do something constructive for the benefit of our people.
> *Malcolm X, in Malcolm X: The Last Speeches* (Dyson, 21).

Malcolm's position was that the divergent points of contention that the people who would join the organization aspired to, would be treated as branches of the same organizational tree. This ideology led him to apologize to Black leaders and Whites he had once offended. At the same time he himself forgave them. Malcolm's invitation for a multiethnic and heterogeneous organization would begin with his core constituency of Black African Americans. He believed that Blacks had a pressing need to organize and mobilize first since their situation was most dire and immediate. Self sufficiency and pride in ones self were still core principles. In terms of his overall agenda, the fight against American racism was paramount, and hoped to succeed especially if African nations would support him at the United Nations.

The tenets of Malcolm X's ideology which remained consistent with his early childhood life in the Nation of Islam and life after the Nation of Islam, were as follows: a) he believed in God, Christian or Islamic. This was an enduring feature of which the expression thereof changed; b) he believed in uniting people under the rubric of fighting for freedom. The changes which occurred as a result of this tenet were only affected by the composition of those who would be united; c) the criterion of Muslim and Black for instance, shifted to a spectrum of multiple ethnicities and divergent expressions of faith; d) the underlying thread of unity was freedom from oppression, regardless of how it was expressed; e) he believed in politically advancing and in unity for the cause of freedom. While commenting on the political situation of America concerning the assassination of the president had been problematic within the Nation of Islam, this was a tenet he intended to further in his life since he had become independent of the Nation; f) he believed in the unity and self sufficiency of the African people in Diaspora and on the continent. This is evidenced by his repeated call for the newly independent nations of Africa to sponsor his charges of racial discrimination before the Untied Nations; g) he believed that once people have put aside the differences which are essentially superficial, human beings generally want the same things, and one of those things is freedom. These are some of the major tenets of the ideology Malcolm espoused and built towards, before his life was ended abruptly by several fatal bullets fired at him by some of his own people. This is how most of America's prophets have died, yet their dreams continue to linger on.

NOTES

1. Franklin, John Hope, and Moss, Alfred A. Jr. (2000) <u>From Slavery to Freedom: A History of African Americans</u>. New York: McGraw-Hill Co. p. 200. Franklin and Moss report of the better known personalities of whose agency was critical in the resistance to the institution of African en-slavement in America.
2. See C. Eric Lincoln, Mamiya, Lawrence H. (1990). <u>The Black Church in the African American Experience.</u> Durham: Duke University Press. p. 203.
3. Franklin, John Hope, and Moss, Alfred A. Jr. (2000) <u>From Slavery to Freedom: A History of African Americans</u>. New York: McGraw-Hill Co.
   "More than a score of black abolitionists went to England, Scotland, France, and Germany. Among them were Douglass, Brown, Pennington, Garnet, Charles Lenox, Redmond, Nathanial Paul, Ellen and William Craft, Samuel Ringgold Ward, Sarah Parker Redmond, and Alexander Crummell" (202).
4. Berry, Mary Francis, Blassingame, John W. (1982) <u>Long Memory: The Black Experience in America</u>. New York: Oxford University Press. p. 54. The exploits of ancient Africans and blacks like Frederick Douglass and Henry Highland Garnet showed that the intellect of Negroes was equal to that of whites. In this regard, free Negroes pointed to the injustice, hypocrisy and cowardice of whites in barring them from educational institutions and then citing their ignorance as proof of their inequality.
5. *Ibid*. "Blacks wanted political power because they believed it would end racial discrimination and ultimately result in improved economic and social conditions in the black community…They believed political participation would free white Americans from bondage to the practices if racism and inequality and would liberate blacks from their oppression" (143).
6. *Ibid*. "…Garnet and others repeatedly pressed their petitions for suffrage before the New York legislature. They failed each time" (145)
7. *Ibid*. Tell them in language which they cannot misunderstand of the exceeding sinfulness of slavery, and of a future judgment, and of the righteous retributions of an indignant God. Inform them that all you desire is FREEDOM, and that nothing else will suffice. Do this and forever after cease to toil for the heartless tyrants, who give you no other reward but stripes and abuse. If they then commence the work of death, they, and not you will be responsible for the consequences. You had far better die-*die immediately,* than live slaves, and entail your wretchedness upon your posterity. If you would be free in this generation here is your only hope. However much you and all of us may desire it, there is not much hope of redemption without the shedding of blood. If you must bleed, let it all come at once-rather *die freemen than live to be slaves.* It is impossible, like the children of Israel, to make a grand exodus from the land of bondage. The Pharaohs are on both sides of the blood-red waters. (94)
8. C. Eric Lincoln, Mamiya, Lawrence H. (1990). <u>The Black Church in the African American Experience.</u> Durham: Duke University Press.

"…black churches and clergy have also been continually involved in a broad range of political activities stemmed from the tradition of the heritage of black churches, which were based on their own interpretations of Old Testament stories, prophetic pronouncements, and New Testament apocalypse" (202-3).

9. Berry, Mary Francis, Blassingame, John W. (1982) Long Memory: The Black Experience in America. New York: Oxford University Press.

As the war dragged on into the summer of 1862, heavy casualties and growing white resistance to Army service led to a change in the sentiments of many northern whites. They began to sing one of the war's most popular tunes, "Sambo's Right to be Kilt'" (300)

10. *Ibid.* "Those Blacks who were wealthy enough to support such schemes generally opposed them, because they would diminish their own economic and political power" (398).

11. Franklin, John Hope, Moss, Alfred A. Jr.(2000) From Slavery to Freedom: A History of African Americans. New York: McGraw Hill.

Accepting the general tenets of the religion of Islam, the Black Muslims, under the leadership of Elijah Poole, who renamed himself Elijah Muhammad, renounced their faith in the ultimate solution of the race problem in the United States, rejected all names that might imply a connection with white America, and sought complete separation from the white community (465)

12. Malcolm X. (1964)The Autobiography of Malcolm X as Told to Alex Haley New York. Ballantine Books.

The American black man should be focusing his every effort toward building his own business, and descent homes for himself. As other ethnic groups have done, let the black people, wherever possible, however possible, patronize their own kind, hire their own kind, and start in those ways to build up the black race's ability to do for self. That's the only way the American black man is ever going to get respect. One thing the white man never can give the black man is self respect! (281)

13. Chapman, Abraham (ed) (1968) Black Voices: An Anthology of Afro-American Literature. New York: New American Library: Times Mirror.

"Malcolm visited Mecca, and made two trips to Africa. In 1964 he broke with Elijah Muhammad and , formed his own organization – The Organization of Afro-American Unity to concentrate on political rights for black Americans and also organized his own Islamic religious center the Muslim Mosque Inc."(332-33)

14. Some African Americans began to focus their attention on Africa and began to speak of it as their home…

Bibliography

Berry, Mary Francis, Blassingame, John W. (1982) <u>Long Memory: The Black Experience in America</u>. New York: Oxford University Press

Brotz, Howard (Eds.) (1992). <u>African American Social & Political Thought 1850-1920</u>. New Brunswick: Transaction Publishers

Chapman, Abraham (ed) (1968) <u>Black Voices: An Anthology of Afro-American Literature</u>. New York: New American Library: Times Mirror.

Cone, James H. (1975) <u>God of the Oppressed</u>. New York: Seabury Press.

Du Bois, WEB (1998). <u>Black Reconstruction in America 1860-1880</u> New York: The Free Press (original work 1935).

Du Bois, WEB (2004). <u>Darkwater</u> New York: Washington Square Press (Original work 1919).

Du Bois, WEB (1994). <u>The Souls of Black Folk</u> New York: Dover Publications (Original Work 1903).

Dyson, Michael Eric (1995) <u>Making Malcolm: The Myth and Meaning of Malcolm X</u>. New York: Oxford University Press.

Franklin, John Hope, and Moss, Alfred A. Jr. (2000) <u>From Slavery to Freedom: A History of African Americans</u>. (Vol. 1) New York: McGraw-Hill Co.

Huggins, Nathan (1986). <u>Du Bois Writings</u>. New York: The Library of America Press.

Lewis, David Levering (2000). <u>WEB Du Bois The Fight for Equality and the American Century, 1919-1963</u>. New York: Henry Holt and Company

Lincoln, C. Eric, Mamiya Lawrence H. (1990). <u>The Black Church in the African American Experience.</u> Durham: Duke University Press.

Malcolm X. (1964)<u>The Autobiography of Malcolm X as Told to Alex Haley</u> New York. Ballantine Books.

Plummer, Brenda Gayle (1996). <u>Rising Wind: Black Americans And U.S. Foreign Affairs, 1935-1960</u>. Chapel Hill: The University of North Carolina Press.

Shortell, Timothy. (2004) "The Rhetoric of Black Abolitionism." <u>Social Science History</u> Spring 2004.

Chapter 14

Afro-Brazilians in Search of an Ideology: Conflicting Ideologies in Brazil

Dr. Donald J. Bradt III

Dr. Donald Bradt III is an Assistant Professor of Political Science at Lincoln University, the nation's oldest of the Historically Black Colleges and Universities in the United States of America [Fall, 2005]. Dr. Bradt has expertise in South American political activities including political ideologies of black liberation.

Introduction

The main problems that beset Afro-Brazilians[i] are similar to the problems that plague people of African descent in the United States of America: poverty, crime, and police brutality. On the other hand, although the problems are similar, many Afro-Brazilians suffer to a much greater extent, sometimes to an extent that is unimaginable to people living in such developed regions as Japan, North America, or Western Europe in general. The obstacles, fears, and pain that many, if not most Afro-Brazilians are afflicted with can be seen within the context of Africans forced to live for centuries as slaves under a European power, namely Portugal, in one of its colonies, now Brazil. Of course Afro-Brazilians are part of the greater African Diaspora. In fact Brazil has the largest Black population in the Americas.

It is also important to remember that Afro-Brazilians are politically Latin Americans but racially or ethnically Africans in Diaspora. Latin America is on the periphery of the international industrial, financial, and technological core, made up mainly of Japan, North America, and Western Europe. Latin America has for centuries suffered from enormous poverty, greater inequality between the rich and poor, a very small middle class, and an economy very vulnerable to the ups and downs of the world economy. In addition, Latin America as a developing or peripheral region, has suffered from political instability and military dictatorships. This political instability and rule by dictatorship has made it very hard for *indígena* (native Americans), Africans, and many others to obtain their political and civil rights.

On the other hand, Afro-Brazilian culture and the blending of African, indigenous, and European cultures have produced in Brazil a country that has a luster, seductiveness, spirituality and richness that is nowhere else to be found on earth. This is especially true in those regions of Brazil where the African influence is strong such as Salvador, Bahia and Rio de Janeiro. African religions such as Candomblé, Macumba, and Umbanda have infused Brazilian Roman Catholicism with a myriad of Afro-Brazilian traditions, practices and foods. Afro-Brazilian *funkeiros* have combined Afro-Brazilian music and global popular music, such as Hip-Hop and reggae, to form a new idiom (see Sansone, Livio, 2003, *Blackness without ethnicity: constructing race in Brazil*).

Background: Statistical and Identity Interpretation

Brazil is a very large country in terms of its geographical size and its population. With a total land area of 3,286,500 square miles, it is only slightly smaller than Canada and the United States and is the fifth largest country in the world. Brazil has approximately 184,000,000 people and is the fifth most populous country in the world, only surpassed by China, India, the United States, and Indonesia. Most citizens of the United States consider America as synonymous with the United States and "American" as synonymous with United States citizenry. On the other hand, residents of South America, Central America, and non-United States North America also consider themselves as "Americans."

Brazil is a very ethnically diverse country that includes people from African, European, Asian, Arab, and Amerindian descent. The percentages of people who belong to a particular ethnicity are subject to fluctuation and controversy. The discrepancies in percentage of people counted as European versus African is a reflection of the increasing awareness and pride Brazilians of African descent have attained for themselves since the late 1970s. In addition, Afro-Brazilian identity is not often seen in clear-cut terms. Many Afro-Brazilians identify themselves as <u>mulatto</u> or <u>moreno</u> (brown) rather than <u>negro</u> (black) (Burdick, 1995, p. 175). One study elicited 492 ethnic classifications from Brazilian respondents (Sheriff, R., 2001, p. 54). Indeed, ethnicity is often seen as a continuum in which there is a tendency to deny one's "blackness" and emphasize one's "whiteness" among Afro-Brazilians, which is called "whitening" (Brooke, September 24, 1991; Burdick, 1995; Serbin, 1995).

According to the Central Intelligence Agency's *World Factbook* (2005), six percent of the Brazilian population was "black," while "mixed white and black" accounted for 38 percent of the population, "white" accounted for 55 percent, and Japanese, Arab, Amerindian for one percent. The World Almanac and Book of Facts (2005, p. 757) describes Brazil's ethnic composition as "European 55%, Creole 38%, African 6%." However, because ethnic lines of demarcation in Brazil have traditionally been very unclear, some estimate Afro-Brazilians to be 60 percent of the population (Serbin, 1995, p. 185). Galanternick stated in the May 8, 2003 "World Briefing" section of the *New York Times* that nearly half of Brazil's people define themselves as being "black." The latter two estimates of Brazil's ethnic composition may be a result of Afro-Brazilians decreasing need or desire to hide behind the "whitening" tendency of the past. Indeed, concepts such as Black Power, Black Pride, and Afro-Brazilian Empowerment have

164

propelled the political and social progress of Afro-Brazilians in the last decades of the 20th century and into the first decade of the 21st century.

Slavery in Brazil

The Portuguese "discovery" of Brazil occurred in 1500 when Pedro Alvares Cabral landed on the coast of what is now the Northeast Brazilian state of Bahia. Because the Portuguese explorers found no readily exploitable riches such as vast quantities of gold and silver, they had to quickly come up with a way of exploiting the land. The Portuguese "explorers" had previously perfected the combination of sugar plantations and slave labor, as a means for paying back the Crown's investment in their explorations and conquest and as means for enriching themselves, on the islands of Cape Verde, São Tomé, and Principe. The pattern developed on these islands off the coast of Africa was to be replicated on the northeast coast of Brazil.

Portuguese colonization, which centered on what is now Northeast Brazil, was oriented toward the production of exportable agricultural goods from its inception (Wood and Carvalho 1988, p. 20). The first crop of economic importance to be exported from the Portuguese New World (or what now is Brazil) was sugar, produced on a massive, almost industrial, scale in the 1500s. Slaves, mostly from indigenous tribes, planted and harvested the sugar cane early in the 1500s; however, as production grew later in the century, Africans were recruited from the continent and shipped to the New World where they were enslaved in dehumanizing conditions (de Andrade, 1980, pp. 44-46). By the 1580s, there were more African than indigenous slaves along parts of the northeast coast (p. 46).

In Brazil, a growing agro-export economy, initially built around sugar cane production, continued to be primarily powered by African slaves. In fact, slavery was so crucial to the Brazilian economy that it was not abolished until 1888, one year before the birth of the first Brazilian republic in 1889. Despite the short life expectancy of slaves in captivity in Brazil, the importation of slaves was such that at the beginning of the 1800s the Brazilian population was 57 percent African, 12 percent indigenous, 17 percent mixed blood, and 14 percent European (Crow, 1992, p. 518). Until the 1700s, the cultivation, milling, and exporting of sugar in the Northeast formed the core of the Brazilian economy and this economic core was "dominated by the *senhor do engenho* the planter who owned the grinding mill" (Donghi, 1993, p. 35). Successive importations of slaves in the 1600s, 1700s, and 1800s replenished the stock, forced labor decimated by the harsh working and living conditions in the sugar plantations of Northeast Brazil. During the 1500s and 1600s, the import of African slaves was driven by sugar cane cultivation in Pernambuco, Bahia, and Rio de Janeiro. On the other hand, in the 1700s the impetus for the importation of slaves was gold mining, cotton and rice plantations, spice cultivation, laborers, domestics, and artisans. Coffee, a rapidly growing agro-export industry in Brazil, became the main impetus for the slave trade in the 1800s (Mattoso, 1986, pp.12-13).

From the Plantation to the Quilombos

In any case, the Portuguese New World became an awful agro-industrial machine that extracted, and in many cases destroyed, a vast mass of humanity from Africa. According to Mattoso (1986), "between 1502 and 1860 9,500,000 Africans were brought to the Americas, with Brazil the largest importer of black men" (p. 10). In addition to the many slaves who perished in Brazil, many never made it to the "New World." Conditions were horrific for those prisoners aboard the slave ships. Often nearly half of the human "cargo" died (pp. 33-35).

Nevertheless, Africans enslaved in Colonial Brazil did not passively bow down to their self-imposed European masters. Whenever possible, Africans escaped from the plantations, built communities which were often sophisticated and well functioning, based on the precepts of African civilizations. They indeed valiantly fought against their European oppressors who often succeeded in crushing the islands of African civilization standing in the hinterlands of Northeast Brazil. The cry of freedom and empowerment that emanates from a politically rising Afro-Brazilian community in the early 21st century can be traced to the *quilombo*, especially the greatest *quilombo* of all: the Palmares.

During the long history of slavery in Brazil, innumerable slaves managed to escape the plantations and live in the Afro-Brazilian communities called *quilombos*. It was in the *quilombos* that African culture could flourish. Moreover, in some of the better-established *quilombos* there was a hereditary leader, productive animal husbandry, the growing of crops, and trade with other settlements (Conrad, 1983, pp. 366-368). The Palmares were a group of settlements that were begun in the hinterlands of Northeast Brazil in the early 1600s and that thrived while Portugal was enmeshed in a war with Holland over Brazil. As Holland encroached further on the Portuguese colony in the New World, the Portuguese became increasingly concerned that they would lose Brazil. Hence, suppression of the *quilombos* and the return of "runaway" slaves were not priorities for the Portuguese. It is under these conditions that the *quilombos* of the Palmares came to resemble a sovereign country of considerable size containing walled cities of "more than two thousand houses" (*Revista do Instituto Histórico e Geográfico Brasileiro*, in Conrad, p 370).

Because of the ongoing war with Holland and because of the formidable defense of the Palmares, the Portuguese governor of Pernambuco signed a peace treaty with the king of the Palmares in 1678. The peace between the Palmares and the Portuguese ended after the Portuguese turned the tide against the Dutch in Brazil; the Portuguese began a military campaign in 1690 which ended with the capture and execution of the principle Palmares war leader in 1695. After the defeat of the Palmares, some *quilombos* continued to exist. For instance in the

1800s, *quilombos* have been noted in the Rio de Janeiro area, in Maranhão, and in the Amazonas (pp.381-389, Conrad, 1983).

By middle of the 1800s, the sugar industry in Brazil's Northeast region became less dependent on slave labor; moreover, the growing cultivation of cotton, also centered in the Northeast region, was mainly dependent on wage laborers and sharecroppers (de Andrade, 1980, pp. 78-79). On the other hand, coffee production in southern Brazil was growing rapidly and needed an ever-increasing number of slaves. In the 1600s and 1700s squatters settled vast areas of the Brazilian hinterland (Forman, 1975, p. 26). Hence, by the 1800s there was a sizable free peasantry that included freed mulattos and blacks (pp. 27-28).

Nevertheless, slavery had become so integral a part of Brazilian life that the institution had become pervasive in both the countryside and towns of Brazil. Crow (1992) states that in the 1800s before abolition, "over one half of the country's seven million inhabitants were slaves . . . [S]laves peddled their wares in the streets and supported their master in this fashion" (p. 533). In 1889, one year after the abolition of slavery in 1888, the emperor was deposed. The overthrow of empire and the installation of a republic was in part a consequence of the political power of landowners, especially the coffee growers of São Paulo, who were angered by abolition (Crow, p. 552; Hagopian, 1996, p. 38).

The Myth of Racial Democracy in Brazil

Between the 1930s and the 1970s, many Brazilians saw their country as a "Racial Democracy" in which blurred color lines fostered a high degree of ethnic tolerance. Many Brazilians saw their "Racial Democracy" as a model to be emulated by the rest of the world. Certainly, ethnic relations in Brazil were a model of tolerance in comparison with the fascist regimes that existed in Germany and Italy prior to the end of World War II and in comparison with the pre-Civil Rights era United States and apartheid South Africa. On the other hand, if Brazil's "Racial Democracy" fostered a degree of tolerance, it did not foster equality. "Racial Democracy" also retarded Afro-Brazilian consciousness raising, social activism, and empowerment.

Proponents of the idea that Brazil was a "racial democracy" argued that slavery in Brazil was less harsh than in other countries (see Tannebaum, Frank, 1947, *Slave and Citizen*). More recent literature, however, disputes the idea that Brazilian slavery was any less harsh than slavery in the United States (See Conrad, Robert Edgar, 1983, *Children of God's Fire*, pp. xvi-xvii and Thomas Skidmore, 1974, *Black into White: Race and Nationality in Brazilian Thought*, p. 217). And in fact, Brazilian slaves were forced to wear iron masks as punishment. Furthermore, suicide among Brazilian slaves was at least as common as it was in the United States. Although many slaves gained free status before the abolition of slavery in 1888, slaveholders were quick to free sick and elderly slaves (Degler, 1971, p. 71). Forman (1975) explains that the "agrarian population of colonial Brazil was comprised of three elements: masters, slaves, and an 'inchoate mass of humanity'. . . which lacked in social and economic organization and lived on the furthest margins of Brazilian society" (p. 29).

Early Stages of Race Ideologies

Abolition, however, did not lead to many positive changes in the ex-slave's life. Once freed, the ex-slaves were quickly incorporated into the lowest rung of commercial agriculture in Brazil. The ex-slave was still completely dependent on the plantation, "continued to live in straw huts or slave quarters . . . to work at hoeing from sunup to sunset" (de Andrade, 1980, p. 80). On the other hand, in exchange for a parcel of land, so-called bondage squatters placed "themselves under the protection of the owner; they did not enjoy any government guarantees" (p. 77) but lived completely under the landowners' rule. The remnants of slavery and other coercive forms of labor would continue to affect Afro-Brazilians for at least another century. As Forman (1975) states, slavery's "incumbent traditions of patronage and paternalism have come to characterize the entire system of socioeconomic relations in Brazil" (p. 21).).

Some Elements of White Supremacist Mentality

Those newly freed Afro-Brazilians, who were not incorporated into the agricultural economy of the Northeast, traveled southward and most often found themselves jobless and in extreme poverty. Abolition in 1888 coincided with a large increase in immigration from Europe, making the situation of the ex-slaves more difficult, especially in the South and Southeast of Brazil where coffee growers often sought immigrant labor. European immigration to this part of Brazil was motivated by an elitist racist policy known as "whitening." This policy reflected the Euro-Brazilian elite's racist belief that Brazil's development was hindered by the presence of Afro-Brazilians and that Europe's power and wealth derived from its "whiteness." Between 1889, a year after abolition, and into the 1910s, much of Brazil's government and academic establishment promoted a white supremacist ideology. "Whitening" was offered an answer to Brazil's ethnic "predicament." This idea, which increasingly gained acceptance during the first half of the 20th century, rested upon three assumptions: one, "white superiority"; two, that the "black population" is in decline because of low birth rates, higher levels of disease, and social pathologies; and three, that the population was becoming "lighter" since "whiter genes were stronger and in part because people chose partners lighter than themselves" (Skidmore, 1974, 64-65). By the 1930s, the Euro-Brazilian elite was satisfied that Brazil's "problem was being solved" (p. 173). Indeed, either because of immigration, or social pressure to "pass" as "white," or intermarriage, Brazil's official population statistics show that the country went from being majority "non-white" in 1890 to majority "white" in 1950 (pp. 44-45).

168

Equally important to Brazil's discourse on ethnicity were the writings of the Brazilian sociologist in the 1930s Gilberto Freyre. Freyre emphasized the contributions of African cultures to Brazilian culture in his 1933 book *Casa Grande e Senzala* (see Freyre, Gilberto, 1956, *The Masters and Slaves*, second English language edition, translated by Samuel Putnam). Freyre's works represent an important turning point in Brazil's perception of its ethnic diversity in that many Brazilians began to see the African presence in the country as a strength rather than a weakness. Freyre's works stimulated the idea of Brazil as a "racial democracy."

Indeed, in some ways Brazil of the 1930s, 1940s, and even 1950s was a paragon of benign "race" relations compared to that of the United States. The strict and blatant segregation of "races" so emblematic of Southern United States and parts of the Northern United States during the same period did not exist in Brazil. Upward mobility of people of African descent, especially those considered to be "mulattos," was fairly common. If Brazil can be considered as historically a bastion of "racial" tolerance, it has not been a bastion of "racial" equality. It has been said that Brazilians are not color blind, but they see many more color distinctions than North Americans (Degler, 1971, p. 102). It has also been said that in Brazil "money 'whitens,'" however, "it takes a good deal to whiten a full-blooded Negro, even in Bahia" (p. 105) which is in the Northeast region of Brazil and is majority Afro-Brazilian.

Moreover, ethnic prejudice sometimes rears its ugly head in quite obvious forms in the South and Southeast part of Brazil, even if not enforced by laws as in the Jim Crow Southern United States. And discrimination exists in Northeastern Brazil where demographics would seem to militate against it. Although "color and class so closely coincide" (Degler, 1971, p. 112), there is evidence that in the area of basic accommodations and commerce that color plays at least as much a role in the allocation of services than does class, especially in such Southern regions as São Paulo (p. 106).

According to Fernandes (1969, 134-138), old forms of racism endured after abolition and the Euro-Brazilian elite engaged in selective cooptation, protection, and selective advancement opportunities for blacks and mulattos. Hence, Brazil's "racial democracy" was a myth that was necessary to "the normal functioning of institutions, and to the stability of the social order of the nation" (p. 138).

If the "racial democracy" myth did reinforce the nation's status quo, it did not bolster consciousness raising, pride, and a sense of empowerment among Afro-Brazilians. It did just the opposite: it negated or at least delayed by decades the development of a civil rights movement, black power movement, and black pride movement. Degler (1971, p. 177) stated that, "in all of Brazilian history there have never been Negro rights organizations of any significance" such as the NAACP, CORE, or SNCC" (p. 177). The fact that unlike in the United States, in which historically there were only two ethnicities, Brazil's many distinctions and categories among the Afro-Brazilian population tended to sap strength and unity from it.

Moreover, according to Fernandes (1969) the racial democracy myth "was a source of obstruction and stagnation that undermined or destroyed the trends of innovation and democracy in social relations" (141). To the degree that there was any successful organizing, it was in the South of Brazil where prejudice and discrimination were strongest (Degler, 1971, p. 179). Michael G. Hanchard states: "Many white elites, regardless of their perspective (left, center, or right) believed in the ideology of racial democracy and considered Brazilian society to be plagued with class conflict and inequality, not racial problems" (diaspora.northwestern.edu). Thus, what we have in Brazil is classism that downplays racism, and this overlooks the former – two ideologies in conflict.

Dictatorship, Democracy, and the "Lost Decade" of the 1980s

In the United States during the 1950s and 1960s, the Civil Rights movement was mobilizing on the mass and elite levels. The most obvious and severe forms of ethnic discrimination were disappearing in a rapidly changing United States. In Brazil, on the other hand, economic and political instability set the stage for the 1964 military coup. In the wake of the coup, political participation, freedom of expression, and organizing efforts by activists and reformers were all sharply curtailed. Debate concerning ethnicity and equality would have to be put on hold for at least a decade.

In 1974, the military government initiated a new policy known as *distensão* or decompression; by 1978 the government launched *abertura* or political opening. Both of these policies, especially *abertura*, allowed for greater political participation and freedom of expression among the Brazilian people (for a fuller discussion of the politics during Brazilian military rule, see Maria Helena Moreira Alves, *State and Opposition in Military Brazil*, 1985). It was in 1978, that Movimento Negro Unificado (MNU) the country's first explicitly political African organization was founded. According to Hanchard, the movement Negro Unificado (M.N.U.) translated in English as the United Black Movement, "sought to raise awareness of the plight of Afro-Brazilians in Brazil" because the historical legacy of slavery and the ongoing practices of racial discrimination in education, health care, housing and administration of civil rights created gross disproportionate representation among the poorest and most oppressed of Brazil. Among the founders on M.N.U. are activists like Flavio Carranca, Hamilton Cardoso, Milton Barbosa, Rafael Pinto, to mention a few.

In 1985, Brazil's first civilian president in more than two decades took office. During the 1980s, throughout Latin America, military regimes were leaving power and the hopeful era of redemocratization was beckoning. On the other hand, the 1980s were years of deepening despair in the economic sphere. In August 1982, Mexico announced it could not service its large debt load. This set off what was known as the "debt crisis" in which developing countries around the world could not pay the interest on their international debt. Latin America, including Brazil, was particularly hard hit. Although people were free

170

to vote and participate in other forms of political expression, their governments were severely constrained in their ability to meet people's demands. Latin American governments, including Brazil, had to appeal to the International Monetary Fund (IMF) for loans so that they could pay the interest on the huge debts that they owed international financial institutions. The IMF usually lent money so that the countries could get by, but only with strict conditions or "conditionality." This conditionality often meant that governments could not provide social programs and services to their people. The debt crisis connotes the lost decade not only because governments were very constrained for what they could do for their people but also because the debt crisis led to the worst economic crisis in Latin America since the Great Depression of the 1930s. People could vote; however, the immediate and pressing problem of most people during the 1980s had to have been feeding themselves and their families.

In Brazil, the economic recovery in the 1990s from the "lost decade" of the 1980s was slow and halting. Hence, it was a daunting environment for the Afro-Brazilian groups that blossomed in the 1990s and that sought to raise the consciousness and level of political participation of Afro-Brazilians during the decade. Moreover, the problems that Afro-Brazilians and other poor Brazilians confronted were truly difficult. Poverty and a huge gap between, on one hand, the small middle class and very wealthy, and on the other, the vast numbers of very poor makes Brazil very difficult to govern, to live in, to be African in. With regard to the two Brazils, Goldstein (2003) states, "Brazil has an incredibly vibrant consumer culture that caters to the middle and upper classes, that the majority cannot possibly adhere to" (p. 88).

Afro-Brazil within the Context of a Divided Brazil

Unfortunately, because the two Brazils live in two different worlds culturally, economically, socially, and politically, violent conflict is one of the primary means by which the two worlds communicate. Linz and Stepan (1996) state that in the midst of recurring economic and political crises after the democratic transition in 1985, "Constitutionalism and rule of law--never strong in Brazil's highly unequal society--weakened further . . . . [T]he police and the legal system are virtually not present concerning the detection and prosecution of rural violence against the poor" (pp. 167, 175). Linz and Stepan also note that in 1990, in New York City 7.8 citizens were killed in exchanges of fire with police, in the line of duty, for every police officer killed, while in greater São Paulo the ratio was about 40 to one (p. 176). Afro-Brazilians are over represented in prison even when controlling for social class (Sansone, 2003, p. 28). According to Sheriff (2001, p. 13), in Brazil 3.5 million Africans are in jail which is more than any other country.

Because of class and ethnic tensions, it appeared as if Brazil had slipped into a low-intensity war, especially in some urban areas of the country. According to Scheper-Hughes and Hoffman (1995), "[I]n Brazil, a poor, ragged kid running along an unpaved road in a <u>favela</u> (shantytown) or playing in a field of sugar cane is just a kid" (p. 139). However, many children are drawn to the city center to participate in the informal economy, beg, or steal in order to help support their families or themselves (pp. 141-142). Within the context of rising poverty, crime, and lawlessness that has plagued Brazilian cities, the street kids are seen as an embarrassment, at best, and a threat, at worst. According to Scheper-Hughes and Hoffman,

> The Federal Police reported that close to 5,000 children were murdered in Brazil between 1988 and 1990. Few of these deaths were considered worthy of investigation, which is hardly surprising given that police officers are themselves perpetrators of many of these crimes . . . Brazilian journalist Gilberto Dimenstein . . . emphasized the complicity of off-duty policemen, hired killers, and store owners. Typically it is store owners who pay to have 'undesirable' adolescents and children eliminated. A similar conclusion was reached by the Sao Paulo chapter of the Brazilian Bar Association. (pp. 146-147)

Jeffrey (1995) cites a Brazilian congressional study that counted 180 different death squads in Rio de Janeiro, 15 of which exclusively target children. In addition, he states, "according to a recent investigation by the Brazilian congress, from 1990 to 1993, 4,611 children--3,781 of them black--were murdered in Brazil" (p. 155). Moreover, Scheper-Hughes and Hoffman note that street children are murdered in small cities such as Bom Jesus which has a population of 50,000 (pp. 146-147).

However, it has been in the city of Rio de Janeiro that the murder of street children and an explosion of crime in general have been most notable. There were "500 killings in the month of April 1989" (Braun, 1991, p. 91). In 1991, Brooke (August 12, 1991) noted the increase in kidnappings in the city by quoting Rio de Janeiro police's director of the anti-kidnapping unit as stating "Kidnapping has become banal" (p. A7). Roberto Campos, a Rio de Janeiro congressman, dubbed the city "The New Bosnia" in "reference to the estimated 70,000 people murdered here in the last decade" (Brooke, October 25, 1994, p. A4). Braun states "Brazilian sociologists are reporting that the violence is increasingly based on social class differences, and that many of the poor are now seeing the killings as an act of social justice" (p. 91). By 1994, Brooke (November 6, 1994) reported that

> The President turned to the army after mounting crime made it clear that the government of Rio de Janeiro had lost control of most of the city's 400 shantytowns. In recent weeks, patrols by the state police have been met by drug gangs firing automatic rifles and by slum residents burning buses and building street barricades . . . 'Rio de Janeiro is living a climate of urban guerrilla warfare' the city's Roman Catholic Archbishop . . . complained after last week after drug traffickers forced several churches to suspend evening programs. (p. 4)

172

It was also in Rio de Janeiro that the internationally notorious slaying of eight street children occurred in July 1993 on the steps of the Candelaria Church. Usually such acts occur with impunity, but because of the international attention the incident received, four men, three of them police, were charged. Eventually one was convicted (Schemo, May 1, 1996) and three others were acquitted (Reuters, December 11, 1996). In the mid-1990s within the context of more Afro-Brazilians being elected to office, Afro-Brazilian organizations became more assertive and visible. Afro-Brazilian leaders were pointing out that "blacks were the primary victims of Brazil's poverty and human rights abuses, which included street children, trafficking in women, and the violence from the growing drug trade" (Telles, 2004, p. 51). In May 1996, President Cardoso made a series of proposals to curb human rights abuses, key of which was to subject military police officers to civilian courts. However, the president did not have enough support in Congress to get this important provision passed. Schemo (December 12, 1997) reported on the continuing violence in Rio de Janeiro:

> Four beggars sleeping under the awning of a furniture store were shot dead shortly after dawn here on Tuesday . . . [A] civic group here found that killing by the police rose to an average of 32 a month in 1996 from 16 a month the previous three years. The latest killings occurred amid a wave violence. On Tuesday a grenade blew up on a city bus when a man tried to rob a passenger, killing them both. A police sweep of one slum yielded a cache of 30 weapons, including artillery and a land mine. (p. A6)

More recently, at least 30 people, including a seven year old and some teenagers were killed. According to Rohter (April 2, 2005), "the secretary of public security for the state of Rio de Janeiro, Marcelo Itagiba, strongly hinted that the gunmen were military police officers angered by a recent campaign to crack down on police violence and corruption" (p. 3A).

In 1989, the top 10 percent of Brazil's economically active population (EAP) received 52.23 percent of the nation's income while the bottom 50 percent of the EAP received a meager 10.94 percent of the national income (Cacciamali, 1997, p. 221; Camargo & Barros, 1993, p. 63). Extremes of income and wealth have created a country in which one sector of society lives in a modern, well-developed, wealthy nation and the other sector of society lives in a squalid, underdeveloped, desperately poor nation. In fact,

> a leading Brazilian economist, Edmar Bacha, has called Brazil 'Belinda,' an amalgam of Belgium and India. A small consumer society, with people living well as one does these days in Belgium, exists amid India, a mass of 'pariahs' as a minister of our military government call them 15 years ago. (Torrens, 1995, p. 190)

The bottom half of the population ekes out a precarious living often at the margins of society. According to Carmago and Barros (1995), "half the economically active population earned less than US $70 a month in 1989" (p.60). For the bottom decile (10 percent) of the economically active population that only earned 0.65 percent of the national income in 1989 (Cacciamali, 1997, p. 221), unspeakable misery and want can only characterize their condition. Pope John Paul II spoke in October 1991 about "the contrasts between the two Brazils: one is highly developed, strong, and launched on the path of progress and riches; the other is seen in untold zones of poverty, suffering, illiteracy and marginalization" (Cowell, October 15, 1991, p. A15). Shellenberger and Danaher (1995) state "there are an estimated 7 million to 10 million Brazilian children who have been abandoned to fend for themselves on the streets" (p. 2).

Nash (February 16, 1993) stated that "an estimated 65 million people of Brazil's 150 million live below the poverty line, defined as half or less of the family income needed for a minimal level of food and shelter" (p. A9). Barros, Mendoca, and Rocha (1995) calculated the poverty rate in Brazil's urban areas in 1990 to be about 29 percent (p. 254). Most poor households are "headed by men aged between 25 and 40 who regularly work 40 hours a week or more" (Camargo & Barros, 1993, p. 64). Because of the lack of social services and a social infrastructure, "being poor in Brazil is a particularly perverse condition" (p. 61). Jeffrey (1995) avers that "almost a third of Brazil's children suffer from stunted growth and social scientists have identified a whole new race of dwarfs growing up in the teeming favelas [shantytowns]" (p. 157). The hunger and malnutrition that affects 32 million of Brazil's people (Couto Soares, 1995, p. 13) along with poor sanitation kill approximately 300,000 children a year in Brazil (Shellenberger & Danaher, 1995, p. 2). Although more education is needed for "good" jobs, the quality of education in public schools is very poor and in some cases worsening because of budget cuts" (Sansone, 2003, p.33).

As the Brazilian economy grew rapidly between 1950 and 1980, mainly propelled by capital-intensive industrialization, many Brazilians came from the countryside into the cities looking for work. However, "only some of the swelling urban labor force provoked by this industrialization found work in the 'modern' urban sectors . . . . [M]ost of those without modern sector jobs were informally employed (i.e., without a legal contract) and self-employed" (Urani, 1998, p. 206). According to a survey of the metropolitan area of Salvador, Bahia, Sansone (2003) reports "the workplace is described as a place in which racism is extremely strong by almost 70 percent of my informants" (p. 52). Most of those who are classified as self-employed or informally employed survive at the margins in the streets of Brazil selling inexpensive goods and services. Braun (1991) states "the informal sector is made up of people doing anything to survive . . . . [I]n Rio they are street vendors selling T-shirts, drugs, sex, a gamut of personal services" (p. 84). In 1990, of the labor force of persons aged 15 years and older, 41.57 percent were in the formal sector, 27.81 percent were in the informal sector, 25.32 percent were self-employed, and 5.30 percent were unemployed (Urani, p. 224). According to Sansone (2003, p. 28), Brazil's huge "informal" sector is made up of mainly Afro-Brazilians.

Thus, many who come to such urban industrial areas as São Paulo and Rio de Janeiro from rural areas or poorer regions such as the Northeast find only an

174

urbanized version of the poverty that they left. For instance, in São Paulo, Nash (February 16, 1993) quotes Suely De Cunto of the São Paulo Center for Screening and Guidance as stating that many "people have given up hope of finding work . . . . [T]he vast majority, entire families, are now living on the street" (p. A9). For those children separated from their families because of violence, poverty, or neglect, a nightmare of drugs, violence, and prostitution awaits them in the "informal economy" of Brazil's streets. According to anthropologist Nancy Scheper-Hughes, "food and affection exchanged for sex is common among Brazilian street kids, the majority of whom are initiated into sex by nine or ten years of age in the big cities" (Scheper-Hughes & Hoffman, 1995, p. 143). It is in Rio de Janeiro where the two Brazils are most closely and vividly juxtaposed in both coexistence and conflict. Braun (1991) writes of Rio de Janeiro as a city in which "luxury hotels line Avenue Atlantica" while within blocks "homeless families live on mattresses or beneath highway viaducts . . . two blocks of Paris along the beach with Ethiopia surrounding it" (p. 90).

According to Sheriff (2001) no one in Brazil disputes that it "has one of the most unequal distributions of wealth in the world—the debate on racial democracy has thus centered . . . on what role racial identity plays if any in the structuring of this inequality" (pp. 5-6). Sheriff reports that Afro-Brazilians are behind their Euro-Brazilian counterparts in such measures as "infant mortality, health, education, employment, occupation, income, and life expectancy" (p. 6). Perhaps most telling is that Sheriff reports that even when Afro-Brazilians have socioeconomic advantages such as college education they still lag behind Euro-Brazilians. An Afro-Brazilian with a college education generally has less income than a Euro-Brazilian with a junior high education (p. 6).

Regional and Ethnic Inequality

When the nation's economic system is structured along racial or ethnic lines, racism is at work. One's class depends, first and foremost, on one's racial identity. In Brazil disparities of income and wealth tend to mirror ethnic differences. Those Brazilians with darker skin tend to have less income and wealth. Darker skinned Brazilians tend also to have less access to quality health care. These disparities are most glaring in the Northeast region, where many if not most of the people are from African origin. According to Wood and Carvalho's (1988) extensive study of inequality in Brazil, people in the Central Northeast region of Brazil had a life expectancy of 49.0 years while those in the South region of the country had a life expectancy of 67.8 years during the period, 1970-1980 (p. 92). Therefore, during that period,

> The life expectancy rate among the poor in the Central Northeast . . . is equivalent to that recorded in Africa in 1965/70. It roughly corresponds to expectation at birth in Western Europe in the 1860s . . . . The average length of life among the most affluent household in the South approximates the relatively

low mortality achieved in Western European countries between 1940 and 1950. (p. 94-95)

Willumsen (1997) found that by 1990 this picture had little changed; the Northeast region of the country had a life expectancy of 51.57 years while the South region had a life expectancy of 66.96 years. Moreover, the infant mortality rate in the Northeast was double that in the South, while the Northeast had a poverty rate of 51.2 percent compared to the South's poverty rate of 20.6 percent (p. 243). The poverty of the Northeast represents an historical echo from the repressive Portuguese sugar plantation economy that had its beginnings in the 1500s and its decline in the 1800s as monocrop export agriculture came to be centered around the growing of coffee in the South region of the country near Sao Paolo. With regard to average regional income per capita, the Southeast region had the highest level of per capita income with 140 percent of the national average while the Northeast region's per capita income was only 46 percent of the national average in 1990. Interestingly, the corresponding percentages of national per capita income for the Southeast and Northeast were 149 and 45 percent, respectively, in 1960 (p. 251). Although income inequality markedly worsened between 1960 and 1990 for all regions, in 1990 the Northeast had the highest income inequality while the South had the lowest (pp. 253-254).

The Northeast region also has a higher percentage of dark skinned individuals than the South and Southeast. For instance, Salvador in the state of Bahia, the "capital of Black Brazil," has a population that is 80 percent Afro-Brazilian (Brooke, September 24, 1991). In any case, "Brazilian blacks remain scarce in the upper levels of government, business and management" (Schemo, October 18, 1996, p. A13) and stories of ethnic discrimination are numerous even in the "black capital" Salvador (Brooke, September 24, 1991). Wood and Carvalho (1988, p. A4), working with 1980 data, found that with regard to infant mortality rates, "race remains a statistically significant variable even after the model controls for household income, mother's education, region of the country, and access to piped water" (pp. 150-151). In the Southern state of Santa Catarina, mainly populated by the descendants of German and Italian immigrants, officials have gone to great lengths to discourage the immigration of the dark skinned and poor from other regions of Brazil in a vain attempt to preserve a kind of regional apartheid (Brooke, May 4, 1994).

Afro-Brazil in the 21st Century: Reasons for Cautious Optimism

During the 1990s, a number of organizations were created to promote the political, cultural, and social well-being and empowerment of Afro-Brazilians. Many of these organizations were so-called nongovernmental organizations (NGOs) that were funded, at least in part, from Europe and the United States. In addition, the 1990s became known as the era of globalization especially as the

176

decade grew to a close. Globalized images from the Internet and satellite television often showed Africans especially from the United States and Jamaica in the vanguard of popular culture and fashion. This changed the image of Africans in Brazil and how young Afro-Brazilians viewed themselves. The internationalization and globalization of ethnic politics and culture in Brazil was furthered by the strategies used by Afro-Brazilian NGOs. Although they were active in domestic politics in such projects as trying to get the Brazilian government to enforce that part of the Brazilian 1988 Constitution that made racism illegal, much of their effort was focused on the activities of international conferences and international organizations such as the United Nations, the World Bank, and the Inter-American Development Bank.

By the mid-1990s according to Burdick (1995), "Brazil's black consciousness movement, a loosely linked collection of nearly 500 organizations, is now active in almost every state in the country" (p. 174). In addition to the MNU, some of the more notable organizations include Ilê Aiyê, an Afro-Brazilian Carnaval school founded in 1974 in Salvador, Bahia as a reaction to the exclusion of Afro-Brazilians in Carnaval, Black Soul in Rio de Janeiro and São Paulo as an expression of Afro-Brazilian culture, and the Palmares Cultural Foundation founded in 1988 (Telles, 2004). These and a myriad of other organization tried to teach a younger generation about its history and refashion what was then a distorted image of Afro-Brazilians (Burdick, 1995, p. 174).

On the legal and political front within Brazil, Afro-Brazilians organizations faced an uphill battle. For instance between 1988 and 1998, there were only three convictions based on the anti-racist clauses of the 1988 Constitution. There was some reason to be optimistic, however. A 1992 ruling that a man was fired for racist reasons garnered significant media attention, and accusations that TV Globo, the giant Brazilian media conglomerate, was racist led to a TV Globo show about an Afro-Brazilian middle class family (Telles, 2004, p. 52). Also during the decade, it was becoming evident that many Brazilians were realizing that the racial democracy myth was just that, a myth. Moreover, in academia ethnicity went from being a marginal concern to one of the "fastest-growing topics of scholarly interest" (p. 53). And although by the end of the decade the federal government of Brazil did nothing concrete in the area of affirmative action, state and local governments and as well as some private sector companies developed affirmative action policies (p. 58).

By reaching beyond Brazil's borders, the Afro-Brazilian movement was able to gain greater influence on the government back home. Unlike in previous reports to the United Nation's Committee for the Elimination of Racism (CERD), in 2001 "the Brazilian government admitted to contemporary racism" (Telles, 2004, p. 62). The greatest change in the level of attention paid to the issue of racism by Brazilian society and the Brazilian government came in the events leading up to, during, and immediately after the United Nation's Conference on Racism in Durban, South Africa in September 2001. Although the Brazilian government refused to hold a regional conference in the lead up to

Durban, it did decide in late August 2001 that its presence at the main conference would be quite substantial (pp. 65-69). Moreover, the Brazilian Foreign Ministry decided that it "would no longer ignore or deny racial issues as it had in the past but rather it would commit major efforts and resources to Durban" (p. 70). Immediately preceding and during the Durban conference, there was an unprecedented amount of media coverage on Durban and on race in general. (p. 71).

As parameters of the political debate concerning Afro-Brazilians and their role in the country's political, economic, and social sphere was becoming more a function of international politics, the role and value of Afro-Brazilian culture was undergoing a radical transformation because of globalization. The Internet, other new forms of communication and technologies, and the new mindset that was emblematic of these technologies produced a new cultural atmosphere in this peripheral country that was so dependent on the core, especially the United States. Certainly, the African Diaspora, in the United States and in other regions of the world, had a very notable place in the firmament of the global media. As this firmament shone above this large, but developing, often politically unstable country, it could not have failed to have an effect—no matter what one thinks of the impact of globalization on authentic cultures around the world. As Sansone (2003) states, "Global commodification purges certain variation and cultural difference, but it also has an upside. Globalization can increase the status of certain cultural expressions that, up to that moment had enjoyed poor recognition at home" (p. 92). Thus in Brazil, aspects of African cultures "once something to be exorcised, have acquired status in both popular and highbrow culture" (p. 89). Moreover, symbols and ideas from the United States such as "black nationalism to black beauty products, the models used in black hair advertisements, and the slogan 'black is beautiful'" have changed Brazil in very palpable ways. This became clear when the magazine *Black Race* quickly sold out its first run of 200,000 copies at the newsstands exploding the myth in the Brazilian publishing industry that such a magazine would not sell (Schemo, October 18, 1996, p. A13).

In the realm of governmental policies, Durban led to a sudden sea change. For instance, the Ministry of Agrarian Development announced that 20 percent of all administrative positions would go to Afro-Brazilians with this percentage rising to 30 percent by 2003. The State of Rio de Janeiro announced that 40 percent of admissions to state universities be reserved for Afro-Brazilians after having announced earlier in the year that at least 50 percent of admissions be reserved for graduates of public schools. The Ministry of Justice and the Federal Supreme Court announced that 20 percent of its staff and consultants be Afro-Brazilians as well the staff of its subcontractors. In the aftermath of Durban, even the elitist Foreign Ministry moved to provide 20 scholarships for Afro-Brazilians studying to become diplomats (Telles, 2004, pp. 72-73). Nevertheless, a Euro-Brazilian backlash led the Rio de Janeiro state legislature to back down and reduce the quota for Afro-Brazilians to 20 percent of admissions.

Conclusion

The Afro-Brazilian people have made monumental gains since 1888, most especially within the last ten years. Nevertheless, the achievement of equality remains a distant goal. This goal will not be achieved until major structural changes in the Brazilian political economy have been accomplished. According to almost all calculations of the GINI coefficient, usually used to measure income inequality, Brazil has the worst income inequality on earth. Similarly in the area of inequality of wealth, Brazil leans toward the extreme. It may be true that one of the effects of globalization is to raise the awareness and esteem of Afro-Brazilians. And if true, this should be celebrated. Nevertheless, it is probably naïve to think that this alone will significantly improve the condition of most Afro-Brazilians. Unfortunately, in a country with already great inequality and great poverty, salaries are down and industrial and public sector jobs are disappearing (Sansone, 2003, p. 26).

Discrimination puts an extra burden on Afro-Brazilians, no matter their social class. On the other hand, the class divide, the existence of two very different Brazils, exacerbates discrimination. The result of economic inequality, which affects all Brazilians regardless of ethnicity, and the result of discrimination towards Afro-Brazilians is an odious and foul concoction that mars the Brazilian landscape. The vast inequalities and discrimination that produce street children, the growth industry of kidnapping middle and upper class people, and the warfare over land in the countryside are variables that could very well worsen ethnic discrimination in the coming years. Vast inequalities of wealth and income and massive poverty can only worsen the condition of belonging to an ethnicity that is subject to prejudice. Class and ethnicity are tightly bound together in Brazil; thus, inequality and discrimination must both be addressed.

In order to begin to address the structural imbalances in Brazil's political economy, a far-reaching land reform should be considered. Land reform would provide farms for the poor and middle class, thus, relieving some of the tremendous demographic and social pressures that Brazil's cities confront. In the United States in the 1860s, the Homestead Act was passed. The Homestead Act served to ensure an equitable distribution of land in the country and, thus, maintain the United States' vaunted middle class which was a main source of political stability as the country industrialized. A land reform in Brazil could open up opportunities for Afro-Brazilians and provide a safety valve for cities with overtaxed services and inadequate physical and human infrastructures.

Although affirmative action is vulnerable to political pressures and to backtracking, affirmative action can provide social and economic mobility to Afro-Brazilians in a society in which class fissures are immense and mobility is improbable. Because the vast disparities between economic and social classes affect Afro-Brazilians most acutely and because these disparities contribute to a society, which often devours the weak of any ethnicity, affirmative action programs that target class are also appropriate. For instance, those state universities that have admissions quotas for graduates of public schools stanch two pathologies: the vast class divide and ethnic prejudice that is endemic to Brazil.

One sign of hope in recent years has been the increase in the number of elected and appointed officials who are Afro-Brazilian. Many of them have been elected from the ranks of the Partido dos Trabalhadores (PT) or Workers Party. As Telles (2004) states, "Most of the black movement leadership seems to be from the Workers Party, as is the leadership of most social movement organizations" (p. 74). The Workers Party sent two Afro-Brazilians to Brazil's constituent assembly, including Benedita da Silva, the first Afro-Brazilian woman ever elected to national office. In the early 1990s, three Afro-Brazilians were elected as governor in the states of Espirito Santo, Rio Grande do Sul, and Sergipe. And in 1994, an Afro-Brazilian was elected to head Brazil's largest trade union. Currently, many Afro-Brazilian members of Brazil's congress are from the Workers Party. Within one year after his election as president in 2002, Luís Inácio Lula da Silva of the Workers Party or "Lula," picked Afro-Brazilians to be Minister of Culture, Minister for Social Assistance and Promotion, Minister of Environment, and a justice on the Supreme Court.

The election of Lula, after three unsuccessful tries, as president put fear into the hearts of many Brazilian elites. His Workers Party promised to radically transform economic and political structures so that the Brazil's workers and masses would benefit more from a Brazilian economy marked so long by vast inequalities. As things turned out, his presidency did not lead to immediate radical changes. In fact, financial markets were pleased by the new administration's emphasis on cutting budget deficits. Any Brazilian government will be faced with international and domestic constraints. Brazil has a relatively small economy that is situated on the periphery of the international political-economic system in which Japan, the United States, and Western Europe dominate. Brazil is dependent on access to global financial markets in order to obtain capital to make its economy grow. Workers Party politician Benedita da Silva, who is the first female Afro-Brazilian to be elected to national office in the form of the Constituent Assembly, the first female Afro-Brazilian elected to the national senate, the first female Afro-Brazilian to be a governor of a state, and who served in Lula's cabinet as Minister for Social Assistance and Promotion decried the fact that "There are 32 million hungry people in our country. We have entire families of unemployed living below freeways" (Shellenberger, 1995, p. 246). On the other hand, recognizing Brazil's place in the international world economy, she states, "We want international investment, we want to open up to the world market" (p. 246).

There are domestic initiatives that the Workers Party can undertake. It could initiate large-scale land reforms. It can deepen affirmative action programs and protect those already in place. Nevertheless, Lula's Workers Party is burdened by domestic political constraints that cloud the prospects for reform. The party is a minority party in the Brazilian congress and has to work with smaller parties to get things done; however, as this is being written many of those parties allied to the Workers Party are embroiled in scandals. The problems of Afro-Brazilians and other poor Brazilians can only be solved when the rest of the world takes an interest in Brazil and its people. Hence, it is fitting to close with this exhortation by Benedita da Silva, "We would specifically like to create more exchange between black businesspeople in the U. S. and here in Rio" (Shellenberger, 1995, p. 248).

Questions for Class Discussion

1. What ideologies could one glean in Afro-Brazilian struggle for survival?
2. Discuss the merits and demerits of coups.
3. Discuss the concept of "moral reparations." Is it possible? What are its possible merits?
4. If globalization is an ideology, whose ideology is it? Is there such a thing as a global ideology?

REFERENCES

Alves, M. H. M. (1985). State and opposition in military Brazil. Austin, TX: University of Texas Press.
Barros, R., Mendonca, R., & Rocha, S. (1995). Brazil: Welfare, inequality, poverty, social indicators, and social programs in the 1980s. In N. Lustig (Ed.), Coping with austerity: Poverty and inequality in Latin America (pp. 237-274). Washington, DC: Brookings Institution.
Braun, D. (1991). The Rich get richer: The rise of income inequality in the United States and the world. Chicago: Nelson-Hall Publishers.
Brooke, J. (1991, September 24). Bahia journal: If it's 'Black Brazil,' why is the elite so white? The New York Times, p. A4.
Brooke, J. (1994, November 6). Brazil's army joins battle in lawless Rio: Gangs rule the slums, instigating the move. The New York Times, p. 4.
Burdick, J. (1995). Brazil's black consciousness movement raises black awareness. In M. Shellenberger & K. Danaher (Eds.), Fighting for the soul of Brazil (pp. 174-183). New York: Monthly Review Press.
Cacciamali, M. C. (1997). The growing inequality in income distribution in Brazil. In M. J. F. Williams & E. G. da Fonseca (Eds.), The Brazilian economy: Structure and performance in recent decades (pp. 215-234). Miami: North-South Center Press.
Camargo, J. M., & Barros, R. (1993). In M. D. G. Kinzo (Ed.), Brazil: The challenges of the 1990s (pp. 60-77). London: The Institute of Latin American Studies, University of London and British Academic Press.

Central Intelligence Agency. Updated on 2005 June 2. *The World Factbook*. Retrieved from http://www.cia.gov/cia/publications/factbook/geos/br.html#People.

Court in Brazil acquits 3 of killing street children. (1996, December 11). Reuters.

Couto Soares, M. C. (1995). Who benefits and who bears the damage under World Bank/IMF-led policies. In M. Shellenberger & K. Danaher (Eds.), Fighting for the soul of Brazil (pp. 8-16). New York: Monthly Review Press.

Cowell, A. (1991, October 15). Pope challenges Brazil leaders on behalf of poor. The New York Times, p. A15.

Conrad, R. E. 1983. Children of God's Fire: A Documentary History of Black Slavery in Brazil. Princeton: Princeton University Press.

de Andrade, M. C. (1980). The land and people of northeast Brazil (D. V. Johnson, trans.) Albuquerque, NM: University of New Mexico Press.

Degler, C. N. (1971). Neither Black nor White: Slavery and Race Relations in Brazil and the United States. New York: The Macmillan Company.

Fernandes, F. (1969). The Negro in Brazilian Society. Edited by P. B. Eveleth. (J. D. Skiles, A. Brunel, & A. Rothwell, Trans.) New York: Columbia University Press.

Forman, S. (1975). The Brazilian peasantry. New York: Colombia University Press.

Freyre, G. (1938). Casa Grande e Senzala. Edited by Schmidt. Rio de Janeiro.

- - - . (1956). The Masters and the Slaves: A Study in the Development of Brazilian Civilization (2nd ed.). (S. Putnam, Trans.) New York: Alfred A. Knopf.

Galnternick, M. (2005, May 8). World Briefing-Americas: First Black Supreme Court Judge. The New York Times, p. A6.

Goldstein, D. M. (2003). Laughter Out of Place: Race, Class, Violence, and Sexuality in a Rio Shantytown. Berkeley: University of California Press.

Hagopian, F. (1996). Traditional politics and regime change in Brazil. Cambridge: Cambridge University Press.

Jeffrey, P. (1995). Targeted for death. In M. Shellenberger & K. Danaher (Eds.), Fighting for the soul of Brazil (pp. 154-162). New York: Monthly Review Press.

Linz, J. J., & Stepan A. (1996). Problems of democratic transition and consolidation: Southern Europe, South America, and post-communist Europe. Baltimore and London: John Hopkins University Press

Mattoso, K. M. D. Q. (1986). To Be a Slave in Brazil: 1550-1888. (A. Goldhammer, Trans.) New Brunswick, NJ: Rutgers University Press.

Nash, N. C. (1993, February 16). Brazil seeks to revive its economic miracle, lying in ruins. The New York Times, p. A9.

Revista do Instituto Hiistórico e Geográfico Brasileiro. (1876). In Conrad, R. E. 1983. Children of God's Fire: A Documentary History of Black Slavery in Brazil, (pp. 369-377). Princeton: Princeton University Press.

Rohter, L. (2005, April 2). String of street shootings kill 30, including youths, in Rio suburb. The New York Times, p. 3A.

Sansone, L. (2003). Blackness without Ethnicity: Constructing Race in Brazil. New York: Palgrave MacMillan.

Schemo, D. J. (1996, May 1). Rio ex-officer is convicted in massacre of children. The New York Times, p. A5.

Scheper-Hughes, N., & Hoffman, N. (1995). Kids out of place. In M. Shellenberger & K. Danaher (Eds.), Fighting for the soul of Brazil (pp. 139-151). New York: Monthly Review Press.

Serbin, K. (1995). Pastoral agents movement raises black awareness. In M. Shellenberger & K. Danaher (Eds.), Fighting for the soul of Brazil (pp. 184-188). New York: Monthly Review Press.

Shellenberger, M. (1995). Black, Female and *Favelada*: Benedita Speaks. In M. Shellenberger & K. Danaher (Eds.), Fighting for the soul of Brazil (pp. 244-248). New York: Monthly Review Press.

Shellenberger, M., & Danaher, K. (1995). Introduction. In M. Shellenberger & K. Danaher (Eds.), Fighting for the soul of Brazil (pp. 1-7). New York: Monthly Review Press.

Sheriff, R. E. (2001). Dreaming Equality: Color, Race, and Racism in Urban Brazil. New Brunswick, NJ: Rutgers University Press.

Tannebaum, F. 1947. Slave and Citizen: The Negro in the Americas. New York: Vintage Books.

Telles, E. E. (2004). Race in Another America: The Significance of Skin Color in Brazil. Princeton: Princeton University Press.

Torrens, J. S. (1995). The role of liberation theology. In M. Shellenberger & K. Danaher (Eds.), Fighting for the soul of Brazil (pp. 189-196). New York: Monthly Review Press.

Urani, A. (1998). The effects of macroeconomic adjustment on the labor market and on income distribution in Brazil. In A. Berry (Ed.), Poverty, economic reform, and income distribution in Latin America, (pp. 205-234). Boulder, CO: Lynne Reinner Publishers.

Willumsen, M. J. F. (1997). Regional disparities in Brazil. In M. J. F. Williams & E. G. da Fonseca (Eds.), The Brazilian economy: Structure and performance in recent decades (pp. 235-260). Miami: North-South Center Press.

Wood, C. H., & Carvalho, J. A. M. D. (1988). The demography of inequality in Brazil. Cambridge: Cambridge University Press.

World Almanac Education Group. (2005). The World Almanac and Book of Facts, 2005. New York: Author.

Chapter 15

Black Nationalism: An Angle of Vision

By Gayle T. Tate

Introduction

Since the fiery speech by Henry Highland Garnet in 1843, "Address to the Slaves," Black nationalism has generated a great deal of interest. The interest, however, did not fully address the fact that Garnet's speech was a connection to earlier nationalist thought. This direct linkage can be traced to David Walker whose pamphlet in 1829, "Appeal to the Coloured Citizens of the World" shaped the beginnings of Black nationalism. Originally, the nationalist direction of Walker's pamphlet was submerged under its impassioned rhetoric of radical agitation. The bond between the two works was more discernable, however, when Garnet published a compendium including his speech and Walker's pamphlet in 1843. By doing this, Garnet also established himself in the tradition of Black nationalism. For it was Walker, along with Robert Alexander Young, Maria W. Stewart, and Reverend Lewis W. Woodson, that gave Black nationalism its definitive form. They defined and clarified, under the rubric of collective elevation, the themes of freedom, justice, the role of women in conflict, and the universality of the Black liberation struggle. Additionally, they established Black nationalism's four primary ideological constants of religion, racial unity, cultural history, and the philosophy of self-determination. This article will discuss the early Black nationalist themes as well as those fundamental ideological properties that nurtured its evolution.

Black nationalism of the 1830s embraced the political realities, aspirations, and destiny of Black Americans. Thus, the vision of Black people as a self-determined nation was always juxtaposed to the realities of their political plight in America. Black nationalism was no small feat for the intensity of these political realities – racism and segregation – were largely dependent upon, although not always, the concentration of Black Americans within a specified geographic location. Against this backdrop, Black nationalism clarified, defined, and analyzed the political struggle and suggested a specific course of action. As an ideology, Black nationalism also mirrored the pithy disillusionment of the Black experience in America. That experience, one of suffering and resistance, was embedded into the Black consciousness. Black nationalism, then, sought to capture the essence of pathos and hope that spoke to the sojourn of Blacks in America.

Many factors contributed to the development of Black nationalism as an ideology. First, kinship ties of common African descent bound Blacks to each other in the new alien land. Second, the institution of slavery and the racial discrimination of free Blacks made all Blacks suffer under the common yoke of oppression. While slaves were physically and economically tied to their masters, free Blacks endured legal constraints and racial prejudice daily.[1] Still another ingredient that fostered their unity was their yearning for freedom. All Blacks, whether slave or free, were linked in a common struggle for liberation. More importantly, however, Blacks wanted the opportunity to determine their own destiny. Reverend Lewis Woodson, who some have dubbed, "the father of Black nationalism" urged Blacks to "settle themselves in communities in the country, and establish society, churches, and schools of their own."[2]

In the early 1800s, Black Americans were victimized by both Northern racism and Southern slavery. Southern slavery was totally dependent upon Black servile labor. Without this economic base, the system would have collapsed. The master-slave relationships that were built upon the economic system of slavery were maintained by absolute authority. The psychological component of reducing slave, in white minds, to stereotypical images of inferiority also served to buttress the system. Thus, the economic foundation tied Blacks to the land for the surplus value they produced; and the psychological element served as justification for the continuous exploitation.[3] On the other hand, Northern racism had greater subtleties and was infinitely more complex. While Blacks looked to the North for its promises of freedom, Northern racial discrimination severely confined their freedom and opportunities. These Northern restrictions included employment opportunities, housing, suffrage, civil and legal rights, admission to public facilities, and the use of public conveyances.[4] Northern segregation and Southern slavery created two social structures, one black and one white. In the South, the overall oppression was clearly definitive and the oppressor had a face. Northern racism, however, was much more depersonalized and hid behind the ambiguities of federal, state, and local institutions and customs. These harsh political and social realities contributed to the nationalist cause.

Black Nationalist Thought

Collective elevation was the crux of Black nationalist thought. Viewed also as moral upliftment, it was the commitment of Black Americans to spiritually improve themselves.[5] But the concept held a deeper meaning. Collective elevation was also seen as the spiritual regeneration of the race and the first step toward full equality in American society. Moreover, moral improvement was only possible as one developed a sense of Black consciousness. This heightened sense of political and spiritual awareness nurtured community ambition and engendered development through education. The challenge to oppression followed this enlightened process. The idea of freedom transcended the psychological and emotional boundaries to become a call for action.

186

Collective elevation was both an individual and group moral task. Black Americans essentially saw their uplift as group members. While individual accomplishments validated Black claim to full citizenship, by themselves, however, they did not serve to move the group forward. It was rather the collective strivings of the entire group that would make full equality possible for the individual. Woodson believed this transmutation of the Black psyche was necessary for freedom and equality:

> To produce a moral revolution, such as is needed in our case, has ever been found a work of the greatest difficulty, even when every facility for its accomplishment was afforded. But how much more difficult must it be with us, when a thousand obstacles are thrown in the way.[6]

While collective elevation was the thrust of nationalist thought, freedom and liberation emerged as its overriding themes. The freedom concept held the idea of emancipation because Black Americans wanted to be free from both Southern bondage and Northern oppression. Nationalists, such as Maria W. Stewart, saw little difference between the condition of slaves and free Blacks, believing that free Black "conditions but little better that that."[7] The idea of liberation for Black Americans, however, contained the same sentiments of liberty and equality that inspired the American revolutionaries: "... our souls are fired with the same love of liberty and independence with which your souls are fired."[8] Black nationalism was an acknowledgement of Black Americans as an oppressed people and liberation was their desire to be free from that oppression. Inspired by other struggles, "all the nations of the earth are crying out for Liberty and Equality,"[9] liberation was the inherent belief of a wronged people waging a righteous struggle.

Although the primary focus of Black nationalism was on freedom and liberation, it was the realities of slavery and oppression that provided its internal dynamism. The stimuli of Southern slavery and Northern racism consistently gave Black nationalism its passion. Moreover, this same stimuli forged the bond of racial unity for a suffering people in a hostile environment. Racial unity provided the strength to surpass the oppression and collectively protest the political plight of Black Americans. Nationalism encouraged this challenge against oppression by diminishing the power of the slaveholding class and, at the same time, mythologizing the collective powers of the slaves. The slaves' power, ever present, was merely lying dormant waiting for their collective consciousness to be awakened. Shoring up their strength was the coming Messiah. Still, the faith of the believers held fast to the idea that the Messiah would one day appear. This Messiah, "the man we proclaim ordained by God, to call together the black people as a nation in themselves."[10] would arouse the slaves to battle and guide Blacks in their liberation struggle to victory.

The tenets of justice and wisdom turned on both a religious and worldly realm in Black nationalism. Containing intertwining sacred and secular chords, justice and wisdom were derived both from human reasons and God" law. Justice was the moral principle guiding human conduct, imbuing them with the knowledge of right and wrong. Entering the sacred realm, justice was the understanding and wisdom that God gave humankind. For nationalists, their sense of justice was their connection to the Deity. It was that special quality that placed the human species on a higher plateau than other forms of animal life. All actions, then, both virtuous and political, must follow principles of morality and conform ultimately with God's law. Slavery not only violated human reason but destroyed the spiritual union of Blacks with God. Young proclaimed slavery to be "contrary to the knowledge of justice, as hath been implemented of God in the souls of man..."[11] Thus, any war waged against this system would be in keeping with God's law. The abolition of slavery was not a only political cause, but a moral right as well.

Morality was also central to the material world-view of antebellum Black women and was at the core of their political activism. Black women viewed their morality, aspirations, and political commitment all through a religious prism. It was their spiritual consciousness that defined the parameters of their political action. For them piety and the freedom cause were one. With their spiritual rebirth, Black women saw moral regeneration paving the way to economic and political opportunities. With the recognition of limited material opportunities, Black women developed a keen sense of political realities. Thus, Black women with economic and political aspirations confronted, the social conditions of Blacks fired with new energy to ""lead the cause of his(her) brethren." The religious reverence of Black women was essential in directing the path of the struggle. Their sanctity was further buttressed by their unity as sisters. Maria Stewart constantly admonished Black women that "till we become united as one, and cultivate among ourselves the pure principles of piety, morality and virtue,"[12] would they be morally victorious.

To play a decisive role in the freedom cause, Black women were urged to go beyond the traditional roles of antebellum women. ""How long shall the fair daughters of Africa be compelled to bury their minds and talents beneath a load of iron pots and kettles?"[13] The mushrooming of Black female benevolent and literary associations, for mutual aid, moral improvement, and political development, in the early 1800s testified to Black women's commitment for community improvement. In this early period, there were societies founded by working-class women as well as women with means, all mirroring the participation of Black women in varied phases of Black struggle. As early as 1793, the Female Benevolent Society was founded by a group of Black women for the express purpose of mutual relief.[14] While early female benevolent societies reflected and imitated white female societies of the period, the emphasis on racial consciousness, self-improvement, and social responsibility were paramount in Black female associations.[15] This focus was in keeping with the central theme of collective elevation in the Black community. It was the growth of these female societies in the 1800s, followed by antislavery societies founded by Black women in the 1830s, that reflected the continuous commitment of Black women to social reform in general and the Black liberation struggle in particular.

188

Black women were not only charged with the moral responsibility of developing their human potential, but the additional task of training all of the descendents. Thus, education which has always been germane to the Black experience proved also to be important in Black nationalism. For Black women, it was crucial because the employment opportunities were limited to field work, domestic service, seamstress, and elementary education. The realities of life for the Black woman placed her in triple jeopardy due to her race, gender, and economic circumstances. Stewart, one of the first females of any color to speak from the public platform, was acutely aware of the racism and sexism peculiar to Black women in American society. She charged Black women with the moral responsibility of distinguishing their talents so that the world could assess and measure their accomplishments. The recognition for their accomplishments would also restore their dignity which had been stripped away under slavery and racism. But their talents and gifts could then be passed on to their descendents providing intellectual continuity. These inter-generational achievements would earn the respect of nations. Stewart implored Black women to "O, ye daughters of Africa, awake! awake! arise! No longer sleep nor slumber, but distinguish yourselves. Show forth to the world that ye are endowed with noble and exalted faculties."[16]

Stewart saw a connection between America's domestic policy of racism, sexism, and slavery and its emerging foreign policy toward the new republic of Haiti. In her eyes, America's failure to recognize the birth of Haiti, which culminated a fierce revolutionary struggle, and at the same time, support other revolutionary causes world-wide, was hypocritical. Undoubtedly, America's failure to recognize this new Black government added zeal to Black nationalism. Moreover, because early nationalism had a profound recognition for the universality of the Black liberation struggle, this failure on America's part denoted racism to the nationalists. Stewart, in her lecture at the Franklin Hall, in Boston, in 1832, was highly critical of America's foreign policy:

> We know that you are raising contributions to aid the gallant Poles; we know that you have befriended Greece and Ireland; and you have rejoiced with France, for her heroic deeds of valor. You have acknowledged all of the nations of the earth, except Haiti.[17]

The Haitian Revolution of 1804 sparked Black nationalism in America. The slave uprising that eventually culminated in Haitian independence did much to encourage Black Americans in their own liberation struggle. Although Haiti became the first Black government in the Western Hemisphere, its vision of becoming the center of pan-Africanism never materialized. Still, the raw courage of the slaves and the mere existence of the Black government was enough for Black Americans to celebrate. At the same time, it restored their faith in their own capabilities of self-government while nourishing their embryonic pan-Africanism. "But what need have I to refer to antiquity, when Haiti, the glory of the blacks and terror of tyrants, is enough to convince the most avaricious and stupid of wretches...."[18] Black Americans also saw some

189

similarities between the two struggles. Haitians were Black descendents from Africa; were brought to the Western Hemisphere as slaves; and had liberated themselves from oppression. Black Americans were also brought to the West as African slaves and were fighting for self-emancipation. For Stewart, the battle lines were clearly drawn; "Many will suffer for pleading the cause of oppressed Africa, and I shall glory in being one of her martyrs..."[19]

Black Americans, glorifying in the victory of the African descendents against their oppressors, received much encouragement from the new Haitian government. This support in addition to the Haitian emigrant plans of Black Americans served to infuse pan-Africanist thought in Black nationalism. Henri Christophe, the enlightened ruler of Haiti, 1811-1820, noted for hiss famous laws and decrees, agreed to a resettlement plan with Prince Saunders. Saunders, an early Haitian emigrant from America, had formerly worked under Christophe in the Haiti ministry of education.[20] Under the plan Black Americans would settle in Haiti with the Haitian government underwriting their relocation. The assassination of Christophe, in 1820, put a temporary stop to all emigration efforts. Immediately thereafter, however, Prince Saunders entered into negotiations with Christoph's successor, Alexander Petion, who also favored Black American emigration. To demonstrate his commitment to the plan, Petion emphasized employment for Black emigrants. In Haiti, Black Americans saw a Black sanctuary as well as an opportunity for economic prosperity. Support for Haitian emigration was drawn principally from New York City and Philadelphia. Roughly 13,000 free Blacks emigrated to Haiti between 1824-28.[21] Despite the enthusiasm, this emigration plan was largely unsuccessful in that many Black emigrants suffered innumerable hardships in Haiti, employment did not materialize for many, low-wage employment for many others, and some returned wearily to America. Emigration fever would not die, however, nor did Black Americans relinquish their ties to Haiti. In the 1850s, a turbulent time in racist America, emigration was again rekindled.

Emigrationism contained the hope, longing, and acute disillusionment of the political plight of Black Americans. It was one of the most volatile issues in Black nationalism and has always been resurrected in times of despair. Even for those Black Americans formerly opposed to emigration plans, Haiti was a symbol of freedom. David Walker vehemently opposed all colonization efforts, and perceived them as, "a plan to get those of the coloured people, who are said to be free, away from among those of our brethren whom they unjustly held in bondage...."[22] Yet, with a profound recognition of a weary warrior, Walker responded to hopeful emigrants with sensitivity. For those who wanted a new life in freedom, Walker implored, "... go to our brethren, the Haytians, who, according to their word, are bound to protect and comfort us."[23] Seeking solace and freedom, when the tides of racism peaked and Black Americans suffered despair, they looked beyond America's shores for their dignity.

Emigrationism, the resettlement of Blacks beyond American borders, was one of the ways in which Black Americans sought to uplift themselves. It co-existed with those themes of freedom, justice, and the role of Black women in struggle, in determining the political direction of Black Americans. These themes did not always co-exist harmoniously, but were determined by the political fluidity of the times. Black Americans consistently refortified their struggle with shifting priorities and directions to meet the contemporary political currents. Due to the urgency of the time, there was a noted strident militancy inherent in Black nationalism and there were reasons why this was so. The early Black nationalists, such as Young, Walker, Stewart, and Woodson were young men and women that represented a new generation in the free Black community that openly acknowledged violence as a necessary part of struggle. Just as importantly, they also believed that Blacks must direct their liberation cause themselves. If others were allowed to plead their cause, they would also determine its political direction. The military, then, inherent in Black nationalism reflected the need for a collective Black agenda. But nationalists who were articulate, charismatic, and forceful, were impatient with others who lacked political clarity on the conditions of Black Americans. Black nationalists, never exclusively Black in their world-view, recognized self-determination as connoting responsibility, commitment, and political action. By drawing on their bi-cultural history of Africa and America, they fashioned ideological components that became the vehicles for shoring up the dignity of Black Americans as well as the impetus for social change. The genesis for the ideological components evolved from the freedom struggle of Black Americans.

Ideological Components

Religion

Black religion, with its transcendental and temporal functions, was found in the slave community. With dual purposes, Black religion addressed the psychological needs for survival in the material world as well as freedom in the after life. Religion was not peculiar to the Black slaves' presence in America. For Africans had had prior exposure to Christianity, Islam and traditional African religious systems. In all of them, religion was the foci of life. It was this ethos, this historical memory, that traversed the seas with the Africans in the middle-passage and, undoubtedly, aided their survival in the new world. Black religion is a union of several qualities. It is the merging of the traditional African belief systems; the spiritual life of the slave community shaped by slavery; and white Christianity, all providing a holistic balm for the Blacks' total existence. This religious experience was shaped, too, by the physical distance of many of the slave communities on the larger plantations from the domiciles of the planters. This separation gave the slaves space to retain their African spirituality. At the same time, the temporal function of religion, which is the criticism of societal norms, was being expressed in the form of resistance. Varied forms of resistance included work stoppage, destroying equipment, "hush harbor meetings," conspiring with fugitives, and escaping as ways of protest.[24] Resistance, the highest stage of societal criticism, was rooted in the slaves' spiritual commitment to freedom. Resistance in the form of Black rebellions was also the fusion of religion and the desire for liberation. The slaves' sense of spirituality, then, was strengthened the more they faced white oppression.[25] The retention of this spirituality, of understanding the very essence of life through religion, was carried into freedom, the Black Church, and Black protest.

Black religion has always served a dual function within the Black community. And the Black Church, due to its autonomous position in the Black community, has maintained that duality. Although recognized for its Africanization of Christianity, the early Black church consistently sounded the clarion call of protest of the political plight of Black Americans. Providing a sanctuary for the weary and challenging political repression has been its primary functions and the two factors are inseparable. The need for sanctuary and freedom is carried forward by the "prophetic tradition" of the Black Church. With the Black minister as spiritual messenger, "The Black Church maintains a clear prophetic tradition... This tradition brings into judgement not only the institutions of society (such as political structures), but the institutional church as well."[26]

The religious world-view of the slave became an ideological component of Black nationalism. This spirituality of life that endures oppression and, yet, contests it in all forms, was the sustaining force of Black nationalism. Early Black theologians supported the political and religious direction of nationalists by merging nationalism with theology. God, a benevolent Deity, was one who provided both justice and equality for all people. By executing good Christian deeds, one could hope to achieve divine grace. These deeds regenerated individual spirituality that led first to the rebirth of the individual and then ultimately the race itself.[27] It was the collective elevation of the Black race that would initially be achieved through moral regeneration. The spirituality of this process provided the needed incentive and commitment in the Black community. Political protest and challenges to the evil system of slavery were synonymous with the achievements of justice, virtue, and divine grace. Decidedly guiding this righteous course, God would avenge His people and set them free.

Even though Black nationalism moved into the secular community in the 1830s, and began to be spearheaded by secular leaders, early nationalists were fundamentally pious. In their angle of vision there remained a connection between religious and political struggle: "The Lord has a suffering people, whose moans and groans at his feet for deliverance from oppression and wretchedness, pierce the very throne of Heaven, and call loudly on the God of Justice, to be revenged."[28]

Racial Unity

Racial unity, the cornerstone of Black nationalism, was the belief and feeling that Blacks must align themselves against common oppression. The crux of racial unity was to unite Blacks regardless of social class, geographic

192

location, and disparate political positions found within the Black community. Focusing on the Shared experiences of traditions, history, and suffering, Blacks were defined as a people. Inherent in racial unity was also the concept that all Blacks had a common racial destiny. The belief, implicitly, was that the past and present had largely been determined by racism, but Blacks themselves could shape their future.

Early evidences of racial consciousness was manifest in the slave community both in the shared culture as well as the collective resistance to bondage. The mixtures of languages, institutions, and religions of the African slave didn't alter their common world-view of life itself. It was this outlook of being one with nature that forged a common bond. The contact with Euro-American culture, sharpened by the realities of the slave experiences, enhanced their sense of racial consciousness. Slaves quickly learned that their survival depended upon the extent to which they supported each other. The cohesiveness of the slave community was more clearly seen in the emerging slave culture with its religious worship, extended non-familial bonding, music, folktales, and child-rearing practices. It was in this way the community was able to objectify its oppression and enhance the individual's psychological self-worth despite harsh circumstances. Members of the slave community also secretly aided fugitives and escapees from the plantations. The closeness of the slave community members can be readily observed in the fugitives' flight patterns. In many cases, fugitives merged with the maroon settlements in the mountainous or swampy regions near plantations, particularly, if family members were still in bondage. Others mingled with the free Black population of the South that had settled near plantations hoping to set family members free. Still others that escaped North and to Canada returned to aid the escapes of family members and friends. These flight patterns not only demonstrate strong kinship ties but also a common bond based on the commonality of oppression as well as racial identity.

Racial solidarity became an effective political instrument in the antebellum Black community. There were several pragmatic realities that sustained the concept of racial unity as a political force for Blacks. For one, free Blacks never constituting more than 14 percent of the total Black population, were dispersed over the entire nation. Carrying the early protest efforts mainly by themselves, Blacks needed a unifying force. There was none more compelling than uniting under the umbrella of racial solidarity. The experience of witnessing racial oppression daily heightened the self-awareness of free Blacks. Secondly, racial cohesiveness was an effective way of dealing with diverse social classes that were starting to emerge in the Black community. The 1830s brought with it a small Black elite, who, while economically experiencing some success were still the victims of racial discrimination and limited social opportunities. The indignities they suffered also propelled the ideal of racial unity forward. Racial unity also served to unite free and enslaved Blacks, so that the struggle of free Blacks was always dependent upon the resistance of the slaves. Equally important was that slave resistance fueled Black protest forward. At all stages of development, racial unity provided the rationale for struggle and remained the underpinnings of Black protest.

Nationalists sought racial unity as the key to freedom. Blacks, in combining their efforts, would challenge American racism. Yet, racial unity was seen through different prisms. Young saw it providing a renewal of spirit that would unite Blacks as a people world-wide. Walker saw racial unity as necessary for the abolition of slavery. The primary focus of Stewart was upon unity as the foundation for all moral and intellectual achievements. "I am of a strong opinion, that the day on which we unite, heart and soul, and turn our attention to knowledge and improvement, that day the hissing and reproach among the nations of the earth against us will cease."[29] On the other hand, Woodson's concern was for the dispersed Black population. He saw the need for a general convention to bring together the collective wisdom of Black Americans. Undoubtedly, modeling his convention after the National Negro Convention Movement which had fallen into disarray by 1838, Woodson believed that type of forum best to encourage and sustain racial unity.[30] All nationalists, however, yielded that the crux of racial unity was for Black Americans to determine their own political struggle.

The element of racial solidarity spearheaded the development of the Black Church and other separatist organizations in the Black community. In one way, they were responding to the acute segregation in America that circumscribed their lives; in another, they responded to their own needs for self-government and freedom to define their own potential. For those nationalists who did not yield to the temptation to emigrate to countries governed by Black leaders, segregated, autonomous institutions fulfilled those nationalist sentiments. It was with the latter sense of purpose that Blacks built their organizations that were expressions of their nationalism. Black leadership did emerge from these organizations which provided much of the sustenance to the early Black community. With nationalist leaders Blacks began to determine their political direction.

Cultural History and the Philosophy of Self-determination

One of the most prodigious efforts of Black nationalism was the restoration of the dignity of Afro-Americans through the retrieval of African history. This recovery was important to both the psychological and political consciousness of Afro-Americans. Nationalists held a cyclical view of history asserting that just as Blacks ruled the ancient world, so they would once again. They argued that Africans, having long excelled in the arts and sciences, provided the foundation for western civilization. It was the African genius, in fact, that nurtured the foundation of Greek civilization. Nationalists further contended that African history proved the capabilities of Afro-Americans in self-determination. They pointed to the great African empires of Mali, Songhay and Ghana that not only substantiated African legislative ability but also validated the African capacity for self-government. Nationalists further contended that the greatness of

194

African history had been suppressed in order to continually exploit her descendants around the world.

> When we take a retrospective view of the arts and sciences – the wise legislators – the Pyramids, and other magnificent buildings – the turning of the channel of the river Nile, by the sons of Africa or of Ham, among whom learning originated, and was carried thence into Greece, where it was improved upon and refined.[31]

The center of the African ontological system was the belief that the natural and supernatural worlds represented a continuity to the purpose of life. The material world and the spiritual world "were all united in one comprehensive, invisible system that has its own laws which sustain the visible world and ordinary life for the good of all."[32] This world-view, this harmonious view of the natural order, was brought into conflict with the European political and economic expansionism of the sixteenth and seventeenth centuries. In the clash of technology, which culminated in the repeated raping of Africa's resources, was also the colliding of world-views. African people conquered, displaced, and scattered throughout the world is evidence of two worlds still grappling with competing ideologies.

By bringing their world-view in harmony once again with the universe, Afro-Americans will redeem themselves by once again restoring Africa's place in the sun. To nationalists, redemption was possible because Black enslavement was mutable. Once freed, Afro-Americans would regain their former stature. The enslavement of Afro-Americans had a redemptive value offering spiritual redemption, even a spiritual platform, by which Blacks would challenge their oppression. Psychological benefits provided the healing whereby Blacks could reclaim their history and rescue their dignity. This mutability of their circumstances formed the core of their philosophy of self-determination.

The philosophy of self-determination was the driving force behind Black nationalism. Moreover, it was the pragmatic outgrowth of national expression of Black Americans. For Afro-Americans it meant that they could challenge, protest, and change the political conditions affecting their lives. And they were determined to do so. This expression took shape in the organizations that Afro-Americans founded in the early 1800s. Paramount to the focus on improving the Black community were these organizations' commitment to political protest. Most organizations of this time period served as ancillaries of the Black Church due to the Church's sphere of influence in the Black community. Still, the secular movement extended nationalism to state and national levels. As state and national organizations developed, such as the National Negro Convention Movement (1830) and the State Convention Movement (1835), the spirituality of protest remained central to the fundamental concerns of Black Americans.

Although the decisive force was still the Black church carrying the movement forward, Black organizations added a broader national focus to the political struggle. With national and state level organizations, the emergence of secular leadership was noticeable. Sacred and secular leadership provided continuity to the nationalist movement and enhanced its viability as a method of political protest. On the national level, the most prominent organization was the National Negro Convention Movement. Although founded specifically to deal with the cause of emigration, the movement dealt with the common concerns of emancipation, education, moral reform, and employment plaguing Black Americans.[33] With this focus, the movement hoped to achieve its goal of moral upliftment for all Black Americans. Although the movement had its stops and starts in the 1830s and 1840s, racial uplift was always the primary goal.

Nationalist expression was also evident on the state and local levels as well. The State Convention Movement, initiated in 1835, was an attempt by Black Americans to deal with their political and civil rights on state levels.[34] The practices of racism and the legal proscriptions surrounding the lives of Black Americans varied from state to state. State organizations challenged the legal apparatus of particular states. On the community level, there were a myriad of organizations reflecting a nationalist stance. There were mutual benefit societies, moral improvement societies, antislavery societies, literary and self-improvement associations. These societies and associations, despite their cultural tone, dealt with those real issues in the Black community such as education, self-improvement, morality, financial needs for widows, and abolitionism.[35] It was their commitment to racial upliftment and self-determination that reflected their nationalism.

Conclusion and Summary

Black nationalism evolved from the oppression suffered by Afro-Americans in the early 1800s. At its core, nationalist thought challenged the political and social realities of Black life. For it was the daily confrontation of racism that shaped and defined the nationalist struggle. But Black nationalist thought and expression of that time also emanated from the needs of the Afro-Americans to define themselves as a people. Unquestionably, nationalism was a nurturing philosophy that empowered Blacks to contest injustice and criticize the hypocrisies in American democracy. However, nationalism was also the essence of who they were – their history, culture, and spirituality – as a people.

The ideological beginnings of Black nationalism reflected the assessment of Black Americans of their political plight. The overall theme of collective elevation, i.e., moral upliftment, embodied all of the nationalist strivings of Black Americans. It is with this definitive purpose that Black Americans struggled for their freedom. And the opposing forces were arduous, for racism and slavery was life-threatening to the Black community. Although racial discrimination varied from region to region, and as a result was frustratingly unpredictable, racism was clearly circumscribed oppression. Thus, early ideological beginnings was the clarion call of the nationalists in the Black community for freedom from racist oppression. Nationalists emphasized those

196

themes of justice and liberation to counterpoise those forces of racism and oppression.

Inherent in Black nationalism were the ideological elements that provided its foundation. Religion and spirituality were the sources for its perpetual dynamism. Racial unity formed the underpinnings of nationalist thought and served as positive forces in the Black community uniting all Blacks despite disparate circumstances. Cultural history was the psychological and political reinforcement for a beleaguered people. Shoring up their dignity, it was the belief that the future of Afro-Americans was rooted in their past history of greatness. The pragmatic philosophy of self-determination was the backbone of the movement ensuring its organizational focus of Black Americans defining their struggle for themselves. At the heart of that struggle was Black nationalism giving meaning to the place of Black Americans in the universe.

NOTES

1. Leon F. Litwack, *North of Slavery*, Chicago: The University of Chicago Press, 1961, p. 64; Philip S. Foner, *History of Black Americans*, volume II Westport: Greenwood Press, 1983, pp. 191-3.
2. Augustine, *The Colored Americans*, Schomburg Center for Research in Black Culture, 28 July 1838 (Note: Augustine is Lewis Woodson who used the name as a pseudonym).
3. Eugene D. Genovese. *The World the Slaveholders Made, New York: Vintage Books, pp. 3-10.*
4. Litwack, p. 153.
5. Augustine, *The Colored Americans*, 10 February 1838; and Tate, Gayle T., *Tangled Vines: Ideological Interpretations of Afro-Americans in the Nineteenth Century*, dissertation, City University of New York, 1984, pp. 121-3.
6. Augustine, ibid.
7. Maria W. Stewart, *Productions of Mrs. Maria W. Stewart*, Boston 1835, Lecture delivered at Franklin Hall, Boston, 1832, pp. 51-2.
8. Ibid. P. 19. The pamphlet entitled Religion and the Pure Principles of Morality, the Sure Foundation on Which We Must Build, 1831, has been included in the larger, more comprehensive *Productions*.
9. Ibid, p. 9.
10. Robert Alexander Young, The Ethiopia Manifesto, found in Sterling Stuckey's *The Ideological Origins of Black Nationalism*, Boston: Beacon Press, p. 37.
11. Ibid, p. 34.
12. Stewart, p. 6.
13. Ibid, p. 16.
14. Sterling, p. 105-8.
15. Dorothy Sterling, editor, *We Are Your Sisters: Black Women in the Nineteenth Century*, New York: W. W. Norton & Company, p. 105; Paula Giddings, *When and Where I Enter: The Impact of Black Women on Race and Sex on America*, New

York: Bantam Books, 1984, pp. 49-50; and Dorothy Porter, "The Organized Educational Activities of Negro Societies, 1828-1846" *Journal of Negro Education*, vol. 5 October 1936, pp. 279, 281, 283, 287.

16. Stewart, p. 6.
17. Ibid, p. 19.
18. Walker, p. 21.
19. Stewart, p. 5.
20. Robert Carlisle, *The Roots of Black Nationalism*, New York: Kennikat Press Corp., 1975, pp. 50-4; Foner, pp. 302-3; Vincent Harding, *There Is A River*, New York: Random House, pp. 58-9, 192-3, 214; and Hollis R. Lynch, "Pan-Negro Nationalism in the New World, Before 1862," in August Meier and Elliott Rudwick, editors, *The Making of Black America*, Vol. 1 New York: Antheneum, 1969, pp. 44-45.
21. Carlisle, ibid.
22. Walker, p.47.
23. Ibid, p. 56.
24. Foner, Volume II, Chapter 7, "Slave Resistance in the Antebellum South;" Harding, pp. 103-8; and Angela Davis, "Reflections in the Black Woman's Role in the Community of Slaves" in *The Black Scholar*, Volume 12: No. 12, November/December 1981, pp. 2-15.
25. Gayraud S. Wilmore, *Black Religion and Black Radicalism*, New York: Orbis Books, 2nd edition, 1983, pp. 51-2.
26. William B. McClain, "Free Style and A Closer Relationship to Life," in The Black Experience in Religion, C. Eric Lincoln, editor, New York: Anchor Press, 1974, p. 5.
27. Monroe Fordham, *Major Themes in Northern Black Religious Thought, 1800-1860*, New York: Exposition Press, 1975, pp. 37-41.
28. Walker, p. 48-9.
29. Stewart, p. 15.
30. Augustine, *The Colored American*, 15 December 1837.
31. Walker, p. 19.
32. Wilmore, p. 15.
33. Howard Bell, ed. Minutes of the Proceedings of the National Negro Conventions, 1830-1864; 1830, 1831, 1836 conventions; and Harding, pp. 138-9.
34. Foner, pp. 322-3.
35. Foner, pp. 239-249; Sterling, pp. 104-119; and Porter, p. 288.

SPECIAL BIBLIOGRAPHY

Biko, Steve. "Black Consciousness and the Quest for a True Humanity." *The Challenge of Black Theology in South Africa*. Ed. Basil Moore. Atlanta: John Knox Press, 1974. 36-47.

Cone, James H. *Black Theology and Black Power*. New York: Seabury Press, 1969.

Green, Charles, and Basil Wilson. "The African-American Intellectual and the Struggle for Black Empowerment." *The Western Journal of Black Studies* Vol. 10 (1986): 59-69.

Harris, Norman. "A Philosophical Basis for an Afrocentric Orientation." *The Western Journal of Black Studies* Vol. 16 (1992): 154-59.

Jones, Rhett S. "In the Absence of Ideology: Blacks in Colonial America and the Modern Black Experience." *The Western Journal of Black Studies* Vol. 12 (1988): 31-39.

Karenga, Maulana. "Black Economics." *Introduction to Black Studies*. 3rd ed. Los Angeles: University of Sankore Press (2002): 439-59.

Pityana, Nyameko. "What is Black Consciousness." *The Challenge of Black Theology in South Africa*. Ed. Basil Moore. Atlanta: John Knox Press, 1974. 58-63.

Reed, W. Edward, Erma J. Lawson, and Tyson Gibbs. "Afrocentrism in the 21st Century." *The Western Journal of Black Studies* Vol. 21 (1997): 173-79.

Smith, R. Drew. "Black Religion-Based Politics, Cultural Popularization and Youth Allegiance." *The Western Journal of Black Studies* Vol. 18 (1994): 115-20.

Tate, Gayle T. "Black Nationalism: An Angle of Vision." *The Western Journal of Black Studies* Vol. 12 (1988): 40-48.

Wilson, Le Von E. "Affirmative Action: The Future of Race Based Preferences in Hiring." *The Western Journal of Black Studies* Vol. 16 (1992): 173-79.

ARTICLES

Alkalimar, Abdul H., and Nelson Johnson. "Toward the Ideological Unity of the African Liberation Support Committee." A Position Paper. South Carolina, 1974.

Anderson, Bernard C. "Economic Patterns in Black America." *The State of Black America*. Ed. James D. Williams. New York: National Urban League, 1982. 1-31.

Asante, Molefi Kete. "Racism, Consciousness, and Afrocentricity."*Lure and Loathing*. Ed. Gerald Early. New York: The Penguin Group, 1993. 127-43.

Jones, Rhett S. "Structural Isolation, Race and Cruelty in the New World." *Third World Review* Fall 1978. 34-43.

GENERAL BIBLIOGRAPHY

Asante, Molefi Kete. *The Afrocentric Idea*. Philadelphia: Temple University Press, 1987.

Axtell, James. *The Invasion Within: The Context of Cultures in Colonial North America*. New York: Oxford University Press, 1985.

Blassingame, John W. *The Slave Community: Plantation Life in the Antebellum South*. New York: Oxford University Press, 1979.

Camus, Albert. *The Rebel*. Trans. Anthony Bower. New York: Random House, 1956.

Carlisle, Robert. *The Root of Black Nationalism*. New York: Kennikat Press Corp., 1975.

Carmichael, Stokely, nd Charles Hamilton. *Black Power: The Politics of Liberation in America*. New York: Random House, 1967.

Cone, James. *Black Theology and Black Power*. New York: Seabury Press, 1969.

Conley, Dalton. *Being Black, Living in the Red: Race, Wealth and Social Policy in America*. Berkeley: University of California Press, 1999.

Cruse, Harold. *The Crisis of the Negro Intellectuals: From Its Origin to the Present*. New York: William Morrow, 1967.

Degler, Carl. *Neither Black nor White: Slavery and Race Relations in Brazil and the United States*. New York: Macmillan, 1971.

Fanon, Franz. *Black Skins, White Masks*. Trans. C. L. Markmann. New York: Grove Press, 1967.

Feagin, Joe. *Living with Racism: The Black Middle-Class Experience*. Boston: Beacon Press, 1994.

Franklin, John Hope. *From Slavery to Freedom: A History of Negro Americans*. Chicago: Alfred A. Knopf, Inc., 2000.

Frederickson, George. *White Supremacy: A Comparative Study in American and South African History*. New York: Oxford University Press, 1982.

Garvey, Marcus. *Philosophy and Opinions of Marcus Garvey*. New York: Atheneum Press, 1969.

Gutman, Herbert G. *The Black Family in Slavery and Freedom, 1750-1923*. New York: Vintage Books, 1977.

Gwaltney, John Langston. *Drylongso: A Self-Portrait of Black America*. New York: Vintage Books, 1981.

Harding, Vincent. *There is a River*. New York: Harcourt, 1981.

Jennings, Francis. *The Invasion of America: Indians, Colonialism, and the Cant of Conquest*. New York: Norton, 1976.

Levine, Lawrence W. *Black Culture and Black Consciousness: Afro-American Folk Thought from Slavery to Freedom*. New York: Oxford University Press, 1978.

Marable, Manning. *Blackwater: Historical Studies in Race, Class Consciousness and Revolution*. Athens, Ohio: Black Praxis Press, 1981.

Madhubuti, Haki R. *Enemies: The Clash of Races*. Chicago: Third World Press, 1978.

Myrdal, Gunnar. *An American Dilemma: The Negro Problem in Modern Democracy*. New York: Harpers, 1944.

Ofari, Earl. *The Myth of Black Capitalism*. New York: Monthly Review Press, 1970.

Patterson, Orlando. *The Sociology of Slavery*. Rutherford: Fairleigh Dickinson University Press, 1969.

Raboteau, Albert. *Slave Religion: The "Invisible Institution" in the Ante-Bellum South*. New York: Oxford University Press, 1970.

Rawick, George P. *From Sundown to Sunup: The Making of the Black Community*. Westport: Greenwood, 1972.

Skidmore, Thomas E. *Black into White: Race and Nationality in Brazilian Thought.* New York: Oxford University Press, 1974.

Silberman, Charles. *Crisis in Black and White.* New York: Random House, 1964.

Simons, Margaret C. *Black Economic Programs: An Agenda for the 1990s.* Washington, D.C.: Joint Center for Political Studies, 1989.

Stampp, Kenneth M. *The Peculiar Institutions: Slavery in the Ante-Bellum South.* New York: Vintage Books, 1956.

Stuckey, Sterling. *The Ideological Origins of Black Nationalism.* Boston: Beacon Press, 1972.

Toldson, Ivory, and Alfred D. Pasteur. *Roots of Soul: The Psychology of Black Expressiveness : An Unprecedented and Intensive Examination of Black--Folk Expressions in the Enrichment of Li.* Garden City: Doubleday, 1982.

West, Cornell. *Race matters.* New York: Vintage Books, 1993.

Wilmore, Gayraud. *Black Religion and Black Radicalism.* New York: Orbis Books, 1983.

www.ingramcontent.com/pod-product-compliance
Lightning Source LLC
Chambersburg PA
CBHW061731270326
41928CB00011B/2190